Good Housekeeping

Delicious Dessert Cookbook

Good Housekeeping

Delicious Dessert Cookbook

More than 200 Recipes for Cakes, Cookies, Pastries, Pies, and Tarts

Edited by Susan Westmoreland
Food Director
Good Housekeeping

With the assistance of
Susan Deborah Goldsmith
Associate Food Director

and Elizabeth Brainerd Burge

HEARST BOOKS
A Division of Sterling Publishing, Co.,
NEW YORK

GOOD HOUSEKEEPING

Ellen Levine	Editor in Chief
Susan Westmoreland	Food Director
Susan Deborah Goldsmith	Associate Food Director

A CARROLL & BROWN BOOK
Designed and produced by
Carroll & Brown Limited
20 Lonsdale Road
London NW6 6RD
England

Library of Congress Cataloging-in-Publication Data
Available upon request.

10 9 8 7 6 5 4 3 2 1

Published by Hearst Books
A Division of Sterling Publishing Company, Inc.
387 Park Avenue South, New York, NY 10016

Good Housekeeping is a trademark owned by Hearst Magazines Property, Inc., in USA, and Hearst Communications, Inc., in Canada. Hearst Books is a trademark owned by Hearst Communications, Inc.

www.goodhousekeeping.com

Distributed in Canada by Sterling Publishing
c/o Canadian Manda Group, One Atlantic Avenue, Suite 105
Toronto, Ontario, Canada M6K 3E7

Distributed in Australia by Capricorn Link (Australia) Pty. Ltd.
P.O. Box 704, Windsor, NSW 2756 Australia

Printed in China

ISBN 1-58816-301-6

FOREWORD

Bring a luscious dessert to the table and brighten up everyone's face. It is the part of the meal everyone in the family looks forward to, whether young or old. A simple, sweet offering can conjure up memories of grandmother's apple pie or of a scrumptious double-chocolate birthday cake. Somehow, desserts draw families closer together and so are a welcome guest at all occasions. With that in mind, I'm very pleased to present the *Good Housekeeping Delicious Dessert Cookbook*, containing recipes from the original *Good Housekeeping Step-by-Step Cookbook*.

We start with a basic technique: Want to make a perfect pie crust? Or a fluffy soufflé? Our step-by-step photos will show you the way. With the turn of a page you'll have more recipes—all using the same technique. You'll also find preparation and cooking times and a full nutritional profile with each recipe. As always, every recipe has been thoroughly tested in Good Housekeeping's Test Kitchens.

Whether you're a curious beginner who wants to learn the basics, or an experienced cook or baker in search of culinary inspiration, you'll find the desserts, cookies, and cakes that you want to make. With photos to instruct and entice, the recipes range from Old-Fashioned Apple Dumplings to Butterscotch Crème Brûlée to a Triple-Layer Mocha-Almond Torte.

Enjoy the recipes, the photos, the wealth of "Know-How" information and cooking tips. Our aim at Good Housekeeping is to give you the sort of information and recipes that make cooking a pleasure.

Susan Westmoreland
Food Director
Good Housekeeping

CONTENTS

◆

PIES AND TARTS 57

◆

COOKIES AND CAKES 75

The following guidelines are ones that no cook should be without. Keeping food in good condition isn't difficult and shouldn't be daunting. But a safe kitchen does call for a few precautions. Here, we outline safety essentials, including the right way to handle raw meats, and how long you can safely store a range of foods.

GOLDEN RULES OF FOOD SAFETY

• Keep a clean kitchen. Any area can harbor harmful bacteria, so always wash and dry your hands before handling food. Frequently wash kitchen towels, cloths, and sponges. Rinse fresh fruits and vegetables before eating. Wash cutting boards, knives, and other utensils with hot soapy water after every use – especially after handling raw meat and poultry. Wash cutting boards occasionally with a solution of 1 tablespoon bleach per 1 gallon water to sterilize them.
• Don't put cooked meat (or any ready-to-eat food) on a plate that has come in contact with raw meat, poultry, or fish.
• To kill harmful bacteria that may be present in raw eggs it's essential to cook them thoroughly. A thermometer is the safest method for checking doneness. For a visual check, egg yolks and whites until firm and set.
• It's unwise to cook foods in stages. Don't start to cook food, stop, and then return to it later. Even when food is stored in the refrigerator between cooking periods, safe temperatures might not be maintained and bacteria may develop.
• Refrigerate leftovers as soon as possible. Do not leave at room temperature longer than 2 hours. Divide large amounts among small, shallow containers for quicker cooling.

WRAP IT UP

Aluminum foil This provides optimal protection, molds easily, and can withstand extreme temperatures. The heavy-duty version is ideal for long-term storage.
Freezer paper This old-fashioned favorite protects food from freezer burn and is very easy to label.
Plastic bags Food storage bags are intended for room-temperature or refrigerated foods. Freezer bags are the thickest and sturdiest, and can even endure a quick zap in the microwave for defrosting and warming.
Plastic wrap The best offer a tight seal and protect food against moisture loss and odor transfer. Thinner wraps often cling better and are ideal for leftovers and brief microwave reheats (but should not be in direct contact with food when microwaved). For freezer storage, choose a heavy plastic wrap intended for that purpose.

PANTRY STORAGE

Unless otherwise noted, these pantry staples fare best in a cool, dry place.
Baking powder Once opened, keep it well sealed and it should be effective for up to 6 months. To test it, add 1 teaspoon to 1 cup hot water; it should bubble vigorously.
Bread crumbs Store dried bread crumbs in the pantry up to 6 months, or – for better flavor – refrigerate up to 2 years.
Honey It will last indefinitely; if it has crystallized, place opened jar in bowl of hot water. Stir until crystals dissolve.
Olive oil Keep in a cool, dark place up to 6 months. Don't buy more than you can use; it may become rancid, especially if stored in a warm place.
Pancake syrup This will keep up to 9 months (after that, syrup thins and flavor weakens). It can also be refrigerated. Pure maple syrup should be refrigerated after opening, or can be frozen. Store in glass jars, not plastic or metal containers.
Peanut butter Unopened, it will last for a year in your cupboard. Refrigerate after opening to avoid rancidity.
Spices and dried herbs Keep in lightproof containers in a cool place up to 1 year.
Vegetable oil Store in a cool, dark place (for 6 months).

THE RIGHT WAY TO REFRIGERATE

• Make sure your refrigerator temperature remains between 33° and 40°F.
• To prevent spoilage, keep foods on a rotating system. Place new items at the back of the shelves and move older purchases to the front.
• Date all leftovers so you know how long you've had them.
• If you're unsure whether a food is safe to eat, discard it.
• Keep eggs in their carton so they don't absorb other food odors. For the same reason, store cheese, cream, milk, yogurt, margarine, and butter tightly closed or covered.

FREEZER FACTS

• Frozen foods retain their color, texture, and nutrients better than foods preserved by other methods.
• Check the temperature of the freezer with a freezer thermometer to be sure that it is at 0°F. (Higher temperatures will draw moisture from the food, resulting in a loss of texture and taste.)
• It's time to defrost whenever there is ½ inch of frost on the sides of the freezer. If the frost has not solidified into hard ice, a plastic scraper makes light work of this job.
• Don't overload your freezer or add more than 2 pounds of food for each cubic foot of space in a 24-hour period. Either will cause temperature changes that may damage food.
• To avoid ice crystals, color or texture changes, or freezer

burn, seal foods in airtight containers, or wrap them tightly in a wrap intended for freezer storage.

• Small "piece" foods such as individual appetizers (e.g., tartlets, phyllo triangles), drop cookies, or strawberries keep best when "tray," or "dry," frozen. This method freezes foods so they remain separate and you can remove only as many as you need. Simply spread the unwrapped food on a baking sheet; freeze just until firm, then package in zip-tight plastic bags. Tray-freezing is also ideal for firming foods such as cakes and pies so packaging material will not adhere to them.

• Liquid and semiliquid foods must be stored in leakproof containers; leave headspace for expansion of liquid during the freezing process (for wide-mouth containers, leave ½ inch for pints and 1 inch for quart cartons; for narrow-mouth containers, leave ¾ inch for pints and 1½ inches for quarts).

• Don't freeze soft cheeses, sour cream, custard, and pumpkin pies – they'll become watery or may separate.

• Label and date food packages, and note the weight of meats and poultry and number of portions.

• Prepare frozen foods right after thawing; growth of bacteria can occur rapidly in thawed foods left at room temperature.

BLENDING AND MIXING OPTIONS

Blenders and food processors can be used for similar tasks, but they each have their own advantages. The blender makes silky sauces, and smooth drinks, a food processor is better at chopping, shredding, and grating and can make pastry dough in a flash. For whipping cream, beating egg whites, and mixing cake batters, an electric mixer does the job best. A handheld mixer is convenient because it's light and can be moved around the kitchen, but holding it can be tiring. A heavy-duty standing mixer easily handles large amounts of thick batter, and frees you up to do other things

FOR THE OVEN

Baking results depend on how long the food bakes and at how high a temperature, and the dimensions of the vessel. Many materials will do the job: enameled cast-iron is easy to clean and transmits heat well; stainless steel is durable and inexpensive; and heat-resistant glass and glass-ceramic can go directly from the freezer or refrigerator to the oven. For most cakes, shiny metal pans will yield the most delicate crusts.

Baking dish A large, fairly shallow, coverless oval or rectangular dish with sides about 2 inches high; usually made of glass or ceramic. Choose a variety in different sizes.

Baking pan Like a baking dish, but made of metal; the sides of this pan are 1½ to 2 inches high. Essential: an 8" by 8" square; a 9" by 9" square; a rectangular 13" by 9" pan.

Cake pan No baker should be without an assortment of round cake pans (8-inch and 9-inch), plus several square and rectangular baking pans. Depending on your baking

needs, also consider the following: springform pan (9" by 3" and 10" by 2½" are useful sizes).

Pie plate The standard size is 9 inches; deep-dish plates are 9½ inches. Glass, dark metal, or dull metal pans make the best piecrusts – crisp and nicely browned.

Tart pan This shallow pan with fluted sides and a removable bottom comes in all shapes and sizes; 11" by 1" and 9" by 1" round pans are especially useful. Tartlet pans (1¾-inch to 4-inch) are nice for individual desserts.

Other baking equipment Jelly-roll pan (15½" by 10½", with low rim all around); baking sheets (with low lip on one or more edges); muffin pan; custard cups (6-ounce capacity).

HOW TO MEASURE PANS

To measure the size of a baking dish or pan, measure across the top of the dish from inside edge to inside edge. Measure depth on the inside of the pan as well, from the bottom to the top of the pan.

PAN SUBSTITUTIONS

Cakes and breads are usually baked in metal baking pans. But in a pinch, you can substitute a glass or ceramic dish – just reduce the oven temperature by 25 degrees, since cakes bake faster in these materials than in metal. That way, the outside of the cake won't be over-baked before the center is cooked.

PAN VOLUMES	
PAN SIZE	APPROXIMATE VOLUME
2½" by 1¼" muffin pan cup	¼ cup
8½" by 4½" by 2½" loaf pan	5 to 6 cups
8" by 8" by 1½" baking pan	1½ quarts
9" by 9" by 1½" baking pan	2 quarts
9" by 1" pie plate	1 quart
11" by 7" by 1½" baking pan	2 quarts
13" by 9" by 2" baking pan	3½ quarts
15½" by 10½" by 1" jelly-roll pan	2½ quarts

COOKING BASICS <u>KNOW-HOW</u>

ALL THE RIGHT MEASURES

Careful measuring of ingredients means you'll get consistent results every time you prepare a recipe. For liquids, always measure in a glass or plastic cup designed for liquids, with a pouring lip. Read the measurement at eye level; for accurate results, place the cup on a flat surface. For dry ingredients, use a stainless steel or plastic cup that can be leveled off. These come in graduated sets of 1 cup, ½ cup, ⅓ cup, and ¼ cup; some sets also include ¾ cup and ⅔ cup measures. Measuring spoons, metal or plastic, come in sets of
1 tablespoon,
1 teaspoon,
½ teaspoon,
¼ teaspoon, and,
sometimes,
⅛ teaspoon.

Measuring spoons

Liquid measuring cups   Dry measuring cups

MEASURING FLOUR

1 Flour tends to pack down during storage. Stir the flour to loosen and aerate it before measuring.

2 Lightly spoon flour into a dry measuring cup (don't use the cup to scoop flour, and don't pack or shake the measuring cup).

3 Level the top with the straight edge of a knife or metal spatula. If the recipe calls for 1 cup sifted flour, sift flour, then measure. If it says 1 cup flour, sifted, you should measure and then sift.

MEASURING SHORTENING

1 If not using sticks, spoon the shortening into a dry measuring cup. With the back of a spoon, pack firmly into the cup.

2 Use the blade edge (not the flat side) of a knife or metal spatula to level off the shortening.

MEASURING BROWN SUGAR

For the most accurate results, always pack brown sugar firmly into a dry measuring cup before leveling off. It should hold its shape when turned out of the cup.

HINTS AND TIPS

• When measuring syrupy foods (e.g., molasses, honey, corn syrup), first coat the measuring spoon or liquid measuring cup with vegetable oil; the syrup will easily slip out.
• Check the volume of a soufflé dish by measuring water into the dish, to the top of the dish.
• When measuring ingredients, don't hold the cup or spoon over the bowl of other ingredients in case of spillage.
• For ingredients like nuts, coconut, and chopped dried fruits, fill a dry measuring cup and level with your fingers.
• Margarine and butter math: 1 stick = 8 tablespoons = ½ cup = ¼ pound (4 ounces).

USING SOURED MILK

If buttermilk is not on hand, don't worry. It's easy to make a "soured" milk that can stand in for buttermilk in any recipe. In a glass measuring cup place 1 tablespoon fresh lemon juice or distilled white vinegar, then pour in enough regular milk to equal 1 cup. Stir and let stand for about 5 minutes to thicken before using.

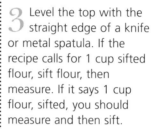

CUT TO SIZE

Chop To cut food into small, irregular pieces about the size of peas. Roughly cut up food, then mound pieces in a pile. Hold the handle of a chef's knife with one hand and the tip with the other, and chop with a rocking motion.
Mince To cut food into tiny irregular pieces, less than ⅛ inch. Proceed as for chopping, but cut food smaller.
Dice These are small, uniform cubes of about ¼ inch in size. To dice, first cut food into matchsticks or shreds. Bundle pieces together; slice crosswise into uniform cubes.
Julienne These are thin matchsticks about 2 inches long. First cut food into slices about 2 inches long and ⅛ inch thick. Stack slices; cut lengthwise into ⅛-inch-wide sticks.

EMERGENCY SUBSTITUTIONS

Baking powder For each 1 teaspoon called for, substitute ¼ teaspoon baking soda and ½ teaspoon cream of tartar (make fresh for each use).
Cake flour For each 1 cup called for, use 1 cup minus 2 tablespoons all-purpose flour.
Light brown sugar For each 1 cup, substitute 1 cup granulated sugar and 1 tablespoon molasses; or use dark brown sugar.
Pine nuts Use walnuts or almonds.
Vanilla extract Use brandy or an appropriate flavored liqueur.

DESSERT UTENSILS

Apple corer This cylindrical tool neatly cores apples as well as pears. Buy the larger size so you don't miss any core.
Cooling racks Have 2 or 3 if you bake a lot of cakes or cookies. Avoid racks with large gaps between the wires.
Decorating bag For decorating cakes and pies and forming spritz cookies and beautifully shaped pastries.
Egg beater This hand-powered mixer can also be used for whipping cream. Crank gears spin the metal beaters.
Ice cream maker They come as manual and electric; used for ice cream, sorbet, and frozen yogurt.
Juicer A device to extract fruit or vegetable juices – from a simple ridged cone onto which a halved citrus fruit is pressed to elaborate electric models used for carrot juice.
Melon baller Besides scooping perfect globes of melon, this tool cores apples and pears. A large one is most useful.
Mixing bowls A set of these all-purpose bowls is invaluable. Typically made of stainless steel, glass, or plastic, they range from tiny to 8 quarts. Avoid using plastic bowls to beat egg whites.
Pastry blender The metal wires on this tool cut the cold fat into flour for pastry without warming it, as your hands would.
Pastry brush Used to brush doughs with butter or egg and apply glazes to baked goods; great for dusting off excess flour. Wash right after using (especially at the base of the bristles);

dry thoroughly. When buying, look for well-anchored bristles.
Rolling pins Heavy pins, hardwood or marble, work best for rolling dough out smoothly, with less effort. Don't wash wooden pins in the dishwasher.
Toothpicks Great for testing cakes and quick breads for doneness.
Zester Pulled across citrus fruit, it removes only the outer peel, avoiding the bitter pith underneath.

SMALL VOLUME EQUIVALENTS

SPOONS	CUPS	FLUID OUNCES
1 tablespoon/3 teaspoons		½ fl oz
2 tablespoons	⅛ cup	1 fl oz
4 tablespoons	¼ cup	2 fl oz
5 tablespoons + 1 teaspoon	⅓ cup	2⅔ fl oz
6 tablespoons	⅜ cup	3 fl oz
8 tablespoons	½ cup	4 fl oz
10 tablespoons + 2 teaspoons	⅔ cup	5⅓ fl oz
12 tablespoons	¾ cup	6 fl oz
14 tablespoons	⅞ cup	7 fl oz
16 tablespoons	1 cup	8 fl oz

LARGER VOLUME EQUIVALENTS

CUPS	FLUID OUNCES	PINTS/QUARTS
1 cup	8 fl oz	½ pint
2 cups	16 fl oz	1 pint
3 cups	24 fl oz	1½ pints/¾ quart
4 cups	32 fl oz	2 pints/1 quart
6 cups	48 fl oz	3 pints/1½ quarts
8 cups	64 fl oz	2 quarts/½ gallon
16 cups	128 fl oz	4 quarts/1 gallon

OVEN TEMPERATURES

Celsius	Fahrenheit	Gas	Description
110°C	225°F	¼	Cool
120°C	250°F	½	Cool
140°C	275°F	1	Very low
150°C	300°F	2	Very low
160°C	325°F	3	Low
170°C	325°F	3	Moderate
180°C	350°F	4	Moderate
190°C	375°F	5	Moderately hot
200°C	400°F	6	Hot
220°C	425°F	7	Hot
230°C	450°F	8	Very hot

VOLUME

Metric	Imperial	Metric	Imperial
25 ml	1 fl oz	500 ml	18 fl oz
50 ml	2 fl oz	568 ml	20 fl oz/1 pint
75 ml	2½ fl oz	600 ml	1 pint milk
100 ml	3½ fl oz	700 ml	1¼ pints
125 ml	4 fl oz	850 ml	1½ pints
150 ml	5 fl oz/¼ pint	1 litre	1¾ pints
175 ml	6 fl oz	1.2 litres	2 pints
200 ml	7 fl oz/⅓ pint	1.3 litres	2¼ pints
225 ml	8 fl oz	1.4 litres	2½ pints
250 ml	9 fl oz	1.5 litres	2¾ pints
300 ml	10 fl oz/½ pint	1.7 litres	3 pints
350 ml	12 fl oz	2 litres	3½ pints
400 ml	14 fl oz	2.5 litres	4½ pints
425 ml	15 fl oz/¾ pint	2.8 litres	5 pints
450 ml	16 fl oz	3 litres	5¼ pints

SPOONS

Metric	Imperial
1.25 ml	¼ tsp
2.5 ml	½ tsp
5 ml	1 tsp
10 ml	2 tsp
15 ml	3 tsp/1 tbsp
30 ml	2 tbsp
45 ml	3 tbsp
60 ml	4 tbsp
75 ml	5 tbsp
90 ml	6 tbsp

US CUPS

Cups	Metric
¼ cup	60 ml
⅓ cup	70 ml
½ cup	125 ml
⅔ cup	150 ml
¾ cup	175 ml
1 cup	250 ml
1½ cups	375 ml
2 cups	500 ml
3 cups	750 ml
4 cups	1 litre
6 cups	1.5 litres

WEIGHT

Metric	Imperial
5 g	⅛ oz
10 g	¼ oz
15 g	½ oz
20 g	¾ oz
25 g	1 oz
35 g	1¼ oz
40 g	1½ oz
50 g	1¾ oz
55 g	2 oz
60 g	2¼ oz
70 g	2½ oz
75 g	2¾ oz
85 g	3 oz
90 g	3¼ oz
100 g	3½ oz
115 g	4 oz
125 g	4½ oz
140 g	5 oz
150 g	5½ oz
175 g	6 oz
200 g	7 oz
225 g	8 oz
250 g	9 oz
275 g	9¾ oz
280 g	10 oz
300 g	10½ oz
315 g	11 oz
325 g	11½ oz
350 g	12 oz
375 g	13 oz
400 g	14 oz
425 g	15 oz
450 g	1 lb
500 g	1 lb 2 oz
550 g	1 lb 4 oz
600 g	1 lb 5 oz
650 g	1 lb 7 oz
700 g	1 lb 9 oz
750 g	1 lb 10 oz
800 g	1 lb 12 oz
850 g	1 lb 14 oz
900 g	2 lb
950 g	2 lb 2 oz
1 kg	2 lb 4 oz
1.25 kg	2 lb 12 oz
1.3 kg	3 lb
1.5 kg	3 lb 5 oz
1.6 kg	3 lb 8 oz
1.8 kg	4 lb
2.25 kg	5 lb
2.7 kg	6 lb

MEASURES

Metric	Imperial
2 mm	1/16 in
3 mm	⅛ in
5 mm	¼ in
8 mm	⅜ in
10 mm/1 cm	½ in
1.5 cm	⅝ in
2 cm	¾ in
2.5 cm	1 in
3 cm	1¼ in
4 cm	1½ in
4.5 cm	1¾ in
5 cm	2 in
5.5 cm	2¼ in
6 cm	2½ in
7 cm	2¾ in
7.5 cm	3 in
8 cm	3¼ in
9 cm	3½ in
9.5 cm	3¾ in
10 cm	4 in
11 cm	4¼ in
12 cm	4½ in
12.5 cm	4¾ in
13 cm	5 in
14 cm	5½ in
15 cm	6 in
16 cm	6¼ in
17 cm	6½ in
18 cm	7 in
19 cm	7½ in
20 cm	8 in
22 cm	8½ in
23 cm	9 in
24 cm	9½ in
25 cm	10 in
26 cm	10½ in
27 cm	10¾ in
28 cm	11 in
29 cm	11½ in
30 cm	12 in
31 cm	12½ in
33 cm	13 in
34 cm	13½ in
35 cm	14 in
37 cm	14½ in
38 cm	15 in
40 cm	16 in
43 cm	17 in
46 cm	18 in
48 cm	19 in
50 cm	20 in

DESSERTS

Anyone who has tasted a warm, fluffy soufflé, perfectly creamy custard, or a tender fruit shortcake knows that there's an art to great dessert making. The following time-honored tricks will help you master all the right methods. Because let's face it, every occasion is sweeter when a spectacular dessert is involved.

COOKING WITH FRUIT

Choosing the best fruit Choose ripe (but not mushy) fruit that's in season. When selecting fruit, the heavier it feels in your hand, the juicier and better tasting it will be. Smell it: If there's no aroma, there will be little flavor. Feel it: Fruit should yield slightly to gentle pressure. To ripen fruit, store it at room temperature in a dark place, or speed the process by placing it in a paper bag containing a whole lime.

Reasons to rinse Pesticides, waxy coatings, or even bacteria can linger on the skin of fruit, so rinse it well before using. (Don't forget to scrub citrus fruit if you're going to use the peel.) Never soak fruit in water, however; this leaches out flavor and encourages rotting. Instead, wash it quickly with gently running water, and dry immediately. Unless they are very sandy, avoid washing soft berries such as raspberries and blackberries, since they tend to become waterlogged.

A spoonful of sugar The sweetness of individual fruits can vary greatly, depending on ripeness, variety, and growing conditions, so you may need to adjust the amount of sugar called for in a recipe. Simply taste the fruit, or the fruit mixture, before cooking and adjust the sugar as necessary.

Prevent discoloration When exposed to air, tannins and enzymes in fruits such as apples, peaches, pears, and bananas cause them to turn brown. To prevent this, rub the fruit with a cut lemon, or briefly place it in a bowl of water with approximately 2 tablespoons of lemon juice added.

Cook it gently When you want to retain the shape and texture of a fruit, cook it gently just until it's tender. For poaching, keep the water at a low simmer. Sauté fruit only until it softens and begins to release its juices.

CREAMY CUSTARD EVERY TIME

Don't overbeat the eggs Overbeating can make the custard foamy and cause bubbles to appear on the surface as it bakes. Beat the eggs just till yolks and whites are blended.

Easy does it Custards, both baked and stove-top, require gentle heat so they don't separate. For silky stove-top custards, use low heat and stir constantly to prevent boiling (and

subsequent curdling). Cook baked custards in a water bath – a larger pan of hot water. This method insulates them from the oven's direct heat so they cook evenly, without separating.

Is it ready? Overbaked custards may separate and turn watery. Remember that the custard is done even if the center is still jiggly; it will firm as it cools. To check, insert a knife ½ inch into the custard about 1 inch from the center; it should come out clean. A stove-top custard is ready when it's thick enough to coat a spoon well. Run your finger across the spoon; it should leave a track (see page 46).

Be careful with cooling Always remove the baked custard promptly from its water bath (otherwise, it will continue to cook), and then cool. Cool stove-top custards with a piece of plastic wrap pressed directly on top so a skin doesn't form.

SOUFFLÉ SUCCESS

• It's easier to separate eggs when they're cold, so separate them straight from the refrigerator, but let the whites stand 30 minutes before beating for maximum volume.

• Perfectly beaten egg whites are a must for a light, fluffy texture; beat the whites until they're stiff but not dry.

• The best way to blend: Mix in one third of the beaten egg whites to lighten batter. Add the remaining whites, half at a time, gently folding into the batter with a rubber spatula.

• Soufflés rely on a blast of quick, even heat to rise properly, so it's essential that the oven is heated to the correct temperature before baking. Only keep the oven door open for an instant when you put in the soufflé, and open it as little as possible during baking.

• Be sure to set the soufflé dish on a low rack in the oven so the mixture has plenty of room to rise.

• How to tell when the soufflé is done? It should be puffed and golden with a slightly soft, barely set texture.

• Come and get it! For the most dramatic presentation, call everyone to the table *before* you take the soufflé out of the oven; cool air will start to shrink it in 3 to 5 minutes.

Preparing soufflé dishes

Use butter, margarine, or nonstick cooking spray to grease soufflé dishes, then sprinkle with just enough sugar to coat dishes lightly.

Folding in egg whites

Using a rubber spatula, gently fold one third of beaten egg whites into mixture. Then fold in the remaining egg whites, half at a time.

MAKING CHOUX PASTRY

This light, airy pastry is used for cream puffs and éclairs.
Beware of boiling Bring the water with the margarine or butter to a full boil, but don't let the water simmer away, or you'll have a dry dough.
Egg essentials For best results, use room-temperature eggs (they'll blend better and rise higher). Add the eggs to the batter one at a time, beating well after each addition to incorporate them thoroughly.
The heat is on Shape and bake choux pastry immediately, while it is still warm, for maximum expansion and lightness.
Go for the gold Pale, underbaked puffs will be raw inside and may collapse after they're removed from the oven. Aim for a rich, golden color.
Get a jump on entertaining Unfilled puffs freeze beautifully in zip-tight plastic bags; simply recrisp them in the oven.

High-rising choux puffs produce – and retain – a lot of steam as they bake. To help them dry into a golden-crisp shell, use a paring knife to cut a small slit into the side of each puff as soon as they come out of the oven.

PUFF PASTRY BASICS

• When buying frozen puff pastry, check the ingredients on the package. The best brands contain only flour, butter, salt, and water.
• Frozen puff pastry thaws very quickly, making it handy for last-minute treats. Figure on 10 to 20 minutes' thawing time.
• When cutting puff pastry dough, be sure your knife or pastry wheel is very sharp – clean cuts will ensure maximum puffing. Always cut straight down, never at an angle, or the dough will puff unevenly as it bakes.
• If you don't want puff pastry to rise too much, prick it in several places with a fork before baking.
• Save puff-pastry trimmings; they can be rerolled and used to make quick desserts (see page 38).
• Puff pastry demands a quick blast of heat at the beginning of baking; this melts the butter while it converts the water in the dough to steam, making it rise. To ensure that your oven is hot enough, preheat it at least 20 minutes ahead.

PHYLLO FACTS

• Fragile and tissue-thin, phyllo dries out quickly and becomes unusable, so keep it covered with plastic wrap until you are ready to use it. Any phyllo you don't use can be refrigerated, well wrapped, up to 2 weeks.

• Frozen phyllo will keep for 3 to 6 months; thaw overnight in the refrigerator. Never refreeze thawed phyllo dough, or it will become dry, brittle, and crumbly.
• Fresh phyllo dough, available at some specialty food stores and Greek and Middle Eastern markets, can be refrigerated, well wrapped, for 5 days, or frozen up to 3 months.
• Before baking, brush phyllo layers with a thin coating of melted margarine or butter for extra flavor and a crisp, golden crust – and to help guard against drying.
• Let phyllo bake until deep golden; this gives it a toasted flavor and a wonderfully crisp crust.
• Phyllo pie crusts and cups can be baked a day ahead. Store them in airtight containers, and recrisp (if necessary) in the oven before filling and serving.

GETTING TO KNOW GELATIN

• What exactly is gelatin? It's an odorless, tasteless, and colorless thickening agent derived from beef and veal bones; some gelatin is a by-product of pig skin.
• For best results, measure carefully. Too much gelatin makes a mixture rubbery; with too little, it will not set firmly.
• To soften gelatin, sprinkle it over a small quantity of cold liquid; leave it without stirring for 5 minutes, or until it softens and swells to a spongy consistency that will dissolve smoothly when heated. The mixture to which dissolved gelatin is added must be warm enough to prevent the gelatin from immediately setting and clumping.
• Dissolve gelatin completely during heating, but never let the mixture boil, or its setting ability will diminish. Stirring is essential to prevent the mixture from lumping or separating.
• When adding fruit to gelatin, keep the pieces small – gelatin will pull away from larger pieces. Raw pineapple, kiwifruit, and papaya contain enzymes that break down gelatin.
• To quick-chill gelatin, set the bowl in a larger bowl of ice water, stirring frequently with a rubber spatula, just until the mixture begins to mound but is not lumpy. (Don't try to speed this process in the freezer; the mixture may crystallize.)
• Once set, molded gelatin desserts have to be loosened from the mold. To do this, lower the base of the mold into a bowl of warm water and leave for 10 seconds (no longer, or the gelatin may melt). Place the serving plate on top of the mold, quickly invert it, and shake to release the dessert.
• Gelatin math: 1 envelope = about 2½ teaspoons (¼ ounce) powdered gelatin; 1 envelope will set up to 2 cups of liquid.

To check that all the gelatin crystals have fully dissolved, lift a little of the gelatin in a spoon – there should be no visible crystals.

MAKING THE MOST OF MERINGUE

A simple mixture of beaten egg whites and sugar, meringue is essential to any dessert repertoire. There are two basic types of meringue: soft and hard. The consistency depends on the proportion of sugar to egg whites. Soft meringue has less sugar and is most often used as a swirled topping for pie. Hard meringue has more sugar; it's piped into shapes such as disks or shells (to cradle fruit or cream fillings) and baked to a crisp, brittle finish.

Properly beaten egg whites form stiff (but not dry) peaks. When the beaters are lifted from the bowl, the peaks hold their shape.

If under- (or over-) beaten, egg whites will be too soft and syrupy and will not hold their shape during the baking process.

For better blending and a light, fluffy texture, it's important to add the sugar to the softly beaten whites gradually – two tablespoons at a time – and to make sure it is completely incorporated. Continue beating on high speed until the mixture forms stiff, glossy peaks. To ensure that the sugar has completely dissolved, follow the foolproof test at right.

Rub a little meringue mixture between your thumb and finger to make sure all the sugar has dissolved; it should feel smooth, not gritty.

Tricks of the trade
• Don't make meringues on a humid or rainy day; they will absorb too much moisture from the air and end up soggy or "weeping" (exuding little beads of moisture).
• If adding ingredients such as ground nuts, be sure to fold them in gently to avoid deflating the egg whites.
• To give meringue extra crispness and a pretty sparkle, sprinkle with granulated sugar before baking.
• Is it done yet? A soft topping is ready when the peaks are brown; hard, crisp meringue will sound hollow when tapped.
• Let hard meringues dry completely in the oven for crisp results. They'll have a gummy texture if removed too soon.
• Meringue pies are best served within a few hours of baking; hard meringues can be stored up to a week in an airtight container.

ALL ABOUT ICE CREAM

STORE-BOUGHT
• A sticky container most likely means the product has thawed, leaked, and been refrozen; choose another carton.
• For easier serving, soften ice cream in the refrigerator about 30 minutes. For speedier results, microwave rock-hard ice cream at medium-low for about 30 seconds.
• The container should be well sealed to prevent the ice cream from absorbing odors from other foods, or forming ice crystals on its surface. It's a good idea to place a sheet of plastic wrap directly against the surface of the ice cream to seal it from air. Reseal the container tightly after opening.
• Low-fat ice creams and frozen yogurt melt faster than full-fat varieties. So prechill serving bowls, or add the scoops at the very last minute – or you may end up with a milky puddle over warm pies or hot, bubbling cobblers.

HOMEMADE
• For the creamiest texture (and a maximum yield), make and chill the ice-cream mixture the day before you plan to freeze it (the chilled mixture will also freeze faster).
• Fill ice-cream machines only two-thirds full – the mixture expands as it freezes and needs room to incorporate air.
• A fresh-frozen mixture thaws quickly, so handle it as little as possible before getting it into the freezer.
• If using an old-fashioned-style churn, add more ice and salt as needed (the faster the freezing process, the smoother the texture of the ice cream).

ICE-CREAM CLINIC (HOW TO AVOID...)
Lumpy mixture Chances are the mixture was too warm when the freezing process began. This increases churning time, which creates a less-smooth texture, as well as the likelihood of flecks of butter forming. A better approach? Make sure the mixture is completely cooled (either slowly in the refrigerator or more quickly in an ice-water bath) before churning.
Grainy texture Pitfalls that prevent smooth results: Sloppy measuring (never add extra water or alcohol to the mixture); churning the mixture too slowly (to help avoid this, add ice and salt when necessary to an old-fashioned-style churn to keep the mixture cold); or simply storing the finished ice cream too long.
Bland taste The most common culprit is a lack of sweetener. (However, if you're making sorbet, it's also possible that you didn't add enough lemon juice, which brightens the flavor.) To avoid this, taste the mixture prior to freezing and sweeten as necessary. You can also enhance the taste by allowing ice cream to "ripen" in the freezer for at least four hours before serving; this helps it fully develop its flavor and texture.
Ice crystals These occur in ice cream that has been stored for too long (a practice that also creates a thick, heavy texture). To prevent ice crystals, add 1 envelope unflavored gelatin for each 6 cups liquid in the ice cream base. Let the gelatin soften in ¼ cup of the liquid, then heat until the gelatin dissolves and stir it into the rest of the liquid.

FRUIT SALADS

When fruit is in its peak season, there's no better way to show it off than with a fabulous fruit salad. Choose fully ripe fruit, then treat it simply: A little sugar brings out its flavor; a touch of an acidic ingredient (such as wine or citrus) brightens it. Serve your favorite after a rich meal or at a special brunch.

1 Prepare coconut: Preheat oven to 350°F. With hammer and screwdriver or large nail, puncture 2 eyes of coconut. Drain coconut liquid; discard. Bake coconut 15 minutes.

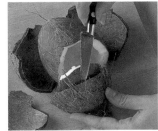

2 Remove coconut from oven and wrap in kitchen towel. With hammer, hit coconut to break into large pieces. With paring knife, pry coconut meat from shell.

3 With paring knife or vegetable peeler, peel outer skin from coconut meat. With large holes of grater or vegetable peeler, shred 1 cup coconut (reserve remainder for use another day).

AMBROSIA

◆◆◆◆◆◆◆◆◆◆◆◆◆

Prep: 40 minutes
Bake: 15 minutes
Makes 10 servings

1 fresh coconut
1 ripe pineapple
6 navel oranges

4 Prepare pineapple: Cut off crown and bottom from pineapple. Stand pineapple upright on cutting board; with large chef's knife, slice off rind and remove eyes. Cut pineapple lengthwise into quarters. Cut out core. Cut each quarter lengthwise in half; slice into chunks. Place in large bowl.

5 Prepare oranges: With paring knife, cut off ends from oranges; stand on cutting board and slice off rind, removing all white pith.

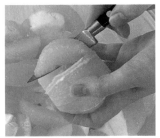

6 Holding oranges over pineapple in bowl, cut sections and add to bowl. Squeeze juice from membranes into bowl; discard membranes. Add coconut to fruit in bowl; toss gently to combine.

EACH SERVING: ABOUT 105 CALORIES, 1g PROTEIN, 19g CARBOHYDRATE, 4g TOTAL FAT (3g SATURATED), 0mg CHOLESTEROL, 25mg SODIUM

FRUIT AND WINE CUP

Prep: 10 to 15 minutes   *Makes 4 servings*

⅓ cup white wine (for strawberries) or red wine (for peaches)

2 tablespoons sugar

1 pint strawberries, hulled and each cut in half, or 2 cups peeled sliced peaches (3 to 4 peaches)

In small bowl, mix white or red wine and sugar until sugar dissolves. Place strawberries or peaches in 4 goblets. Pour wine mixture over fruit.

Each serving: About 60 calories, 0g protein, 12g carbohydrate, 0g total fat, 0mg cholesterol, 0mg sodium

FRUIT WITH MARSALA CREAM AND TORTILLA CRISPS

Prep: 25 minutes   *Cook: 6 to 8 minutes*
Makes 4 servings

⅓ cup sugar

½ teaspoon ground cinnamon

2 flour tortillas (7 inches each)

Vegetable oil

1 pint strawberries

2 medium kiwifruit

2 medium peaches

½ cup heavy or whipping cream

2 tablespoons confectioners' sugar

1 tablespoon sweet Marsala wine

◆ In small shallow bowl, mix sugar and cinnamon. Cut each tortilla into 6 triangles. In 10-inch skillet, heat ¼ inch oil over medium heat; add tortilla triangles, a few at a time, and cook, turning once, until golden. Drain on paper towels. Immediately toss in sugar mixture; set aside. If not using right away, store triangles in tightly covered container.

◆ Hull strawberries and cut each in half. Peel kiwifruit and cut into bite-size chunks. Peel and slice peaches. Place fruit in 4 dessert bowls.

◆ Prepare Marsala cream: In small bowl, with mixer at medium speed, beat heavy cream and confectioners' sugar until soft peaks form; gradually beat in Marsala. Spoon Marsala cream alongside fruit; serve with tortilla crisps.

Each serving: About 325 calories, 3g protein, 47g carbohydrate, 15g total fat (7g saturated), 41mg cholesterol, 100mg sodium

BLUEBERRY-MANGO SALAD

Prep: 15 minutes   *Makes 6 servings*

1 tablespoon sugar

1 tablespoon dark rum

1 tablespoon fresh lime juice

2 large mangoes, peeled and diced

1 pint blueberries

In medium bowl, combine sugar, rum, and lime juice. Add mangoes and blueberries; toss to coat.

Each serving: About 95 calories, 1g protein, 24g carbohydrate, 0g total fat, 0mg cholesterol, 5mg sodium

SUMMER FRUIT BASKET

Prep: 1 hour 20 minutes   *Makes 16 servings*

1 oblong watermelon, about 20 pounds, chilled

2 large navel oranges

½ cup sugar

1 medium pineapple

1 pint strawberries

4 large kiwifruit

2 medium nectarines

½ pound red seedless grapes

Green florist wire, herb sprigs, clear thread or nylon fishing line, and tiny nontoxic flowers such as baby's breath and sweetheart roses for handle (optional)

◆ Prepare watermelon basket: With sharp knife, cut lengthwise slice about 2 inches from top of watermelon. Scoop out pulp from both sections; cut into bite-size chunks. Place 10 cups watermelon in large bowl (save remainder for another day). Cut a thin slice of rind from bottom of watermelon shell, if needed, so it will stand level. Cut scalloped edge around rim of watermelon shell.

◆ With vegetable peeler, remove peel from 1 orange. In blender, process peel with sugar until peel is finely chopped. Cut white pith from orange; cut peel and pith from remaining orange. Cut sections from oranges. Cut off crown and bottom from pineapple. Cut off rind; remove eyes. Cut pineapple lengthwise into quarters; cut out core. Cut pineapple into bite-size chunks. Hull strawberries; cut each in half if large. Peel kiwifruit; cut into bite-size chunks. Cut nectarines into wedges.

◆ Place fruit in bowl with watermelon. Add grapes and orange sugar and toss to mix. Fill watermelon shell with fruit; cover with plastic wrap and refrigerate until ready to serve.

◆ Meanwhile, if you like, make a handle for basket: Cut florist wire into three 18-inch lengths. Wrap herb sprigs completely around wire; secure with clear thread. Tuck in flowers. Wrap with damp paper towels and plastic wrap; refrigerate. To serve, loosely twist wires together and insert ends into watermelon basket.

Each serving: About 115 calories, 2g protein, 29g carbohydrate, 1g total fat, 0mg cholesterol, 5mg sodium

POACHED FRUIT AND COMPOTES

Poaching is an easy and classic way to transform firm fresh or dried fruits into a deliciously succulent dessert. The fruit first gently simmers in a sugar syrup; the flavorful poaching liquid is then reduced to create an even richer syrup that will accompany the fruit. In these recipes we've infused the syrup with spices, herbs, and citrus peel to complement different fruits. Try serving any leftover fruit for breakfast.

HONEY-POACHED PEARS AND ORANGES

Prep: 30 minutes plus chilling   *Cook: 35 to 45 minutes*
Makes 8 servings

½ cup honey	8 firm, ripe pears (about
¼ cup sugar	4¼ pounds)
2 tablespoons fresh lemon	4 small navel oranges
juice	1 small lemon, sliced
6 whole cloves	Mint leaves for garnish

1 In 5-quart Dutch oven or saucepot, stir together honey, sugar, lemon juice, cloves, and *4 cups water*. Peel pears. With melon baller, remove cores from bottom of pears; do not remove stems. Immediately place pears in honey mixture, turning to coat. Heat to boiling over high heat.

2 Reduce heat to low; cover and simmer 10 to 20 minutes, until pears are tender when pierced with knife. With slotted spoon, transfer pears to large bowl. Meanwhile, with paring knife, cut peel and white pith from oranges; discard.

3 To poaching liquid, add oranges; heat to boiling over high heat. Reduce heat to medium-low; simmer, uncovered, 5 minutes, turning occasionally.

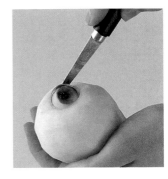

4 With slotted spoon, add oranges to bowl with pears. Heat poaching liquid to boiling over medium-high heat; cook 10 minutes, uncovered, to reduce slightly. Pour hot syrup over fruit. Cool slightly. Cover and refrigerate, turning fruit occasionally, at least 3 hours, until well chilled. To serve, stir in lemon slices. Garnish with mint sprigs.

HONEY

One of the first sweeteners known to man, honey is made by bees from flower nectar. It is available in three forms: comb honey, complete with the wax honeycomb, which may also be eaten; cream or spun honey, which is finely crystallized; and liquid honey, which is free of crystals. The flavor of honey varies according to the flower it comes from; in general, the darker the color, the stronger the flavor. Kept covered in a cool, dark place, honey will last indefinitely. If it crystallizes, it can be liquefied by standing the opened jar in a bowl of hot water. When measuring honey for cooking, oil the cup or spoon first so the honey slips out easily.

EACH SERVING: ABOUT 260 CALORIES, 2g PROTEIN, 67g CARBOHYDRATE, 1g TOTAL FAT (0g SATURATED), 0mg CHOLESTEROL, 0mg SODIUM

AUTUMN FRUIT COMPOTE

Prep: 20 minutes plus chilling
Cook: 35 to 40 minutes
Makes 8 servings

1 medium orange
1 medium lemon
4 medium Golden Delicious or Jonagold
   apples, peeled, cored, and each cut
   into 16 wedges
1 package (8 ounces) mixed dried fruit
   (with pitted prunes)
½ (8-ounce) package dried Calimyrna figs
¼ cup dried tart cherries or cranberries
½ cup sugar
1 cinnamon stick (3 inches)

◆ With vegetable peeler, remove peel
from orange and lemon in 1-inch-wide
strips. Squeeze 2 tablespoons juice
from lemon.

◆ In 4-quart saucepan, heat orange
and lemon peels, lemon juice, apples,
mixed dried fruit, figs, dried cherries,
sugar, cinnamon stick, and *3 cups water*
to boiling over high heat, stirring to
dissolve sugar. Reduce heat to low;
cover and simmer 15 to 20 minutes,
until apples are tender. Cool slightly.

◆ Pour fruit mixture into bowl; cover
and refrigerate at least 4 hours to
blend flavors. Serve chilled or at room
temperature.

**Each serving: About 225 calories,
1g protein, 55g carbohydrate, 0g total fat,
0mg cholesterol, 40mg sodium**

HERB-POACHED PEACHES

Prep: 20 minutes plus chilling
Cook: 35 to 40 minutes
Makes 8 servings

4 large lemons
½ cup sugar
1 bay leaf
3 thyme sprigs
8 firm, ripe peaches (about 3 pounds)
2 tablespoons peach jam
1 small lemon, thinly sliced,
   for garnish

◆ Grate peel from 1 large lemon.
Squeeze ½ cup juice from large lemons.

◆ In 5-quart Dutch oven or saucepot,
stir together lemon peel, lemon juice,
sugar, bay leaf, 2 thyme sprigs, and
4½ cups water.

◆ Peel peaches. As each peach is
peeled, immediately place in lemon-
juice mixture, turning to coat
completely to help prevent darkening.

◆ Heat peach mixture to boiling over
high heat, stirring to dissolve sugar.
Reduce heat to low; cover and simmer
5 to 10 minutes, until peaches are
tender. With slotted spoon, transfer
peaches to large bowl.

◆ Heat poaching liquid to boiling
over high heat; cook, uncovered, about
15 minutes, until liquid is reduced to
about 1½ cups. Stir in peach jam until
dissolved. Pour hot syrup over peaches
in bowl. Cool slightly.

◆ Cover and refrigerate, turning
peaches occasionally, at least 4 hours,
until well chilled.

◆ To serve, discard bay leaf. Serve
peaches with syrup; garnish with lemon
slices and remaining thyme sprig.

**Each serving: About 140 calories,
1g protein, 38g carbohydrate, 0g total fat,
0mg cholesterol, 0mg sodium**

LEMON-ANISE POACHED PEARS

Prep: 20 minutes plus chilling
Cook: 40 to 50 minutes
Makes 8 servings

2 medium lemons
8 firm, ripe pears (about 4¼ pounds)
1 cup sugar
2 tablespoons whole star anise or
   2 cinnamon sticks (3 inches each)
1 small navel orange, thinly sliced, for
   garnish

◆ Squeeze juice from 1 lemon into
8-quart Dutch oven. Thinly slice
remaining lemon. Peel pears. With
melon baller, remove cores from
bottom of pears; do not remove stems.

◆ Add pears, lemon slices, sugar, star
anise, and *6 cups water* to Dutch oven.
Heat to boiling over high heat, stirring
to dissolve sugar. Reduce heat to low;
cover and simmer 10 to 20 minutes,
until pears are tender. With slotted
spoon, transfer pears to large bowl.

◆ Heat poaching liquid to boiling
over high heat; cook, uncovered,
15 minutes, or until reduced to about
3 cups. Pour hot syrup over pears.
Cool slightly. Cover; refrigerate,
turning occasionally, at least 4 hours,
until pears are well chilled. Serve pears
with syrup; garnish with orange slices.

**Each serving: About 250 calories,
1g protein, 65g carbohydrate, 1g total fat
(0g saturated), 0mg cholesterol,
0mg sodium**

STAR ANISE

A star-shaped seed pod from a type of
magnolia shrub, star anise has a mild
licorice flavor and is a common ingredient
in Chinese cooking. It is generally used
whole for its attractive appearance. You
will find star anise in the
spice section of some
supermarkets or in
Asian food
markets.

Fruit Shortcakes

Shortcakes may look fancy, but they're simply biscuits or cakes dressed up with sweet, juicy fruit and thick whipped cream. We have a cake-based summer classic, a strawberry shortcake; a peach and blueberry version; and a giant shortcake showcasing mixed berries. Be sure to serve shortcakes right after they're assembled.

BLUEBERRY-PEACH SHORTCAKES

◆◆◆◆◆◆◆◆◆◆◆◆◆

Prep: 30 minutes
Bake: 16 to 22 minutes
Makes 8 servings

2 tablespoons fresh lemon juice

1 tablespoon cornstarch

1½ pints blueberries (about 3½ cups)

1 cup plus 3 tablespoons sugar

2 pounds peaches (about 6 medium), peeled (see right) and each cut into 8 wedges

3 cups all-purpose flour

4½ teaspoons baking powder

¾ teaspoon salt

10 tablespoons cold margarine or butter

1 cup plus 2 tablespoons milk

1 cup heavy or whipping cream

1 In 3-quart saucepan, mix lemon juice and cornstarch until smooth. Stir in blueberries and ⅔ cup sugar; heat to boiling over medium-high heat. Reduce heat to medium; cook 1 minute. Stir in peaches; set aside.

2 Preheat oven to 425°F. In bowl, mix flour, baking powder, salt, and ⅓ cup sugar. With pastry blender or two knives used scissor-fashion, cut in 9 tablespoons margarine until mixture resembles coarse crumbs.

3 Stir in milk just until mixture forms a soft dough that leaves side of bowl. On lightly floured surface, knead dough 6 to 8 times, just until smooth. With lightly floured hands, pat dough ¾ inch thick.

4 With floured 3-inch round biscuit cutter, cut out shortcakes. With pancake turner, place shortcakes 1 inch apart on ungreased large cookie sheet.

5 Press trimmings together; cut to make 8 shortcakes in all. Melt remaining 1 tablespoon margarine; brush over shortcakes. Sprinkle with 1 tablespoon sugar. Bake 16 to 22 minutes, until golden. In small bowl, with mixer at medium speed, beat cream with remaining 2 tablespoons sugar to soft peaks. With fork, split warm shortcakes in half. Spoon some fruit into each; top with cream, then more fruit.

PEELING PEACHES

Plunge peaches into pan of boiling water for 30 seconds. With slotted spoon, transfer to large bowl filled with ice water to cover; cool. With fingers or small paring knife, slip off skin. If desired, rub peeled peaches with lemon juice to prevent discoloration.

EACH SERVING: ABOUT 610 CALORIES, 8g PROTEIN, 89g CARBOHYDRATE, 27g TOTAL FAT (10 g SATURATED), 45mg CHOLESTEROL, 670mg SODIUM

BERRIES AND CREAM SHORTCAKE

Prep: 25 minutes plus cooling   Bake: 25 to 30 minutes
Makes 10 servings

½ cup margarine or butter, softened	2 large eggs
1 cup plus 1 tablespoon sugar	1 pint blueberries
1½ cups cake flour (not self-rising)	½ pint strawberries, hulled and each cut in half
½ cup milk	½ pint raspberries
1½ teaspoons baking powder	½ pint blackberries
1 teaspoon vanilla extract	¼ cup strawberry jam
¼ teaspoon salt	1 cup heavy or whipping cream

◆ Preheat oven to 350°F. Grease and flour two 8-inch round cake pans.

◆ In large bowl, with mixer at low speed, beat margarine and 1 cup sugar just until blended. Increase speed to high; beat about 5 minutes, until light and creamy. Reduce speed to low; add flour, milk, baking powder, vanilla, salt, and eggs; beat until well mixed, frequently scraping bowl with rubber spatula. Increase speed to high; beat 2 minutes longer, occasionally scraping bowl.

◆ Spoon batter into pans. Bake 25 to 30 minutes, until toothpick inserted in centers of cakes comes out clean. Cool cake layers in pans on wire racks 10 minutes. Remove from pans; cool completely on racks. Meanwhile, in large bowl, gently toss all berries with strawberry jam.

◆ In small bowl, with mixer at medium speed, beat cream with remaining 1 tablespoon sugar until stiff peaks form.

◆ Place 1 cake layer on plate. Spread with half of whipped cream; top with half of fruit mixture. Place second cake layer on fruit mixture; top with remaining cream and fruit.

Each serving: About 385 calories, 4g protein, 50g carbohydrate, 20g total fat (8g saturated), 77mg cholesterol, 265mg sodium

CLASSIC STRAWBERRY SHORTCAKE

Prep: 30 minutes plus cooling   Bake: 30 to 35 minutes
Makes 12 servings

1 cup milk	1 tablespoon baking powder
4 tablespoons margarine or butter	½ teaspoon salt
4 large eggs	3 pints strawberries
1½ cups plus ⅓ cup granulated sugar	2 cups heavy or whipping cream
1½ teaspoons vanilla extract	¼ cup confectioners' sugar
1¾ cups all-purpose flour	Mint sprigs for garnish

◆ Preheat oven to 350°F. Grease 13" by 9" metal baking pan. In 1-quart saucepan, heat milk and margarine over medium heat until margarine melts. Set aside.

◆ In large bowl, with mixer at high speed, beat eggs, 1½ cups granulated sugar, and 1 teaspoon vanilla 2 to 3 minutes, until very thick and lemon-colored. Reduce speed to low. Add flour, baking powder, and salt; beat 1 minute, frequently scraping bowl with rubber spatula. Add hot milk mixture; beat 1 minute longer, or until batter is smooth.

◆ Pour batter into pan. Bake 30 to 35 minutes, until cake is golden and top springs back when lightly pressed. Cool cake completely in pan on wire rack.

◆ Hull and thinly slice strawberries. In large bowl, mix sliced strawberries with remaining ⅓ cup granulated sugar.

◆ Cut cake lengthwise into 3 strips, then cut each strip crosswise into 4 pieces. In small bowl, with mixer at medium speed, beat cream, confectioners' sugar, and remaining ½ teaspoon vanilla until soft peaks form. To serve, place each piece of cake on a dessert plate; top with some sliced strawberries with their syrup, then with some whipped cream. Garnish with mint.

Each serving: About 420 calories, 6g protein, 53g carbohydrate, 21g total fat (11g saturated), 128mg cholesterol, 300mg sodium

WHAT'S IN A NAME?

Probably originating in New England, strawberry shortcake has been an all-American favorite since the 1850s. The most traditional version is made with fluffy, warm baking-powder biscuits, split and buttered, then filled with fruit. The permutations are endless, however. The biscuit may be individual or large, sweeter or richer, buttered or not.... It might not be a biscuit at all, but sponge or pound cake, piecrust, or even sweet, rich bread. Peaches and other berries also make a luscious filling, with ice cream or whipped cream to top it off.

CRISPS AND COBBLERS

These old-fashioned desserts are pure comfort food. What's more, neither crisps nor cobblers require any special ingredients; just choose the best and ripest fruit you can find. It takes mere minutes to make the fruit filling and to mix up the biscuit or crumb topping – then just pop the pan in the oven and dessert is done. Ice cream is perfect on the side.

RHUBARB-STRAWBERRY COBBLER WITH SPICE BISCUITS

◆◆◆◆◆◆◆◆◆◆◆◆◆

Prep: 20 minutes plus cooling
Bake: 20 minutes
Makes 8 servings

1¼ pounds rhubarb, cut into 1-inch chunks (4 cups)
¾ cup plus 1 teaspoon sugar
1 tablespoon cornstarch
1 pint strawberries, hulled and each cut into quarters
1½ cups all-purpose flour
1½ teaspoons baking powder
½ teaspoon baking soda
¼ teaspoon salt
¼ teaspoon ground cinnamon
⅛ teaspoon ground nutmeg
4 tablespoons margarine or butter
¾ cup plus 1 tablespoon heavy or whipping cream

1 In 3-quart saucepan, heat rhubarb and ½ cup sugar to boiling over high heat, stirring constantly. Reduce heat to medium-low; cook about 8 minutes, until rhubarb is tender.

2 In cup, mix cornstarch and ¼ cup water. Stir cornstarch mixture and strawberries into cooked rhubarb; cook 2 minutes longer, or until slightly thickened. Keep warm.

3 Preheat oven to 400°F. Prepare biscuits: In large bowl, mix flour, next 5 ingredients, and ¼ cup sugar. With pastry blender or two knives used scissor-fashion, cut in margarine until mixture resembles coarse crumbs. Add ¾ cup cream; stir just until mixture forms a soft dough that leaves side of bowl. Turn onto lightly floured surface.

4 Knead dough 6 to 8 times, just until smooth. With floured rolling pin, roll dough ½ inch thick. With 3-inch star-shaped cookie cutter, cut out biscuits.

5 Reroll trimmings; cut to make 8 biscuits in all. Pour hot rhubarb mixture into shallow 2-quart casserole or 11" by 7" glass baking dish. Place biscuits on top.

6 Brush biscuits with remaining 1 tablespoon cream; sprinkle with remaining 1 teaspoon sugar. Place sheet of foil under baking dish; crimp edges to form rim to catch any drips during baking. Bake 20 minutes, or until biscuits are golden brown and rhubarb mixture is bubbly. Cool slightly on wire rack, about 15 minutes, to serve warm.

EACH SERVING: ABOUT 315 CALORIES, 4g PROTEIN, 43g CARBOHYDRATE, 15g TOTAL FAT (7g SATURATED), 33mg CHOLESTEROL, 315mg SODIUM

COUNTRY APPLE CRISP

Prep: 30 minutes plus cooling   Bake: 30 to 35 minutes
Makes 8 servings

1 large orange
2½ pounds Golden Delicious
or Cortland apples (about
7 medium), peeled, cored,
and cut into 1-inch slices
½ cup dried cherries or raisins
1 teaspoon ground cinnamon
½ teaspoon salt
¼ teaspoon ground nutmeg

⅓ cup plus ¼ cup packed light
brown sugar
2 tablespoons plus ⅓ cup all-
purpose flour
½ cup quick-cooking or old-
fashioned oats, uncooked
3 tablespoons margarine or
butter

◆ Preheat oven to 425°F. Grate ½ teaspoon peel and squeeze
⅓ cup juice from orange. In shallow 2-quart glass or ceramic
baking dish, toss orange peel, orange juice, apples, next
4 ingredients, ⅓ cup brown sugar, and 2 tablespoons flour.

◆ Prepare topping: In small bowl, mix oats and remaining
⅓ cup flour and ¼ cup brown sugar. With pastry blender or
two knives used scissor-fashion, cut in margarine until mixture
resembles coarse crumbs. Sprinkle over apple mixture.

◆ Bake 30 to 35 minutes, until apples are tender and
topping is lightly browned, covering with foil if necessary to
prevent overbrowning. Cool slightly on wire rack to serve
warm. Or, cool completely to serve later; reheat if desired.

Each serving: About 260 calories, 2g protein, 53g carbohydrate,
5g total fat (1g saturated), 0mg cholesterol, 190mg sodium

NECTARINE AND CHERRY CRISP WITH OATMEAL TOPPING

Prep: 30 minutes plus cooling   Bake: 1 hour to 1 hour 15 minutes
Makes 12 servings

½ cup sugar
3 tablespoons cornstarch
3 pounds ripe nectarines
(about 10 medium), each
cut into 6 wedges
1½ pounds dark sweet
cherries, pitted
2 tablespoons fresh lemon
juice
8 tablespoons margarine or
butter

⅔ cup packed light brown
sugar
1 large egg
2 teaspoons vanilla extract
1½ cups old-fashioned oats,
uncooked
¾ cup all-purpose flour
¼ teaspoon salt
¼ teaspoon baking soda

◆ Preheat oven to 375°F. In large bowl, with wire whisk or
fork, mix sugar and cornstarch. Add nectarines, cherries,
and lemon juice and toss until fruit is evenly coated.
Spoon fruit mixture into 13" by 9" glass baking dish; dot
with 2 tablespoons margarine. Cover with foil; bake 40 to
50 minutes, until fruit mixture is gently bubbling.

◆ Meanwhile, prepare oatmeal topping: In large bowl, with
mixer at medium-high speed, beat brown sugar and
remaining 6 tablespoons margarine, softened, until smooth.
Add egg and vanilla; beat until light and creamy. With
wooden spoon, stir in oats and remaining ingredients until
mixed. Cover and refrigerate until ready to use.

◆ Drop topping by scant ¼ cups over baked fruit. Bake
nectarine crisp, uncovered, 20 to 25 minutes longer, until
topping is browned. Cool slightly on wire rack to serve
warm. Or, cool completely to serve later; reheat if desired.

Each serving: About 325 calories, 5g protein, 58g carbohydrate,
10g total fat (2g saturated), 18mg cholesterol, 170mg sodium

LIGHT PLUM COBBLER

Prep: 20 minutes plus cooling   Bake: 50 to 60 minutes
Makes 10 servings

2½ pounds ripe red or purple
plums (about 10 medium),
each cut into 4 wedges
2 tablespoons all-purpose
flour

½ cup sugar
1¾ cups reduced-fat all-
purpose baking mix
¼ cup yellow cornmeal

◆ Preheat oven to 400°F. In large bowl, toss plums with
flour and sugar. Spoon plum mixture into shallow 2-quart
ceramic or glass baking dish. Cover loosely with foil. Bake
30 to 35 minutes, until plums are very tender.

◆ In medium bowl, mix baking mix and cornmeal with
¾ cup water until just combined. Drop 10 heaping spoonfuls
of batter randomly over baked plums. Bake cobbler,
uncovered, 20 to 25 minutes longer, until biscuits are
browned and plum mixture is bubbling. Cool slightly on
wire rack to serve warm. Or, cool completely to serve later;
reheat if desired.

Each serving: About 200 calories, 3g protein, 43g carbohydrate,
2g total fat (0g saturated), 0mg cholesterol, 240mg sodium

WHAT'S IN A NAME?

It's easy to be confused by the variety of names for
cooked fruit desserts. A *cobbler* is fruit baked with a
biscuit crust, while a *crisp* is baked with a rich crumb
topping. To make a *slump* or *grunt*, spoonfuls of dough
are steamed atop a hot fruit mixture in a saucepot. A
pandowdy is made with fruit topped with pastry; before
the crust is baked completely, it's cut up and pressed
back into the fruit to absorb the juices. *Brown Betty* is a
dessert of fruit (especially apples) layered with buttered
bread crumbs and spices and baked until tender.

BAKED FRUIT DESSERTS

Baking heightens the flavor of many fruits and gives them a pleasing mellow texture. Here we've wrapped apples in pastry to create tempting dumplings; given pears an Italian nuance with sweet Marsala and lemon; and enhanced ripe plums with a crumbly almond topping. These desserts are best served warm, with half-and-half or light cream, or ice cream, if you like.

OLD-FASHIONED APPLE DUMPLINGS

Prep: 40 minutes *Bake:* 35 to 40 minutes

Makes 6 servings

2½ cups all-purpose flour

1 teaspoon salt

8 tablespoons light brown sugar

1 cup shortening

½ cup diced mixed dried fruit

2 tablespoons margarine or butter

1½ teaspoons ground cinnamon

6 small Golden Delicious apples (6 ounces each)

1 large egg, beaten

6 whole cloves

1 In large bowl, mix flour, salt, and 2 tablespoons brown sugar. With pastry blender or two knives used scissor-fashion, cut in shortening until mixture resembles coarse crumbs. Stir in *5 to 6 tablespoons cold water* until dough holds together; set aside. In small bowl, mix dried fruit, margarine, 4 tablespoons brown sugar, and 1 teaspoon cinnamon.

2 Peel apples. With melon baller, remove cores but do not go all the way through to bottom. Press dried-fruit mixture into cavities. Preheat oven to 400°F. Grease 15½" by 10½" jelly-roll pan.

3 Reserve ⅓ cup dough. On floured surface, with floured rolling pin, roll out remaining dough, using a ruler to help push and shape dough into 21" by 14" rectangle. Cut dough into six 7-inch squares.

4 On waxed paper, mix remaining 2 tablespoons brown sugar and ½ teaspoon cinnamon. Roll an apple in sugar mixture. Center apple on a dough square; brush edges of dough with some beaten egg.

5 Bring dough up over top of apple. Press to shape; seal edges. Place dumpling in jelly-roll pan. Repeat with remaining apples, sugar mixture, and dough squares, and more beaten egg, to make 6 dumplings in all.

6 Roll reserved dough ⅛ inch thick. Using knife, cut out as many leaves as possible (see page 61); reroll scraps and cut out more leaves. Score leaves with back of knife to make veins. Brush dumplings with egg. Attach leaves; brush with egg. Press in cloves for stems. Bake dumplings 35 to 40 minutes, until pastry is golden and apples are tender when pierced with knife.

EACH SERVING: ABOUT 730 CALORIES, 7g PROTEIN, 90g CARBOHYDRATE, 40g TOTAL FAT (10g SATURATED), 36mg CHOLESTEROL, 435mg SODIUM

ROASTED ALMOND-CRUST PLUMS

Prep: 15 minutes   Bake: 25 to 35 minutes
Makes 6 servings

1½ pounds ripe plums, each cut in half	¼ cup all-purpose flour
⅓ cup sliced natural almonds	3 tablespoons margarine or butter, softened
⅓ cup packed brown sugar	Vanilla ice cream (optional)

Preheat oven to 425°F. Arrange plums, cut-side up, in one layer in shallow baking dish. In medium bowl, with fingertips, mix almonds and next 3 ingredients until mixture comes together. Sprinkle over plums. Bake 25 to 35 minutes, until plums are tender. Serve hot, with ice cream, if you like.

Each serving: About 205 calories, 3g protein, 31g carbohydrate, 9g total fat (1g saturated), 0mg cholesterol, 70mg sodium

CLAFOUTI

Prep: 20 minutes   Bake: 40 to 45 minutes
Makes 12 servings

1 pound dark sweet cherries, pitted	4 large eggs
⅔ cup all-purpose flour	2 cups half-and-half or light cream
⅓ cup granulated sugar	Confectioners' sugar for garnish
2 tablespoons amaretto (almond-flavor liqueur)	

◆ Preheat oven to 350°F. Grease 10" by 1½" round ceramic baking dish. Place cherries in dish. In blender at low speed, blend flour, granulated sugar, amaretto, eggs, and 1 cup half-and-half 30 seconds. With motor running, gradually add remaining 1 cup half-and-half; blend 30 seconds longer.

◆ Pour egg mixture over cherries in baking dish. Bake 40 to 45 minutes, until custard is set and knife inserted 1 inch from edge comes out clean (center will still jiggle). Serve hot, sprinkled with confectioners' sugar.

Each serving: About 160 calories, 4g protein, 20g carbohydrate, 7g total fat (3g saturated), 86mg cholesterol, 40mg sodium

CHERRY PITTER

This pliers-like tool made from aluminum or stainless steel makes short work of pitting cherries and gives a cleaner result than using a paring knife. It can also be used for pitting olives.

CARIBBEAN BAKED BANANAS

Prep: 10 minutes   Bake: 15 minutes
Makes 4 servings

2 tablespoons dark rum	2 tablespoons margarine or butter, melted
½ teaspoon grated lime peel	½ cup flaked coconut
4 large ripe bananas, cut into ½-inch slices	Vanilla ice cream (optional)
2 tablespoons brown sugar	

◆ Preheat oven to 425°F. In 9-inch pie plate or shallow baking dish, combine rum and lime peel. Add bananas, tossing to coat.

◆ In small bowl, mix brown sugar and melted margarine until smooth. Stir in coconut. Spoon coconut mixture evenly over bananas. Bake 15 minutes, or until coconut is golden brown. Serve hot, with ice cream, if you like.

Each serving: About 280 calories, 2g protein, 46g carbohydrate, 10g total fat (5g saturated), 0mg cholesterol, 100mg sodium

BAKED PEARS WITH MARSALA

Prep: 25 minutes plus cooling   Bake: 40 to 50 minutes
Makes 8 servings

1 medium lemon	½ cup sweet Marsala wine
8 firm Bosc pears	2 tablespoons margarine or butter, melted
2 teaspoons plus ⅓ cup sugar	

◆ Preheat oven to 450°F. With vegetable peeler or small knife, remove peel from lemon in 2½" by ½" strips; squeeze juice from lemon.

◆ With melon baller or small knife, remove cores from bottom of unpeeled pears but do not remove stems. With pastry brush, brush insides of pears with lemon juice, then sprinkle insides with a total of 2 teaspoons sugar.

◆ In shallow 1½- to 2-quart ceramic or glass baking dish, mix lemon-peel strips, Marsala, and ⅓ *cup water*. Place remaining ⅓ cup sugar on sheet of waxed paper.

◆ With pastry brush, brush pears with melted margarine, then roll in sugar to coat. Place pears, cored-ends down, in baking dish. Sprinkle any sugar remaining on waxed paper around pears in baking dish.

◆ Bake pears, basting occasionally with syrup in dish, 40 to 50 minutes, until fork-tender. Cool slightly to serve warm. Or, cool pears completely; cover and refrigerate up to 1 day and reheat to serve warm.

Each serving: About 170 calories, 1g protein, 34g carbohydrate, 3g total fat (2g saturated), 8mg cholesterol, 30mg sodium

RICE PUDDINGS

These creamy, mild-flavored puddings are made of the simplest ingredients – basically rice, milk, and sugar. Short-grain rice such as Italian Arborio gives an especially creamy texture, but regular long-grain rice also makes a delicious pudding. Avoid using parboiled rice, which will never become as soft. Each of these puddings is as comforting served warm as it is cold.

VANILLA RICE PUDDING WITH DRIED CHERRIES

◆◆◆◆◆◆◆◆◆◆◆◆

Prep: 15 minutes plus chilling
Cook: 1 hour 30 minutes
Makes 12 servings

½ **vanilla bean or 1 tablespoon vanilla extract**
6 **cups milk**
¾ **cup sugar**
¾ **cup Arborio rice (Italian short-grain rice) or regular long-grain rice**
½ **cup dried cherries or raisins**
2 **tablespoons dark rum**
¼ **teaspoon salt**
½ **cup heavy or whipping cream**

1 With knife, cut vanilla bean lengthwise in half. Scrape out and reserve seeds from inside of both halves. Place bean halves and seeds in 4-quart saucepan. (If using vanilla extract, stir in with rum in Step 3.)

2 Add milk and sugar to saucepan; heat to boiling over medium-high heat, stirring occasionally. Stir in rice; heat to boiling. Reduce heat to low.

3 Cover; simmer 1¼ hours, stirring occasionally, until very creamy and slightly thickened. Discard vanilla-bean halves. Spoon into large bowl; stir in cherries, rum, and salt.

VANILLA BEANS

The dried pod of an orchid native to Central America, vanilla adds its familiar but intriguing aroma to a vast range of sweet dishes. The bean is usually split before use and the seeds scraped out; both bean and seeds are added to the dish. Pure vanilla extract provides flavor in a more convenient form. Vanillin (unless labeled "natural"), imitation vanilla, and "vanilla flavor" are based on synthetic vanillin, which is strong in flavor and may have a harsh aftertaste. You can make vanilla sugar by placing a split bean in a storage jar with 1 to 2 cups of sugar; leave 24 hours before using. Top up the sugar each time you use some; the bean will last up to 1 year.

4 Cool slightly; cover and refrigerate at least 6 hours. Up to 2 hours before serving, whip cream until stiff peaks form. Fold whipped cream, half at a time, into rice pudding.

EACH SERVING: ABOUT 230 CALORIES, 5g PROTEIN, 33g CARBOHYDRATE, 8g TOTAL FAT (5g SATURATED), 30mg CHOLESTEROL, 110mg SODIUM

LEFTOVER-RICE PUDDING

Prep: 5 minutes   Cook: 25 minutes
Makes 4 servings

2 cups milk	2 tablespoons sugar
1 cup cooked rice	¼ cup raisins or dried cherries
1 cinnamon stick (3 inches) or	(optional)
⅛ teaspoon ground	
cinnamon	

In 3-quart saucepan, heat milk, rice, cinnamon stick, and sugar to boiling over high heat. Reduce heat to medium-low; boil gently 20 minutes, stirring occasionally. Stir in raisins, if using, during last 5 minutes of cooking. Remove from heat. Discard cinnamon stick. Serve warm, or cover and refrigerate to serve cold later.

Each serving: About 150 calories, 5g protein, 23g carbohydrate, 4g total fat (3g saturated), 17mg cholesterol, 60mg sodium

COCONUT RICE PUDDING

Prep: 5 minutes plus standing   Cook: 35 minutes
Makes 6 servings

⅔ cup regular long-grain rice	⅓ cup sugar
½ teaspoon salt	Toasted flaked coconut
1 can (15 ounces)	(optional)
unsweetened coconut milk	

In 3-quart saucepan, heat rice, salt, and *2 cups water* to boiling over medium-high heat. Reduce heat to low; cover and simmer 15 minutes. Stir in coconut milk and sugar. Cook, uncovered, 10 minutes longer, stirring occasionally. Remove from heat. Let stand 20 minutes. Serve warm, or cover and refrigerate to serve cold later. Just before serving, sprinkle with toasted coconut, if you like.

Each serving: About 280 calories, 3g protein, 32g carbohydrate, 17g total fat (15g saturated), 0mg cholesterol, 190mg sodium

COCONUT MILK

Canned unsweetened coconut milk (not to be confused with the thin, milky liquid that drains from a fresh coconut when you crack the shell) is a blend of coconut meat and water processed to a paste and strained. A basic ingredient in Thai and other Asian cuisines, it adds a rich and exotic flavor to soups, sauces, meat and seafood curries, and desserts. Cream of coconut, a richer mixture containing sugar and stabilizers, is used in drinks and desserts. Once opened, canned coconut milk can be refrigerated in an airtight container for up to 1 week or frozen for 6 months.

CREAMY CARDAMOM RICE PUDDING

Prep: 5 minutes   Cook: 1 hour 15 minutes
Makes 6 servings

4 cups milk	½ teaspoon salt
⅓ cup regular long-grain rice	2 large egg yolks
⅓ cup sugar	⅓ cup heavy or whipping
5 cardamom pods	cream

◆ In 5-quart Dutch oven, heat milk, rice, sugar, cardamom, and salt to boiling over medium-high heat, stirring occasionally. Reduce heat to low; cover and simmer 1 hour, stirring occasionally.

◆ In medium bowl, whisk egg yolks with cream. Gradually whisk in 1 cup hot rice pudding. Return mixture to Dutch oven; cook over low heat, stirring constantly, 3 minutes, or until mixture just begins to bubble. Pour into serving bowl. Serve warm, or cover and refrigerate to serve cold later.

Each serving: About 245 calories, 7g protein, 28g carbohydrate, 12g total fat (7g saturated), 111mg cholesterol, 265mg sodium

BAKED CUSTARD RICE PUDDING

Prep: 20 minutes plus cooling   Bake: 1 hour 15 minutes
Makes 8 servings

½ cup regular long-grain rice	3 large eggs
4 strips (3" by 1" each)	½ cup sugar
orange peel	3 cups milk
½ teaspoon salt	1 teaspoon vanilla extract

◆ Preheat oven to 350°F. In 2-quart saucepan, heat rice, orange peel, salt, and *2 cups water* to boiling over medium-high heat. Reduce heat to low; cover and simmer 15 minutes. Remove and discard orange peel.

◆ In large bowl, whisk eggs and sugar until well blended. Whisk in milk and vanilla. Stir in hot rice. Pour mixture into shallow 1½-quart glass baking dish, stirring to distribute rice. Place baking dish in larger roasting pan; carefully pour *boiling water* into roasting pan to come halfway up sides of baking dish.

◆ Bake 1¼ hours, or until knife inserted halfway between center and edge of pudding comes out clean. Remove baking dish from roasting pan; cool on wire rack 30 minutes. Serve pudding warm, or cover and refrigerate to serve cold later.

Each serving: About 180 calories, 6g protein, 27g carbohydrate, 5g total fat (3g saturated), 92mg cholesterol, 205mg sodium

BAKED PUDDINGS

Baked puddings owe much of their charm to their simplicity. We've included a British toffee pudding with a sticky brown-sugar topping; a delicate orange pudding that forms its own sauce; and a rich, rich chocolate pudding. For maximum pleasure, serve warm.

STICKY TOFFEE PUDDING

◆◆◆◆◆◆◆◆◆◆◆◆◆

Prep: 20 minutes plus standing and cooling
Bake: 30 minutes
Makes 12 servings

1 cup chopped pitted dates
1 teaspoon baking soda
10 tablespoons margarine or butter, softened
1 cup granulated sugar
1 large egg
1 teaspoon vanilla extract
2 cups all-purpose flour
1 teaspoon baking powder
1 cup packed brown sugar
¼ cup heavy or whipping cream
Whipped cream (optional)

1 Preheat oven to 350°F. Grease a 13" by 9" broiler-safe baking pan. In medium bowl, combine dates, baking soda, and *1½ cups boiling water*; let stand 15 minutes.

2 In large bowl, with mixer at medium speed, beat 6 tablespoons margarine until creamy. Beat in granulated sugar. Add egg and vanilla; beat until blended.

3 At low speed, add flour and baking powder. Add date mixture and beat until evenly combined (batter will be thin). Pour batter into pan. Bake 30 minutes, or until golden and toothpick inserted in center comes out clean. Meanwhile, in 2-quart saucepan, heat brown sugar, cream, and remaining 4 tablespoons margarine to boiling over medium heat; boil 1 minute. Set aside. Turn oven control to broil.

WHAT'S IN A NAME?

The word "pudding" often describes a creamy, soft stovetop dessert made with milk, sugar, and eggs, and thickened with a starch, such as flour, rice, or cornstarch. It also applies to a wide range of sweet dishes, including bread pudding and steamed or baked cakelike desserts such as plum pudding or the Sticky Toffee Pudding on this page. In England, desserts in general may be referred to as "pudding," although two of the country's best-known puddings are savory: steak and kidney pudding (a pastry crust filled with meat) and Yorkshire Pudding, the traditional accompaniment to roast beef.

4 Spread brown-sugar mixture evenly over hot pudding. Broil at closest position to heat source about 30 seconds, or until bubbly. Cool in pan on wire rack 15 minutes. Serve warm, with whipped cream, if you like.

EACH SERVING: ABOUT 355 CALORIES, 3g PROTEIN, 61g CARBOHYDRATE, 12g TOTAL FAT (3g SATURATED), 25mg CHOLESTEROL, 270mg SODIUM

CHOCOLATE FUDGE PUDDING

Prep: 25 minutes   *Bake:* 40 minutes
Makes 8 servings

1 cup milk
4 large eggs, separated
½ cup plus 2 tablespoons
   granulated sugar
⅓ cup all-purpose flour
3 squares (3 ounces)
   unsweetened chocolate,
   melted

1 teaspoon vanilla
   extract
¼ teaspoon salt
Confectioners' sugar
Vanilla ice cream or whipped
   cream (optional)

◆ Preheat oven to 350°F. Grease 8" by 8" glass baking dish.

◆ In 3-quart saucepan, heat milk to boiling over medium-high heat. Meanwhile, in medium bowl, whisk egg yolks with ½ cup granulated sugar until smooth. Whisk in flour until combined. Gradually whisk hot milk into yolk mixture. Return mixture to saucepan; heat to boiling over medium-high heat, whisking constantly. Reduce heat to low; cook 1 minute, whisking. Remove from heat and whisk in melted chocolate, vanilla, and salt.

◆ In small bowl, with mixer at high speed, beat egg whites until soft peaks form; beat in remaining 2 tablespoons granulated sugar. Whisk one-third of whites into chocolate mixture until smooth; fold in remaining whites (batter will be stiff). Spoon evenly into baking dish.

◆ Place baking dish in roasting pan; carefully pour *boiling water* into roasting pan to come halfway up sides of dish. Bake 40 minutes, or until firm. Sift confectioners' sugar on top. Serve warm, with ice cream, if you like.

Each serving: About 190 calories, 6g protein, 25g carbohydrate, 9g total fat (4g saturated), 111mg cholesterol, 115mg sodium

◆◆◆◆◆◆◆◆◆◆◆◆◆◆◆◆◆◆◆◆◆◆◆◆◆◆

MELTING CHOCOLATE

You can melt chocolate in a heavy saucepan or double boiler on the stove top. The pan must be dry, as moisture will make the chocolate grainy. Melt over low heat, stirring constantly to prevent scorching. To microwave, place 1 to 4 ounces chocolate in a microwave-safe container; cook on Medium (50% power) for 1½ to 2 minutes.

Chocolate melted in the microwave retains its shape, so it won't look melted until it's stirred (above).

◆◆◆◆◆◆◆◆◆◆◆◆◆◆◆◆◆◆◆◆◆◆◆◆◆◆

INDIAN PUDDING

Prep: 30 minutes plus cooling   *Bake:* 2 hours
Makes 8 servings

⅔ cup yellow cornmeal
4 cups milk
½ cup light molasses
4 tablespoons margarine or
   butter, cut up
¼ cup sugar

1 teaspoon ground ginger
1 teaspoon ground cinnamon
½ teaspoon salt
¼ teaspoon ground nutmeg
Vanilla ice cream

◆ Preheat oven to 350°F. Grease shallow 1½-quart glass or ceramic baking dish. In small bowl, stir together cornmeal and 1 cup milk. In 4-quart saucepan, heat remaining 3 cups milk to boiling over high heat. Stir in cornmeal mixture; heat to boiling. Reduce heat to low and cook, stirring often, 20 minutes. Remove from heat. Stir in molasses and next 6 ingredients.

◆ Pour batter into baking dish. Cover with foil. Place dish in roasting pan; carefully pour *boiling water* into roasting pan to come halfway up sides of dish. Bake 1 hour. Remove foil; bake 1 hour longer. Remove from roasting pan; cool on wire rack 30 minutes. Serve warm with ice cream.

Each serving (without ice cream): 245 calories, 5g protein, 34g carbohydrate, 10g total fat (4g saturated), 17mg cholesterol, 265mg sodium

ORANGE PUDDING-CAKE

Prep: 20 minutes   *Bake:* 40 minutes
Makes 6 servings

¾ cup sugar
¼ cup all-purpose flour
⅛ teaspoon salt
1 cup milk
3 large eggs, separated

4 tablespoons margarine or
   butter, melted
¼ cup fresh lemon juice
¼ cup fresh orange juice
2 teaspoons grated orange peel

◆ Preheat oven to 350°F. Grease 8" by 8" glass baking dish. In large bowl, whisk sugar, flour, and salt until combined. Whisk in milk, egg yolks, and next 4 ingredients until smooth.

◆ In small bowl, with mixer at high speed, beat egg whites to soft peaks. Fold one-fourth of orange mixture into whites; fold whites back into orange mixture until evenly combined.

◆ Pour batter into baking dish. Place dish in roasting pan; carefully pour *boiling water* into roasting pan to come halfway up sides of dish. Bake 40 minutes, or until top is golden and set (dessert will separate into pudding and cake layers). Serve warm.

Each serving: About 250 calories, 5g protein, 33g carbohydrate, 11g total fat (3g saturated), 112mg cholesterol, 185mg sodium

Baked custards

Crème brûlée, crème caramel, and flan are nothing more than baked custards with elegant names. They can be varied with a wide range of flavors; here we've used butterscotch, chocolate, basic vanilla, and the surprise ingredient of pumpkin. For best results, take care not to overbake, or the mixture may become watery and start to separate. Baked custards are done even if the centers are still slightly jiggly – remember, they'll firm up as they cool.

Butterscotch crème brûlée

Prep: 20 minutes plus cooling and chilling   *Bake:* 1 hour
Makes 12 servings

3 cups half-and-half or light cream
4 tablespoons margarine or butter
¾ cup plus 2 tablespoons packed light brown sugar

9 large egg yolks
1½ teaspoons vanilla extract
Strawberries for garnish

1 Preheat oven to 325°F. In 2-quart saucepan, heat half-and-half over medium heat until tiny bubbles form around edge of pan.

2 Meanwhile, in heavy 3-quart saucepan, heat margarine and ¾ cup packed brown sugar to boiling over medium heat; boil 2 minutes, stirring constantly. Gradually whisk in warm half-and-half until mixture is completely smooth. Remove from heat. In medium bowl, with wire whisk or fork, beat egg yolks and vanilla until blended.

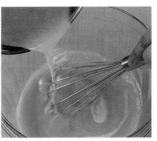

3 Slowly beat half-and-half mixture into egg-yolk mixture until well mixed. Pour into twelve 4-ounce ramekins or custard cups. Place ramekins in small roasting pan; place in oven.

4 Carefully pour *boiling water* into roasting pan to come halfway up sides of ramekins. Bake 1 hour, or just until set (mixture will be slightly soft in center). Remove ramekins from roasting pan; cool on wire rack. Refrigerate at least 3 hours, until well chilled.

5 Up to 4 hours before serving, preheat broiler. Place remaining 2 tablespoons brown sugar in small sieve. With spoon, press brown sugar through sieve over top of chilled custards.

6 Place ramekins in jelly-roll pan for easier handling. With rack in broiler at closest position to heat source, broil crème brûlée 3 to 4 minutes, just until sugar melts. Refrigerate until ready to serve. The melted brown sugar will form a shiny, crisp crust over the custard. Serve within 4 hours, or the crust will lose its crispness. To serve, arrange ramekins on platter and garnish platter with strawberries.

EACH SERVING: ABOUT 220 CALORIES, 4g PROTEIN, 19g CARBOHYDRATE, 15g TOTAL FAT (6g SATURATED), 182mg CHOLESTEROL, 80mg SODIUM

LOW-FAT CRÈME CARAMEL

Prep: 15 minutes plus cooling and chilling   *Bake:* 30 minutes
Makes 8 servings

1½ cups sugar	4 cups low-fat milk (1%)
3 large eggs	1 teaspoon vanilla extract
3 large egg whites	

◆ Preheat oven to 350°F. Grease eight 8-ounce custard cups. In 2-quart saucepan, heat 1 cup sugar and *2 tablespoons water* over medium heat until sugar is melted and a light caramel color. Immediately pour into custard cups.

◆ In large bowl, with wire whisk or fork, beat eggs, egg whites, and remaining ½ cup sugar until well blended. Beat in milk and vanilla; pour into custard cups. Skim foam from tops. Place cups in large roasting pan; place in oven. Carefully pour *boiling water* into roasting pan to come halfway up sides of cups. Bake 30 minutes, or until centers are just set. Remove cups from roasting pan; cool on wire rack. Refrigerate 3 hours, or until well chilled.

◆ To serve, with small spatula, carefully loosen custard from cups and invert each custard onto a dessert plate, allowing caramel syrup to drip from cup onto custard.

Each serving: About 235 calories, 8g protein, 44g carbohydrate, 3g total fat (1g saturated), 85mg cholesterol, 110mg sodium

CHOCOLATE POTS DE CRÈME

Prep: 15 minutes plus cooling and chilling   *Bake:* 30 to 35 minutes
Makes 6 servings

3 squares (3 ounces) semisweet chocolate	2 large egg yolks
2½ cups milk	¼ cup sugar
2 large eggs	1 teaspoon vanilla extract

◆ Preheat oven to 350°F. In 3-quart saucepan, heat chocolate and ¼ cup milk over low heat, stirring frequently, until chocolate is melted; remove from heat. In 2-quart saucepan, heat remaining 2¼ cups milk to boiling over medium-high heat; stir into chocolate mixture. In large bowl, whisk eggs, egg yolks, sugar, and vanilla until well blended. Gradually whisk in chocolate mixture. Pour evenly into six 6-ounce ramekins or custard cups. Place ramekins in roasting pan; place in oven.

◆ Carefully pour *boiling water* into roasting pan to come halfway up sides of ramekins. Cover roasting pan with foil, crimping edges loosely. Bake custards 30 to 35 minutes, until knife inserted halfway between edge and center of custard comes out clean.

◆ Remove foil; remove ramekins from roasting pan. Cool on wire rack. Refrigerate 3 hours, or until well chilled. Serve custards in ramekins.

Each serving: About 210 calories, 7g protein, 22g carbohydrate, 11g total fat (6g saturated), 156mg cholesterol, 75mg sodium

PUMPKIN FLAN

Prep: 15 minutes plus cooling and chilling   *Bake:* 50 minutes
Makes 12 servings

⅓ cup plus ¾ cup sugar	1 can (12 ounces) evaporated milk
8 large eggs	
2 cups milk	¾ teaspoon ground cinnamon
½ (16-ounce) can solid-pack pumpkin (not pumpkin-pie mix)	¼ teaspoon ground ginger
	¼ teaspoon ground nutmeg

◆ Preheat oven to 325°F. In 10-inch skillet, heat ⅓ cup sugar over medium heat, stirring constantly, until melted and a light caramel color. Immediately pour caramel syrup into 9" by 5" loaf pan, tilting pan to cover bottom completely.

◆ In large bowl, with wire whisk or fork, beat eggs and remaining ¾ cup sugar until well blended. Beat in milk, pumpkin, evaporated milk, cinnamon, ginger, and nutmeg until well mixed; pour mixture into loaf pan.

◆ Place loaf pan in 13" by 9" baking pan; place in oven. Caefully pour *boiling water* into baking pan to come halfway up sides of loaf pan. Bake about 50 minutes, until knife inserted in center of flan comes out clean.

◆ Remove loaf pan from baking pan. Cool on wire rack. Refrigerate flan 3 hours, or until well chilled.

◆ To serve, with small spatula, carefully loosen flan from loaf pan and invert onto a chilled large platter, allowing caramel syrup to drip from pan onto flan.

Each serving: About 190 calories, 8g protein, 25g carbohydrate, 7g total fat (3g saturated), 156mg cholesterol, 95mg sodium

SOUFFLÉS

Dessert soufflés are dazzling whether they're baked as puffy individual servings or as one giant soufflé. Despite their mystique, they are amazingly simple – follow our straightforward recipes for guaranteed light and airy results. Be sure to serve soufflés immediately from the oven, before they deflate.

APRICOT SOUFFLÉ

◆◆◆◆◆◆◆◆◆◆◆◆

Prep: 20 minutes plus cooling
Bake: 12 to 15 minutes
Makes 6 servings

1 package (6 ounces) dried apricots (about 1 cup)
¾ cup orange juice
About 2 tablespoons plus ¼ cup sugar
6 large egg whites
½ teaspoon cream of tartar
1 teaspoon vanilla extract

1 In small saucepan, heat apricots and orange juice to boiling over high heat. Reduce heat to low; cover and simmer 10 minutes, or until apricots are softened. In blender or food processor with knife blade attached, blend apricots with any liquid in pan until pureed. Place in large bowl; set aside to cool to room temperature. Preheat oven to 375°F. Grease six 6-ounce soufflé dishes or custard cups; sprinkle with about 2 tablespoons sugar.

2 In large bowl, with mixer at high speed, beat egg whites and cream of tartar until soft peaks form. Beat in vanilla. Beating at high speed, gradually sprinkle in remaining ¼ cup sugar until mixture holds stiff peaks when beaters are lifted.

3 With rubber spatula, gently fold one-third of beaten egg whites into apricot mixture to lighten mixture. Fold in remaining whites, half at a time. Spoon mixture into soufflé dishes.

FRESH PEAR SOUFFLÉ

Prepare Apricot Soufflé as recipe directs, but instead of the apricot-orange juice mixture in Step 1, make pear puree: In 2-quart saucepan, toss 4 cups peeled, coarsely chopped fully ripe pears (5 to 6 pears) with 1 tablespoon fresh lemon juice. Cook over high heat, covered, 15 minutes, or until pears are very tender. Uncover and cook 10 to 15 minutes longer, stirring occasionally, until mixture is almost dry. Transfer to blender or food processor with knife blade attached and blend until pureed. Place in large bowl; cool to room temperature. Proceed as recipe directs.

Each serving: About 165 calories, 4g protein, 39g carbohydrate, 1g total fat (0g saturated), 0mg cholesterol, 55mg sodium

4 With metal spatula held at a 45-degree angle to soufflé, make a domed peak on each soufflé. Place dishes on jelly-roll pan for easier handling. (If not serving right away, soufflés can be refrigerated for up to 3 hours before baking.) Bake soufflés 12 to 15 minutes, until puffed and golden. Serve immediately.

EACH SERVING: ABOUT 150 CALORIES, 5g PROTEIN, 34g CARBOHYDRATE, 0g TOTAL FAT, 0mg CHOLESTEROL, 60mg SODIUM

CHOCOLATE SOUFFLÉ

Prep: 20 minutes plus cooling   Bake: 30 minutes
Makes 6 servings

⅓ cup all-purpose flour
1 tablespoon instant espresso-coffee powder
About 1¼ cups granulated sugar
1 cup milk
3 tablespoons margarine or butter, softened

6 squares (6 ounces) unsweetened chocolate, coarsely chopped
6 large eggs, separated
2 teaspoons vanilla extract
¼ teaspoon salt
Confectioners' sugar for garnish

◆ In 3-quart saucepan, mix flour, espresso powder, and 1¼ cups granulated sugar; gradually stir in milk until blended. Cook over medium heat, stirring constantly, until mixture thickens and boils; boil 1 minute. Remove from heat.

◆ Stir in margarine and chocolate until melted and smooth. Beat in egg yolks all at once until well mixed. Stir in vanilla. Cool to lukewarm. Preheat oven to 350°F. Grease six 8-ounce soufflé dishes; sprinkle lightly with granulated sugar.

◆ In large bowl, with mixer at high speed, beat egg whites and salt to stiff peaks. With rubber spatula, gently fold one-third of beaten egg whites into chocolate mixture; gently fold back into remaining whites. Pour into soufflé dishes. Bake 30 minutes (centers will be fudgy). When soufflés are done, sprinkle with confectioners' sugar; serve immediately.

Each serving: About 485 calories, 11g protein, 60g carbohydrate, 27g total fat (9g saturated), 219mg cholesterol, 240mg sodium

RASPBERRY SOUFFLÉ

Prep: 25 minutes plus cooling   Bake: 20 minutes
Makes 4 servings

3 tablespoons margarine or butter
3 tablespoons all-purpose flour
⅛ teaspoon salt
¾ cup milk
About 5 tablespoons granulated sugar
3 large egg yolks

2 tablespoons orange-flavor liqueur
4 large egg whites
Three ½-pints raspberries
¼ cup red currant jelly
1 teaspoon cornstarch
Confectioners' sugar for garnish

◆ In 2-quart saucepan, melt margarine over low heat. Stir in flour and salt until blended. Gradually stir in milk and cook, stirring constantly, until mixture thickens slightly and boils; boil 1 minute. Remove from heat.

◆ With wire whisk, beat in 3 tablespoons sugar. Rapidly whisk in egg yolks. Cool to lukewarm. Stir in orange liqueur. Preheat oven to 375°F. Grease four 10-ounce soufflé dishes or custard cups; sprinkle lightly with granulated sugar.

◆ In large bowl, with mixer at high speed, beat egg whites to stiff peaks. With rubber spatula, fold one-third of beaten egg whites into egg-yolk mixture; gently fold back into remaining whites. Fold in ½ pint raspberries. Spoon into soufflé dishes; place on jelly-roll pan for easier handling. Bake 20 minutes, or until knife inserted in soufflés comes out clean.

◆ Meanwhile, prepare raspberry sauce: Reserve ½ cup raspberries for garnish. Press remaining raspberries through sieve to remove seeds. In 1-quart saucepan, heat raspberry puree, currant jelly, cornstarch, and remaining 2 tablespoons granulated sugar over medium heat until mixture thickens and boils; boil 1 minute. Keep sauce warm.

◆ When soufflés are done, sprinkle with confectioners' sugar; serve immediately with sauce and reserved berries.

Each serving: About 370 calories, 9g protein, 50g carbohydrate, 14g total fat (4g saturated), 166mg cholesterol, 250mg sodium

HAZELNUT SOUFFLÉ

Prep: 25 minutes plus cooling   Bake: 45 minutes
Makes 6 servings

½ cup hazelnuts, toasted and skinned (see page 94)
About ½ cup granulated sugar
1½ cups milk
4 tablespoons margarine or butter
¼ cup all-purpose flour

4 large egg yolks
2 tablespoons hazelnut-flavor liqueur
¼ teaspoon salt
6 large egg whites
Confectioners' sugar for garnish

◆ In food processor with knife blade attached, process hazelnuts with ¼ cup sugar until very finely ground.

◆ In 1-quart saucepan, heat milk to boiling over medium-high heat. Meanwhile, in 3-quart saucepan, melt margarine over low heat; add flour and cook, stirring frequently, 2 minutes. Whisk in milk; heat to boiling. Cook, whisking constantly, 1 minute. Remove from heat. Whisk in egg yolks, 1 at a time. Stir in ground hazelnut mixture, hazelnut liqueur, and salt. Cool to lukewarm. Preheat oven to 375°F. Grease 2½-quart soufflé dish; sprinkle lightly with granulated sugar.

◆ In large bowl, with mixer at high speed, beat egg whites until soft peaks form. Gradually sprinkle in remaining ¼ cup granulated sugar, beating until mixture holds stiff peaks when beaters are lifted. Fold one-fourth of whites into hazelnut mixture until blended; gently fold back into remaining whites. Pour into soufflé dish. Bake 45 minutes, or until just set. When soufflé is done, sprinkle with confectioners' sugar; serve immediately.

Each serving: 330 calories, 9g protein, 28g carbohydrate, 20g total fat (5g saturated), 150mg cholesterol, 265mg sodium

CHOUX PASTRIES

A stovetop batter, full of eggs, choux pastry puffs up dramatically when baked to give deliciously light, crisp pastries. To ensure crispness, bake until thoroughly golden.

CHOCOLATE CREAM-PUFF RING

◆◆◆◆◆◆◆◆◆◆◆◆◆

Prep: 40 minutes plus standing and cooling
Bake: 40 minutes
Makes 12 servings

Basic Choux Pastry (see page 36)
1 package (12 ounces) semisweet-chocolate pieces (2 cups)
¼ cup plus 1½ teaspoons milk
3 tablespoons margarine or butter
2 large eggs
2 cups heavy or whipping cream
1½ teaspoons light corn syrup
1 pint strawberries

1 Preheat oven to 400°F. Lightly grease and flour cookie sheet. Using 7-inch plate as guide, trace circle in flour on cookie sheet. Prepare Basic Choux Pastry.

2 Drop batter by heaping tablespoons into 12 mounds, inside circle, to form a ring. With moistened finger, smooth tops. Bake 40 minutes, or until golden. Turn off oven; let ring stand in oven 15 minutes. Remove ring from oven; cool on cookie sheet on wire rack.

3 Meanwhile, prepare chocolate mousse filling: In heavy 3-quart saucepan, heat 1½ cups semisweet-chocolate pieces (reserve remaining ½ cup for glaze), ¼ cup milk, and 2 tablespoons margarine over low heat, stirring occasionally, until smooth. Add eggs, one at a time, stirring constantly with wire whisk.

4 Continue whisking chocolate mixture about 5 minutes longer, until slightly thickened. Transfer to bowl, cover surface with plastic wrap, and refrigerate 30 minutes until cool.

5 In large bowl, with mixer at medium speed, beat cream until stiff peaks form. With rubber spatula, fold whipped cream into cooled chocolate mixture, half at a time, until blended.

6 With long serrated knife, cut cooled ring horizontally in half. Spoon chocolate mousse filling into bottom of ring. Replace top of ring. Refrigerate until ready to serve. Prepare glaze: In heavy 1-quart saucepan, heat reserved ½ cup semisweet-chocolate pieces, remaining 1 tablespoon margarine, remaining 1½ teaspoons milk, and light corn syrup over low heat, stirring occasionally, until smooth. Spoon over ring. Fill center of ring with strawberries.

EACH SERVING: ABOUT 445 CALORIES, 7g PROTEIN, 31g CARBOHYDRATE, 34g TOTAL FAT (12g SATURATED), 162mg CHOLESTEROL, 235mg SODIUM

CREAM PUFFS WITH HOT FUDGE SAUCE

Prep: 30 minutes plus standing and cooling   Bake: 40 to 45 minutes
Makes 8 servings

Basic Choux Pastry (see   1 quart vanilla ice cream
   below right)
Hot Fudge Sauce (see
   page 54)

◆ Preheat oven to 400°F. Grease and flour large cookie sheet. Prepare Basic Choux Pastry. Drop batter by slightly rounded ¼ cups, 3 inches apart, onto cookie sheet into 8 large mounds. With moistened finger, gently smooth tops to round slightly.

◆ Bake 40 to 45 minutes, until golden. Remove puffs from oven; with knife, poke a hole into side of each puff to let out steam. Turn off oven. Return puffs to oven and let stand 10 minutes. Transfer puffs to wire rack to cool.

◆ With serrated knife, cut each cooled puff horizontally in half; remove and discard any moist portion inside puffs.

◆ Prepare Hot Fudge Sauce. To serve, place ½-cup scoop vanilla ice cream in bottom half of each cream puff; replace tops. Spoon Hot Fudge Sauce over cream puffs.

Each serving: About 610 calories, 9g protein, 55g carbohydrate, 43g total fat (18g saturated), 176mg cholesterol, 330mg sodium

ÉCLAIRS

Prep: 1 hour plus chilling, cooling, and standing   Bake: 40 minutes
Makes about 24

3 cups milk   Basic Choux Pastry (see right)
6 large egg yolks   3 squares (3 ounces)
1 cup sugar   semisweet chocolate
⅓ cup cornstarch   3 tablespoons heavy or
4 teaspoons vanilla extract   whipping cream

◆ Prepare pastry cream: In 4-quart saucepan, heat milk to boiling over high heat. Meanwhile, in large bowl, whisk egg yolks with sugar until smooth; whisk in cornstarch until combined. Gradually whisk hot milk into yolk mixture.

◆ Return mixture to saucepan; cook over high heat, whisking constantly, until mixture thickens and boils. Reduce heat to low and cook, whisking, 2 minutes.

◆ Remove saucepan from heat and stir in vanilla. Pour pastry cream into shallow dish. Press plastic wrap onto surface of pastry cream to keep skin from forming as it cools. Refrigerate at least 2 hours, or overnight. Preheat oven to 400°F.

◆ Grease and flour large cookie sheet. Prepare Basic Choux Pastry. Spoon batter into large decorating bag fitted with ½-inch round tip. Pipe batter into strips about 3½ inches long and ¾ inch wide, 1 inch apart, onto cookie sheet to make 24 éclairs. With moistened finger, smooth any tails. Bake 40 minutes, or until golden. Transfer to wire rack to cool.

◆ With serrated knife, cut each cooled éclair horizontally in half, leaving one side intact, or, with small knife, make a hole in each end. Whisk pastry cream until smooth; spoon into large decorating bag fitted with ¼-inch round tip. Pipe into éclairs (reserve extra pastry cream for use another day).

◆ In 1-quart saucepan, melt chocolate with cream over very low heat, stirring often; remove from heat. Dip top of each éclair in chocolate mixture, smoothing with small metal spatula if necessary. Let stand until chocolate sets.

Each éclair: 160 calories, 4g protein, 18g carbohydrate, 9g total fat (3g saturated), 95mg cholesterol, 95mg sodium

BASIC CHOUX PASTRY

◆◆◆◆◆◆◆◆◆◆◆◆◆

½ cup margarine or   1 cup all-purpose flour
   butter   4 large eggs
¼ teaspoon salt

1 In 3-quart saucepan, heat margarine, salt, and *1 cup water* over medium heat until margarine melts and mixture boils. Remove from heat. With wooden spoon, vigorously stir in flour all at once until mixture forms ball and leaves side of pan.

2 Add eggs to flour mixture, one at a time, beating well after each addition, until mixture is smooth and satiny. Shape and bake warm batter as directed.

PUFF PASTRIES

Dozens of paper-thin layers of dough and butter make puff pastry light and flaky; we've used frozen puff pastry to create ultra-easy, elegant desserts. The rich, delicate pastry is lovely with a fragrant apple filling for a French-style treat or baked into little fruit-filled bundles for a less formal dessert.

APPLE-ALMOND PASTRY

◆◆◆◆◆◆◆◆◆◆◆◆◆

Prep: 30 minutes plus cooling
Bake: 25 to 30 minutes
Makes 10 servings

1 large egg
½ (7- to 8-ounce) tube or can almond paste
2 teaspoons vanilla extract
3 medium Golden Delicious apples (about 1 pound), peeled, cored, and thinly sliced
2 teaspoons all-purpose flour
1 package (17¼ ounces) frozen puff-pastry sheets, thawed
2 teaspoons sugar

1 In medium bowl, with fork, beat egg. Transfer 1 tablespoon egg to cup; mix in *1 tablespoon water*. Set aside. To egg in bowl, add almond paste and vanilla; with fork, break up almond paste and blend mixture. In large bowl, toss apple slices with flour. Unfold 1 pastry sheet on lightly floured large cookie sheet. With floured rolling pin, roll pastry to about a 13-inch square. (Place damp towel under cookie sheet to help prevent it from moving.)

2 Invert an 11-inch round bowl onto pastry, lightly pressing to make circle. With pastry wheel or sharp knife, trim pastry, leaving 1-inch border around circle; discard trimmings.

3 With small spatula, spread almond mixture to cover 11-inch circle. Arrange apple slices on top. Unfold second pastry sheet on lightly floured surface; roll, mark, and trim as in Steps 1 and 2.

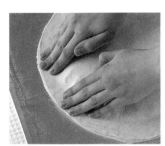

4 Preheat oven to 375°F. With pastry brush, brush some egg mixture in cup on pastry border around apples. Place second pastry circle on top of apples; press all around edge to seal.

5 With tip of sharp knife, cut ½-inch triangles from edge of pastry, about 2 inches apart; discard triangles.

6 Lightly score top crust with curved lines, starting at center and working toward edge (do not cut all the way through). Brush crust with remaining egg mixture in cup; sprinkle with sugar. (Dessert can be prepared to this point and refrigerated up to 4 hours before baking.) Bake pastry 25 to 30 minutes, until crust is golden brown. Cool pastry on wire rack at least 30 minutes before serving.

EACH SERVING: ABOUT 335 CALORIES, 6g PROTEIN, 41g CARBOHYDRATE, 17g TOTAL FAT (3g SATURATED), 21mg CHOLESTEROL, 170mg SODIUM

FRUIT BUNDLES

Prep: 35 minutes plus cooling   Bake: 20 to 25 minutes
Makes 8 servings

¾ cup pitted prunes (about
   4 ounces), coarsely chopped
¾ cup dried apricots (about
   4 ounces), coarsely chopped
¾ cup apple juice
1 tablespoon all-purpose flour
½ teaspoon ground cinnamon

1 medium Golden Delicious
   apple, peeled, cored, and
   cut into ½-inch pieces
¼ cup plus 1 tablespoon sugar
1 package (17¼ ounces)
   frozen puff-pastry sheets,
   thawed

◆ In 1-quart saucepan, heat prunes, apricots, and apple juice to boiling over high heat. Reduce heat to low; simmer 8 to 10 minutes, until fruit is soft and liquid is absorbed. Cool completely; transfer to large bowl. Stir in flour, cinnamon, apple pieces, and ¼ cup sugar.

◆ Preheat oven to 425°F. Unfold 1 pastry sheet on lightly floured surface. With floured rolling pin, roll pastry to a 12-inch square. With sharp pastry wheel or knife, trim edges of sheet; cut square into four 6-inch squares. Spoon one-eighth of fruit mixture onto center of each square.

◆ Brush edges of 1 pastry square with some *water*. Bring corners of pastry square over fruit; gently squeeze and twist pastry together to seal in filling and form a bundle. Fan out corners of pastry. Repeat to make 3 more bundles.

◆ Repeat with second pastry sheet, remaining fruit mixture, and more *water* to make 4 more bundles. Place bundles, 2 inches apart, on ungreased large cookie sheet. (If desired, refrigerate bundles on cookie sheet to bake later in day.)

◆ Brush tops of bundles with *water*, then sprinkle with remaining 1 tablespoon sugar. Bake 20 to 25 minutes, until bundles are puffed and golden. Serve warm or transfer bundles to wire rack to cool.

Each serving: About 415 calories, 5g protein, 65g carbohydrate, 17g total fat (4g saturated), 0mg cholesterol, 205mg sodium

QUICK PUFF-PASTRY DESSERTS

Frozen puff pastry is great to have on hand for impressive no-fuss desserts. When working with puff pastry, remember that clean edges are important for maximum puffing. Use a cookie cutter with very sharp edges or very sharp knife or pastry wheel and cut straight down. If necessary, trim edges of the pastry sheets after you've rolled them out. The following method is easy and adapts to many ideas:

On lightly floured surface, unfold puff-pastry sheet. With cookie cutter, cut out hearts, stars, or other shapes. Or, with sharp knife or pastry wheel, trim edges of pastry sheet and then cut out small squares, rectangles, or triangles. Place on an ungreased cookie sheet and prick several times with a fork.

If desired, sprinkle pastry with a little sugar or a few crushed sugar cubes. Or, brush pastry (tops only) with 1 large egg white beaten with 1 tablespoon water (if egg mixture drips on cut edges, pastry won't puff fully), then sprinkle with finely chopped pistachios or other nuts. Bake 10 to 15 minutes at 375°F, until pastry is puffed and golden. Cool on wire rack.

With serrated knife, carefully split each cooled pastry horizontally in half or thirds. Fill with sweetened whipped cream (flavored with a little liqueur or vanilla extract, if you like), ice cream, berries or other fruit, or Marsala Cream Cheese (see below). Try serving with any of the sauces on page 54.

Marsala cream cheese In large bowl, with mixer at low speed, beat 1 package (8 ounces) cream cheese, softened, with ½ cup confectioners' sugar until smooth. Gradually beat in ¼ cup sweet Marsala wine until blended; set aside. In small bowl, with mixer at medium speed, beat 1 cup heavy or whipping cream until stiff peaks form. Fold whipped cream into cream-cheese mixture. Makes about 1½ cups.

Each tablespoon: About 80 calories, 1g protein, 3g carbohydrate, 7g total fat (4g saturated), 24mg cholesterol, 30mg sodium

Puff-pastry hearts filled with whipped cream cheese, served with hot fudge sauce

Nut-topped puff-pastry rectangles filled with kiwifruit, banana slices, and whipped cream

PHYLLO PASTRIES

Phyllo pastry, purchased fresh or frozen, makes spectacular desserts like our delicate phyllo cups with a fruit-and-ricotta filling. Phyllo dries out quickly; keep it covered until you are ready to use it. Wrap unused phyllo and refrigerate it up to 2 weeks; do not re-freeze thawed dough, or it will become dry and brittle.

PHYLLO CUPS WITH HONEY-RICOTTA AND MIXED BERRIES

Prep: 45 minutes plus draining and cooling
Bake: 12 minutes   Makes 6 servings

2 containers (15 ounces each) part-skim ricotta cheese
6 sheets (about 16" by 12" each) fresh or frozen (thawed) phyllo (about 4 ounces)
2 tablespoons margarine or butter, melted

¼ cup honey
1 teaspoon grated orange peel
1 cup blueberries
1 cup raspberries
1 cup blackberries
Confectioners' sugar for garnish

1 In food processor with knife blade attached, blend ricotta cheese about 1 minute, or until smooth. Place double-thick layer of white paper towels in medium strainer set over small bowl. Spoon ricotta cheese onto paper towels; cover with plastic wrap, place in refrigerator, and let drain at least 2 hours or overnight (whey will drop into bowl and ricotta will thicken).

2 Meanwhile, preheat oven to 375°F. On work surface, stack phyllo sheets one on top of the other. With knife, cut stack lengthwise, then crosswise in half (you will have twenty-four 8" by 6" pieces).

3 Keep phyllo stack covered with plastic wrap to prevent it from drying out while assembling phyllo cups. Lightly brush six 10-ounce custard cups with melted margarine. On work surface, place 2 pieces of phyllo, one on top of the other; brush top piece with some melted margarine. Arrange phyllo in custard cup.

4 Repeat with 2 more pieces of phyllo, placing crosswise over phyllo in cup. Fold phyllo overhang to make pretty edge. Repeat with remaining phyllo and melted margarine to make 6 phyllo cups in all.

5 Place custard cups in jelly-roll pan for easier handling. Bake phyllo cups about 12 minutes, until phyllo is crisp and golden.

6 Cool phyllo cups in custard cups on wire racks about 15 minutes; carefully remove from custard cups. (Phyllo cups can be made 1 day ahead and kept in airtight container.) Just before serving, remove ricotta from refrigerator. Discard whey in bowl. Transfer drained ricotta to same bowl.

7 Add honey and orange peel to ricotta and mix well. In medium bowl, toss blueberries, raspberries, and blackberries. Spoon ricotta mixture into phyllo cups; top with berries. Sprinkle with confectioners' sugar. Serve immediately.

EACH SERVING: ABOUT 370 CALORIES, 18g PROTEIN, 38g CARBOHYDRATE, 16g TOTAL FAT (8g SATURATED), 44mg CHOLESTEROL, 315mg SODIUM

SPICED PEAR STRUDEL

Prep: 30 minutes plus cooling Bake: 40 minutes
Makes 16 servings

3 large pears (1¾ pounds), peeled and thinly sliced	**12 sheets (about 16" by 12"each) fresh or frozen (thawed) phyllo (about 8 ounces)**
½ cup pitted dates, diced	
⅓ cup granulated sugar	
½ teaspoon ground cinnamon	**½ cup margarine or butter, melted**
¼ teaspoon ground ginger	
⅛ teaspoon salt	**Confectioners' sugar for garnish**
¾ cup plain dried bread crumbs	

◆ Grease large cookie sheet. In large bowl, toss pears with next 5 ingredients and ¼ cup bread crumbs.

◆ Cut two 24-inch lengths of waxed paper; overlap 2 long sides about 2 inches. On waxed paper, arrange 1 sheet of phyllo; brush with some melted margarine, then sprinkle with scant tablespoon bread crumbs. (Keep remaining phyllo covered with plastic wrap to prevent it from drying out.) Continue layering phyllo, brushing each sheet with some margarine and sprinkling every other sheet with crumbs.

◆ Preheat oven to 375°F. Starting along 1 long side of phyllo, spoon pears to about ½ inch from edges to cover half of rectangle. From pear-side, roll phyllo, jelly-roll fashion.

◆ Place roll on cookie sheet seam-side down; tuck ends under. Brush with remaining margarine. Cut 16 diagonal slashes in top. Bake 40 minutes, covering with foil during last 20 minutes if necessary to prevent overbrowning. Cool on cookie sheet on wire rack 30 minutes. Sprinkle cooled strudel lightly with confectioners' sugar; serve warm or cold.

Each serving: About 175 calories, 2g protein, 27g carbohydrate, 7g total fat (1g saturated), 0mg cholesterol, 195mg sodium

HONEY-LEMON BAKLAVA

Prep: 30 minutes plus cooling Bake: 1 hour 15 minutes
Makes 24 servings

4 cups walnuts (about 16 ounces)	**10 tablespoons margarine or butter, melted**
1 teaspoon ground cinnamon	**1 cup honey**
¼ teaspoon ground cloves	**1 cinnamon stick (3 inches)**
1 cup sugar	**4 teaspoons fresh lemon juice**
1 package (16 ounces) fresh or frozen (thawed) phyllo (each sheet about 16" by 12")	

◆ Grease 13" by 9" glass baking dish. In food processor with knife blade attached, place first 3 ingredients and ½ cup sugar. Pulse until walnuts are finely chopped; set aside.

◆ Preheat oven to 300°F. Cut phyllo sheets into 13" by 9" rectangles. In baking dish, place 1 sheet phyllo; brush with some melted margarine. (Keep remaining phyllo covered with plastic wrap to prevent it from drying out.) Repeat with 5 more sheets; sprinkle with about 1 cup walnut mixture.

◆ Place 1 sheet of phyllo in baking dish over walnuts; brush with some margarine. Repeat with 5 more sheets of phyllo; sprinkle with about 1 cup walnut mixture. Repeat layering 2 more times, ending with walnuts. Place 1 sheet of phyllo on top of last walnut layer; brush with some margarine. Repeat until all phyllo sheets are used, brushing with remaining margarine.

◆ With sharp knife, cut almost but not all the way through layers to make 24 servings: Cut lengthwise into 3 strips; cut each strip crosswise into 4 rectangles. Then cut each rectangle diagonally into 2 triangles. Bake 1¼ hours, or until golden.

◆ Prepare syrup: About 15 minutes before baklava is done, in small saucepan, heat honey, cinnamon stick, *1 cup water*, and remaining ½ cup sugar to boiling over medium heat; boil 5 minutes, stirring often. Reduce heat to low. Add lemon juice; simmer 5 minutes longer. Discard cinnamon stick; spoon hot syrup over hot baklava. Cool baklava in pan on wire rack at least 1 hour. Let stand at room temperature until ready to serve. To serve, finish cutting through layers.

Each serving: About 305 calories, 4g protein, 34g carbohydrate, 18g total fat (2g saturated), 0mg cholesterol, 150mg sodium

---

PHYLLO NAPOLEONS

Stack 6 sheets (about 16" by 12" each) fresh or frozen (thawed) phyllo (about 4 ounces), lightly brushing every second sheet with melted margarine. With pizza wheel or knife, cut stack lengthwise in half; cut each half crosswise into 6. Bake on cookie sheet at 375°F 10 minutes; cool on sheet on wire rack.

Spread 4 rectangles with half of Marsala Cream Cheese (see page 38) or sweetened whipped cream; top with some berries mixed with jam. Layer with 4 more rectangles, remaining cream cheese, and more berry mixture. Sprinkle remaining rectangles with confectioners' sugar; place on top to make 4 Napoleons.

CREPES AND BLINTZES

These thin pancakes make a lovely dessert when wrapped around sweet fillings. Freeze crepes for up to 4 months, stacked with a sheet of waxed paper between each one. Thaw for about an hour before using. Crepes used for blintzes are made from the same batter but are browned on one side only.

APPLE-CALVADOS CREPES

❖❖❖❖❖❖❖❖❖❖❖❖

Prep: 50 minutes plus chilling batter
Bake: 5 minutes
Makes 6 servings

Basic Crepes
5 tablespoons margarine or butter
3 pounds Golden Delicious apples (6 large), peeled, cored, and diced
½ cup plus 1 tablespoon sugar
¼ cup Calvados or applejack brandy

1 Prepare Basic Crepes. Preheat oven to 400°F. In 12-inch skillet, melt 4 tablespoons margarine over medium-high heat. Stir in apples and ½ cup sugar; cover and cook 10 minutes, or until apples are tender.

2 Uncover and cook about 10 minutes longer, until apples begin to caramelize. Stir in Calvados. Remove skillet from heat.

3 Spread scant ¼ cup filling down center of each crepe. Roll up; arrange in shallow baking dish. Dot with remaining 1 tablespoon margarine; sprinkle with remaining 1 tablespoon sugar. Bake 5 minutes.

BASIC CREPES

❖❖❖❖❖❖❖❖❖❖❖❖

Crepes, made from a smooth egg batter, are used in both sweet and savory dishes. It's important to let the batter rest before cooking; the resting process relaxes the gluten in the flour for tender crepes. This recipe makes about 12 crepes.

Prep: 5 minutes plus chilling   Cook: 20 minutes

3 large eggs	**½ teaspoon salt**
1½ cups milk	**About 4 tablespoons butter,**
⅔ cup all-purpose flour	**melted**

1 In blender at medium speed, mix eggs, milk, flour, salt, and 2 tablespoons melted butter until completely smooth and free from lumps.

2 Transfer to bowl and refrigerate at least 1 hour, or overnight. Whisk batter thoroughly just before using.

3 Heat nonstick 10-inch skillet over medium-high heat; brush lightly with melted butter. Pour scant ¼ cup batter into pan; tip pan to coat bottom. Cook crepe 1½ minutes, or until top is set and underside is lightly browned.

4 With plastic spatula, loosen crepe; turn and cook other side 30 seconds. Slip onto waxed paper. Repeat with remaining batter, brushing pan lightly with butter before cooking each crepe; stack cooked crepes.

Each crepe: About 80 calories, 3g protein, 6g carbohydrate, 4g total fat (2g saturated), 62mg cholesterol, 140mg sodium

EACH SERVING: ABOUT 465 CALORIES, 7g PROTEIN, 65g CARBOHYDRATE, 19g TOTAL FAT (6g SATURATED), 125mg CHOLESTEROL, 390mg SODIUM

CREPES SUZETTE

Prepare Basic Crepes (see page 41). In 10-inch skillet, melt 4 tablespoons margarine or butter with ⅓ cup orange juice, 2 tablespoons sugar, and ¼ teaspoon grated orange peel over low heat. Fold each crepe into quarters; arrange in sauce, turning to coat. Simmer 10 minutes. Pour ¼ cup orange-flavor liqueur evenly over crepes (do not stir).

Heat 1 to 2 minutes. With long wooden match, carefully ignite. When flames subside, transfer crepes to plates. Makes 6 servings.

Each serving: 275 calories, 7g protein, 22g carbohydrate, 16g total fat (6g saturated), 125mg cholesterol, 365mg sodium

CHEESE BLINTZES

Prep: 40 minutes plus chilling batter **Cook:** *20 minutes*
Makes 6 servings

Basic Crepes (see page 41)
2 packages (8 ounces each) cream cheese, softened
1 container (8 ounces) cottage cheese
3 tablespoons confectioners' sugar

¾ teaspoon vanilla extract
1 large egg
Blueberry Sauce (see page 54)
2 tablespoons margarine or butter
Sour cream (optional)

◆ Prepare batter as directed in Steps 1 and 2 of Basic Crepes. While batter is chilling, prepare filling: In medium bowl, with mixer at medium speed, beat cheese, confectioners' sugar, vanilla, and egg until smooth. Cover and refrigerate filling until ready to use.

◆ Cook crepes as directed in Steps 3 and 4 of Basic Crepes, but cook crepe on bottom side only. Stack cooked crepes, browned-side up, between waxed paper. Prepare sauce. Place ¼ cup filling in center of browned side of each crepe. Fold left and right sides over filling and overlap ends to make a package. In 10-inch skillet, heat 1 tablespoon margarine over medium heat. Add 6 blintzes, seam-side down; cook until golden on both sides. Transfer to plates. Repeat with remaining margarine and blintzes. Serve hot with sauce, and sour cream, if you like.

Each serving: About 595 calories, 18g protein, 38g carbohydrate, 42g total fat (23g saturated), 250mg cholesterol, 715mg sodium

CREPES WITH STRAWBERRIES AND CREAM

Prep: 30 minutes plus chilling batter **Cook:** *20 minutes*
Makes 6 servings

Basic Crepes (see page 41)
4 tablespoons granulated sugar
1 pint strawberries, hulled and thinly sliced
1 to 2 tablespoons orange-flavor liqueur

1 cup heavy or whipping cream
1 tablespoon margarine or butter, melted
Confectioners' sugar for garnish

◆ Prepare Basic Crepes, adding 1 tablespoon granulated sugar to batter in Step 1. While batter is chilling, in medium bowl, mix strawberries, liqueur, and 2 tablespoons granulated sugar. Let stand 20 minutes to allow sugar to dissolve and berries to marinate.

◆ In small bowl, with mixer at medium speed, beat heavy cream with remaining 1 tablespoon granulated sugar until soft peaks form. Spoon cream into serving bowl.

◆ Strain syrup from strawberries into small bowl. Stir in melted margarine; use to brush on crepes. Fold each crepe into quarters. Dust crepes lightly with confectioners' sugar. Place strawberries in small serving bowl. Serve crepes with strawberries and whipped cream.

Each serving: About 365 calories, 8g protein, 27g carbohydrate, 25g total fat (14g saturated), 179mg cholesterol, 315mg sodium

BROWN SUGAR CREPES

Prep: 25 minutes plus chilling batter **Cook:** *3 to 6 minutes*
Makes 6 servings

Basic Crepes (see page 41)
12 rounded teaspoons brown sugar

6 teaspoons margarine or butter

◆ Prepare Basic Crepes. Press 1 rounded teaspoon brown sugar through sieve evenly over 1 crepe. Fold crepe into quarters. Repeat with remaining brown sugar and crepes.

◆ In nonstick 10-inch skillet, melt 2 teaspoons margarine over medium-high heat, swirling to coat bottom of pan. Add 4 crepes and cook 30 to 60 seconds per side, until heated through. Transfer to 2 dessert plates. Repeat with remaining margarine and crepes in 2 more batches.

Each serving: About 225 calories, 7g protein, 22g carbohydrate, 12g total fat (5g saturated), 125mg cholesterol, 325mg sodium

Bread puddings

One of the most homey desserts, bread pudding is simply bread baked in a custard of eggs, milk, and sugar. Thrifty cooks make it as a way of using up day-old or stale bread – dry bread soaks up the egg mixture and all the flavors better than fresh bread would. Our Bread and Butter Pudding is an old-fashioned favorite, and we've created new versions with apples and cinnamon, with dried cherries, and with chocolate for a touch of luxury. For the white chocolate called for in our Black-and-White Bread Pudding and White-Chocolate Custard Sauce, you can substitute the equivalent weight in Swiss confectionery bars or white baking bars.

BLACK-AND-WHITE BREAD PUDDING

Prep: 30 to 40 minutes plus standing and cooling
Bake: 1 hour 15 minutes   *Makes* 16 servings

1 loaf (16 ounces) sliced firm white bread
4 cups milk
½ cup sugar
1 tablespoon vanilla extract
½ teaspoon salt
9 large eggs
3 ounces bittersweet chocolate (not unsweetened), grated
3 ounces white chocolate, grated
White-Chocolate Custard Sauce (optional, see below)

WHITE-CHOCOLATE CUSTARD SAUCE

Place 3 ounces white chocolate, finely chopped, in large bowl; set aside. In small bowl, with wire whisk, beat 4 large egg yolks and ¼ cup sugar until combined. In heavy 2-quart saucepan, heat 1 cup milk and ¾ cup heavy or whipping cream to boiling over high heat. Into egg mixture, beat small amount of hot milk mixture. Slowly pour egg mixture back into milk mixture, stirring rapidly to prevent lumping. Reduce heat to low; cook, stirring constantly, about 5 minutes, until mixture thickens slightly and coats back of spoon well. (Mixture should be about 160°F, but do not boil, or it will curdle.) Pour mixture over white chocolate, stirring to combine (white chocolate will not melt completely). Serve sauce warm, or refrigerate to serve cold. Makes about 2½ cups.

Each tablespoon: About 40 calories, 1g protein, 3g carbohydrate, 3g total fat (2g saturated), 28mg cholesterol, 5mg sodium

1 Preheat oven to 325°F. Place bread slices on large cookie sheet; lightly toast in oven 20 to 30 minutes, turning once. Grease 13" by 9" glass or ceramic baking dish.

2 Arrange bread in baking dish, overlapping slightly. In very large bowl, with wire whisk or fork, mix milk, sugar, vanilla, salt, and eggs until blended. Whisk in grated chocolates.

3 Pour milk mixture over bread; let stand 30 minutes, occasionally spooning liquid over bread. Bake, covered, 1 hour. Uncover; bake 15 minutes longer, or until golden. Cool on wire rack 30 minutes. Prepare sauce, if using. Serve pudding warm, or refrigerate to serve cold later.

EACH SERVING: ABOUT 240 CALORIES, 9g PROTEIN, 28g CARBOHYDRATE, 10g TOTAL FAT (5g SATURATED), 128mg CHOLESTEROL, 285mg SODIUM

BREAD-AND-BUTTER PUDDING

Prep: 15 minutes plus standing and cooling   *Bake: 55 to 60 minutes*
Makes 8 servings

4 tablespoons margarine or
  butter, softened
12 slices firm white bread
¾ teaspoon ground cinnamon
3 cups milk

⅓ cup sugar
1½ teaspoons vanilla extract
¼ teaspoon salt
4 large eggs

◆ Preheat oven to 325°F. Grease 8" by 8" glass baking dish. Spread margarine on bread slices. Arrange 4 slices of bread in dish in one layer, overlapping slightly; sprinkle with ¼ teaspoon cinnamon. Repeat, making 2 more layers.

◆ In medium bowl, with wire whisk or fork, mix remaining ingredients until well blended. Pour mixture over bread slices; let stand 10 minutes. Bake 55 to 60 minutes, until knife inserted in center of pudding comes out clean. Cool on wire rack 30 minutes. Serve warm, or refrigerate to serve cold later.

Each serving: About 270 calories, 9g protein, 30g carbohydrate, 13g total fat (4g saturated), 119mg cholesterol, 385mg sodium

LIGHT CHERRY BREAD PUDDING

Prep: 20 minutes plus standing and cooling   *Bake: 1 hour 30 minutes*
Makes 12 servings

4 ounces dried tart cherries
  (¾ cup)
1 loaf (12 ounces) Italian
  bread
6 cups low-fat milk (1%)
¾ cup packed light brown sugar

1 tablespoon vanilla extract
2 teaspoons ground cinnamon
4 large egg whites
3 large eggs
Confectioners' sugar for
  garnish

◆ In 2-quart saucepan, heat dried cherries and *¾ cup water* to boiling over high heat. Reduce heat to low; cover and simmer 10 minutes, or until cherries are tender.

◆ Meanwhile, grease shallow 3-quart casserole. Cut bread into 1-inch-thick slices. In very large bowl, with wire whisk or fork, mix milk and next 5 ingredients until well blended. Drain cherries, adding any liquid to egg mixture. Set cherries aside. Add bread slices to egg mixture; let stand 10 minutes, carefully turning slices occasionally for even soaking.

◆ Preheat oven to 350°F. Arrange enough bread slices in casserole in one layer, pushing slices together, to cover bottom; sprinkle all but ¼ cup cherries over bread. Arrange remaining bread, overlapping slices to fit, on top. Pour any egg mixture remaining in bowl over bread.

◆ Bake bread pudding 1½ hours, or until knife inserted in center comes out clean, covering loosely with foil during last 10 to 15 minutes of baking if top browns too quickly.

◆ Sprinkle pudding with remaining cherries. Dust with confectioners' sugar. Cool on wire rack 30 minutes. Serve warm, or refrigerate to serve cold later.

Each serving: About 240 calories, 10g protein, 42g carbohydrate, 4g total fat (1g saturated), 58mg cholesterol, 270mg sodium

APPLE BREAD PUDDING

Prep: 40 minutes plus standing and cooling
Bake: 1 hour 15 to 30 minutes   *Makes 12 servings*

8 ounces unsliced rich egg
  bread, such as challah, cut
  into 1-inch cubes (6 cups)
3 tablespoons margarine or
  butter
6 large Golden Delicious
  apples (3 pounds), peeled,
  cored, and sliced

1 teaspoon ground cinnamon
½ cup plus ⅔ cup plus
  1 tablespoon sugar
2 tablespoons cornstarch
5 cups milk
5 large eggs
1½ teaspoons vanilla extract

◆ Preheat oven to 350°F. Spread bread cubes in jelly-roll pan; bake 15 to 20 minutes, until lightly toasted. Meanwhile, in 12-inch skillet, melt margarine over medium-high heat. Stir in apples and ½ teaspoon cinnamon; cover and cook 10 minutes. Uncover; stir in ½ cup sugar. Cook, stirring often, 5 to 10 minutes, until apples are lightly caramelized. In cup, mix cornstarch and ½ cup milk until smooth; stir into apples. Reduce heat to low and cook, stirring constantly, 1 minute.

◆ Place half of bread in 13" by 9" glass baking dish. Spoon apple mixture over bread; top with remaining bread. In large bowl, with wire whisk or fork, mix eggs, vanilla, ⅔ cup sugar, and remaining 4½ cups milk until well blended; pour over bread. Let stand 10 minutes, pressing bread into liquid. In cup, combine remaining 1 tablespoon sugar with remaining ½ teaspoon cinnamon; sprinkle over bread.

◆ Place baking dish in larger roasting pan. Carefully pour *boiling water* into roasting pan to come halfway up sides of dish. Bake 1¼ to 1½ hours, until knife inserted in center comes out clean. Cool on wire rack 30 minutes. Serve warm.

Each serving: 325 calories, 8g protein, 53g carbohydrate, 10g total fat (4g saturated), 112mg cholesterol, 205mg sodium

STOVETOP CUSTARDS

These easy stirred custards make simple puddings or form the basis for festive desserts like our trifle, laced with almond liqueur. There are also delicate brown-sugar custards, left alone to cook gently on the stovetop, plus a foolproof method for classic custard sauce.

RASPBERRY-PEAR TRIFLE

Prep: 1 hour plus chilling   **Cook:** 10 minutes
Makes 16 servings

2¼ cups milk
¾ cup plus 3 tablespoons sugar
¼ cup cornstarch
⅛ teaspoon salt
6 large egg yolks
¼ cup almond-flavor liqueur (amaretto)
3 cans (16 ounces each) pear halves in extra-light syrup
1 package (10 ounces) frozen raspberries in light syrup, thawed

1 cup heavy or whipping cream
1 store-bought pound cake (10¾ to 12 ounces), cut into 1-inch cubes
8 pairs amaretti cookies, coarsely crushed (about 1¼ cups)
Fresh raspberries for garnish

1 In 3-quart saucepan, heat 1¾ cups milk and ¾ cup sugar just to boiling over medium heat. Remove from heat. In medium bowl, with wire whisk, mix cornstarch, salt, and remaining ½ cup milk until smooth; beat in egg yolks.

2 Into yolk mixture, stir small amount of hot milk mixture; gradually stir yolk mixture back into milk mixture in saucepan. Cook over medium heat, stirring constantly, until mixture thickens and boils.

3 Remove custard from heat; stir in liqueur. Pour custard into clean bowl. Press plastic wrap onto surface of hot custard to keep skin from forming as custard cools. Refrigerate at least 3 hours, until chilled.

4 Drain pear halves, reserving ⅓ cup syrup. In blender at low speed, blend thawed frozen raspberries with their syrup and reserved syrup from pears. In small bowl, with mixer at medium speed, beat heavy cream, gradually adding remaining 3 tablespoons sugar, until stiff peaks form. Reserve 1 rounded cup whipped cream for garnish.

5 Gently fold remaining whipped cream into chilled custard. In 4-quart glass trifle or serving bowl, place half of cake cubes; top with half of raspberry mixture.

6 Arrange half of pear halves over raspberry mixture. Reserve ¼ cup cookie crumbs for garnish; sprinkle pear halves with half of remaining cookie crumbs.

7 Spread half of custard over crumb layer. Repeat layering. Garnish trifle with reserved whipped cream, fresh raspberries, and reserved cookie crumbs. Cover and refrigerate at least 2 hours or up to 24 hours to blend flavors.

EACH SERVING: ABOUT 375 CALORIES, 6g PROTEIN, 51g CARBOHYDRATE, 15g TOTAL FAT (6g SATURATED), 116mg CHOLESTEROL, 140mg SODIUM

CHOCOLATE PUDDING

Prep: 10 minutes plus chilling   *Cook:* 20 minutes
Makes 8 servings

¾ cup sugar	3 squares (3 ounces)
⅓ cup cornstarch	unsweetened chocolate,
½ teaspoon salt	melted
3¾ cups milk	2 tablespoons margarine or
5 large egg yolks	butter
2 teaspoons vanilla extract	Whipped cream (optional)

◆ In 3-quart saucepan, mix sugar, cornstarch, and salt until blended; gradually stir in milk. Cook over medium heat until mixture thickens and boils, stirring constantly; boil 1 minute, stirring. In small bowl, with wire whisk or fork, beat egg yolks lightly. Into yolks, beat small amount of hot milk mixture.

◆ Gradually pour yolk mixture back into milk mixture in saucepan, stirring rapidly to prevent lumping. Cook over low heat, stirring constantly, about 2 minutes, until very thick (mixture should be about 160°F).

◆ Remove from heat; stir in vanilla, melted chocolate, and margarine. Pour pudding into shallow bowl; press plastic wrap onto surface to prevent skin from forming as pudding cools. Refrigerate at least 4 hours, until chilled and set. Serve with whipped cream, if you like.

Each serving: About 280 calories, 6g protein, 32g carbohydrate, 15g total fat (6g saturated), 149mg cholesterol, 225mg sodium

---

THE PERFECT CUSTARD SAUCE

This classic sauce, also known as "crème anglaise," goes beautifully with pies, tarts, plain cakes, or fruit: In 2-quart saucepan, heat 1¼ cups milk to boiling. Meanwhile, in medium bowl, whisk 4 large egg yolks with ¼ cup sugar until smooth. Gradually whisk hot milk into egg-yolk mixture. Return mixture to saucepan; cook over medium heat, stirring constantly (do not boil), just until mixture thickens slightly and coats back of wooden spoon well. (A finger run across the custard-coated spoon should leave a track.)

Remove from heat; strain through sieve into clean bowl. Stir in 1 teaspoon vanilla extract, 1 tablespoon liqueur or brandy, or ½ teaspoon grated lemon peel. Refrigerate if not serving right away. Makes 1½ cups.

Each tablespoon: About 25 calories, 1g protein, 3g carbohydrate, 1g total fat (0g saturated), 37mg cholesterol, 5mg sodium

---

BROWN-SUGAR SKILLET CUSTARDS

Prep: 10 minutes plus chilling   *Cook:* 1 hour
Makes 6 servings

4 large eggs	2 teaspoons vanilla extract
½ cup packed dark brown	Pinch salt
sugar	3 cups milk

◆ In large bowl, with wire whisk, mix eggs with brown sugar, vanilla, and salt until sugar is dissolved. Whisk in milk.

◆ Fold a kitchen towel in half to line bottom of 12-inch skillet; set six 6-ounce custard cups or ramekins in skillet. Carefully pour milk mixture into custard cups; pour *cold water* into skillet to come halfway up sides of custard cups.

◆ Heat water to boiling over medium heat (it will take about 45 minutes). Cover skillet and remove from heat; let stand 15 minutes. Remove custard cups from skillet and refrigerate at least 2 hours, until chilled, or overnight.

Each serving: About 200 calories, 8g protein, 24g carbohydrate, 7g total fat (4g saturated), 159mg cholesterol, 145mg sodium

---

LEMON PUDDING

Prep: 10 minutes plus chilling   *Cook:* 15 minutes
Makes 6 servings

⅔ cup sugar	2½ cups milk
¼ cup cornstarch	2 large egg yolks
1 teaspoon grated lemon peel	⅓ cup fresh lemon juice
Pinch salt	Assorted berries (optional)

◆ In 2-quart saucepan, with wire whisk, stir sugar, cornstarch, lemon peel, and salt until blended. Stir in a little milk until smooth; stir in remaining milk. Cook over medium-high heat, whisking constantly, until mixture thickens and boils. Boil 1 minute, whisking. Remove from heat.

◆ In small bowl, whisk egg yolks and lemon juice. Into yolks, gradually whisk half of hot milk mixture. Pour yolk mixture back into milk mixture in saucepan, stirring rapidly to prevent lumping. Cook over low heat, stirring constantly, about 2 minutes, until very thick (mixture should be about 160°F).

◆ Spoon pudding into shallow bowl. Press plastic wrap onto surface of pudding to prevent skin from forming as pudding cools. Refrigerate at least 2 hours, until chilled and set. Serve with assorted berries, if you like.

Each serving: About 190 calories, 4g protein, 33g carbohydrate, 5g total fat (3g saturated), 85mg cholesterol, 90mg sodium

GELATIN-BASED DESSERTS

Gelatin works magic, turning simple cream or fruit mixtures into smooth mousses or showpiece molded desserts. We've included a delicately flavored cooked-cream dessert from Italy, two very different mousses, and an elegant Raspberry Charlotte. The golden rules: Always dissolve the gelatin completely during heating, and never allow a gelatin mixture to boil.

PANNA COTTA WITH RASPBERRY SAUCE

◆◆◆◆◆◆◆◆◆◆◆◆◆

Prep: 20 minutes plus chilling
Cook: 15 minutes
Makes 8 servings

1 envelope unflavored gelatin
1 cup milk
½ vanilla bean or
   1½ teaspoons vanilla extract
1¾ cups heavy or whipping
   cream
¼ cup sugar
1 strip (3" by 1") lemon peel
1 cinnamon stick (3 inches)
1 container (10 ounces)
   frozen raspberries in syrup,
   thawed
2 tablespoons red currant jelly
2 teaspoons cornstarch
Fresh raspberries and mint
   sprigs for garnish

1 In 2-cup glass measuring cup, sprinkle gelatin over milk; let stand 5 minutes. Meanwhile, with knife, cut vanilla bean lengthwise in half. Scrape out and reserve seeds.

2 In 1-quart saucepan, heat bean halves and seeds, cream, and next 3 ingredients to boiling over high heat, stirring occasionally. (If using vanilla extract, stir in after removing lemon peel.) Reduce heat to low; simmer, stirring occasionally, 5 minutes.

3 Stir milk mixture into saucepan; heat 2 to 3 minutes, stirring constantly, until gelatin is completely dissolved (do not boil). Remove lemon peel, cinnamon stick, and vanilla bean. Pour mixture into medium bowl set in large bowl of *ice water*.

4 Stir mixture often, 10 to 12 minutes, just until beginning to mound when dropped from spatula. Immediately remove from ice bath.

5 Pour into eight 4-ounce ramekins or custard cups; place on jelly-roll pan for easier handling. Refrigerate at least 4 hours, until well chilled, or overnight.

6 Prepare sauce: Into 2-quart saucepan, press thawed raspberries through sieve. Stir in jelly and cornstarch. Heat to boiling over medium heat, stirring; boil 1 minute. Transfer to bowl; cover and refrigerate.

7 To unmold panna cotta, run warm knife around edge of each ramekin, then tap side of ramekin sharply to break seal; invert onto a dessert plate. Spoon some sauce around each panna cotta and garnish.

EACH SERVING. ABOUT 280 CALORIES, 3g PROTEIN, 23g CARBOHYDRATE, 20g TOTAL FAT (13g SATURATED), 75mg CHOLESTEROL, 35mg SODIUM

CAPPUCCINO MOUSSE

Prep: 30 minutes plus chilling   Cook: 2 to 3 minutes
Makes 8 servings

1 envelope plus 1 teaspoon unflavored gelatin
⅓ cup plus ½ cup milk
1 cup freshly brewed espresso coffee, or 2 tablespoons instant espresso-coffee powder dissolved in 1 cup boiling water

½ cup plus 1 teaspoon sugar
2 tablespoons coffee-flavor liqueur
1⅓ cups heavy or whipping cream
Pinch ground cinnamon
Chocolate-covered coffee beans for garnish

◆ In 1-quart saucepan, sprinkle gelatin over ⅓ cup milk; let stand 5 minutes. Stir in espresso. Heat over low heat, stirring constantly, 2 to 3 minutes, until gelatin is completely dissolved (do not boil). Remove from heat and stir in ½ cup sugar until dissolved. Stir in liqueur and remaining ½ cup milk. Transfer mixture to large bowl.

◆ Set bowl in larger bowl of *ice water*. With rubber spatula, stir often just until mixture mounds slightly when dropped from spatula. Immediately remove from ice bath.

◆ Meanwhile, in medium bowl, with mixer at medium speed, beat 1 cup cream to soft peaks. Fold one-third of cream into espresso mixture until incorporated. Fold in remaining whipped cream. Spoon into 8 coffee cups or 6-ounce custard cups. Cover and refrigerate at least 4 hours, until well chilled, or overnight.

◆ To serve, beat remaining ⅓ cup cream with cinnamon and remaining 1 teaspoon sugar to stiff peaks; spoon a dollop onto each mousse. Garnish with coffee beans.

Each serving: 220 calories, 3g protein, 17g carbohydrate, 16g total fat (10g saturated), 58mg cholesterol, 30mg sodium

MANGO MOUSSE

Prep: 20 minutes plus chilling   Cook: 3 minutes
Makes 8 servings

1 envelope unflavored gelatin
2 large ripe mangoes, peeled and cut into bite-size chunks (about 3 cups)

1 can (15 ounces) cream of coconut
½ cup fresh lime juice

◆ In 1-quart saucepan, sprinkle gelatin over ¼ *cup cold water*; let stand 5 minutes. Meanwhile, in blender at medium speed, blend remaining ingredients until smooth.

◆ Heat gelatin mixture over low heat, stirring constantly, 2 to 3 minutes, until completely dissolved (do not boil). Add to mango mixture in blender and blend until combined. Pour mixture into eight 4-ounce custard cups. Cover and refrigerate 4 hours, until well chilled, or overnight.

Each serving: 225 calories, 3g protein, 16g carbohydrate, 19g total fat (16g saturated), 0mg cholesterol, 5mg sodium

RASPBERRY CHARLOTTE

Prep: 25 minutes plus chilling   Cook: 4 minutes
Makes 8 servings

1 tablespoon plus ¼ cup sugar
2 tablespoons orange-flavor liqueur
1 package (3 to 4½ ounces) sponge-type ladyfingers
1 envelope unflavored gelatin
3 tablespoons fresh lemon juice

2 containers (10 ounces each) frozen raspberries in syrup, thawed
1 cup heavy or whipping cream
Fresh raspberries for garnish

◆ Line 9" by 5" loaf pan with plastic wrap. In 1-quart saucepan, heat 1 tablespoon sugar and *2 tablespoons water* to boiling, stirring to dissolve sugar. Remove from heat; stir in liqueur.

◆ Separate ladyfingers into halves. Lightly brush flat sides of ladyfinger halves with liqueur mixture. Line long sides and bottom of loaf pan with ladyfingers, flat sides in (they will not completely cover bottom).

◆ In clean 1-quart saucepan, sprinkle gelatin over ¼ *cup cold water*; let stand 5 minutes. Heat over low heat, stirring constantly, 2 to 3 minutes, until gelatin is completely dissolved (do not boil). Remove from heat; stir in lemon juice.

◆ In blender at medium speed, blend thawed frozen raspberries until smooth. Into large bowl, press raspberries through sieve; stir in gelatin mixture and remaining ¼ cup sugar. Set bowl in larger bowl of *ice water*. With rubber spatula, stir often, just until mixture mounds slightly when dropped from spatula; immediately remove from ice bath.

◆ In small bowl, with mixer at medium speed, beat cream to soft peaks. Fold one-third of cream into raspberry mixture until completely incorporated; gently fold in remaining cream. Spoon into ladyfinger-lined pan. Cover and refrigerate 4 hours, until well chilled, or overnight.

◆ To serve, trim ladyfingers level with raspberry filling. Unmold charlotte onto serving plate and remove plastic wrap. Garnish with fresh raspberries.

Each serving: About 255 calories, 2g protein, 36g carbohydrate, 11g total fat (7g saturated), 52mg cholesterol, 40mg sodium

Meringues

A mixture of stiffly beaten egg whites and sugar, meringue can be baked into many shapes. For best results, add the sugar very gradually while beating the egg whites, and beat until they stand straight in peaks when the beaters are lifted. Avoid making meringues on a humid day, because they'll absorb moisture from the air and turn soggy. They can be stored for up to a week in an airtight container at room temperature.

Hazelnut dacquoise

Prep: 1 hour 30 minutes plus cooling and chilling
Bake: 45 minutes plus drying in oven   *Makes* 12 servings

1 cup (about 4 ounces) hazelnuts (filberts), toasted and skinned (see page 94)
2 tablespoons cornstarch
1½ cups plus 4 tablespoons confectioners' sugar
6 large egg whites
½ teaspoon cream of tartar
3 cups heavy or whipping cream

1 teaspoon vanilla extract
3 squares (3 ounces) semisweet chocolate, melted and slightly warm
1 tablespoon instant espresso-coffee powder
Chocolate Curls for garnish (see page 123)

1 Preheat oven to 300°F. Line 2 large cookie sheets with foil. Using 8-inch round cake pan as a guide, with toothpick, outline 2 circles on foil on each sheet. In food processor with knife blade attached or in blender, blend hazelnuts, cornstarch, and ¾ cup confectioners' sugar until nuts are ground.

2 In large bowl, with mixer at high speed, beat egg whites and cream of tartar to soft peaks. Sprinkle ¾ cup confectioners' sugar, 2 tablespoons at a time, into egg whites, beating well after each addition, until sugar dissolves and whites stand in stiff, glossy peaks.

3 With rubber spatula, fold hazelnut mixture into egg whites. With metal spatula, spread one-fourth of meringue mixture inside each circle on cookie sheets. Bake meringues 45 minutes. Turn oven off; leave meringues in oven 1 hour to dry.

4 Transfer meringues with foil to wire racks; cool completely. With metal spatula, carefully loosen and remove meringues from foil.

5 Prepare chocolate cream: In small bowl, with mixer at medium speed, beat 1½ cups heavy cream, 1 tablespoon confectioners' sugar, and ½ teaspoon vanilla just to soft peaks. With rubber spatula, fold half of whipped cream into slightly warm melted chocolate just until combined. Fold in remaining whipped cream. Reserve ¼ cup chocolate cream.

6 Prepare coffee cream: In cup, dissolve espresso in 2 tablespoons heavy cream. In small bowl, beat remaining heavy cream and 3 tablespoons confectioners' sugar until soft peaks form. Add espresso mixture; beat until stiff peaks form.

7 On cake stand or plate, place 1 meringue layer; spread with half of chocolate cream. Top with another meringue layer and half of coffee cream. Repeat layering, ending with coffee cream. Spoon reserved ¼ cup chocolate cream on top. Refrigerate dacquoise at least 5 hours, or overnight, for easier cutting. Prepare Chocolate Curls. Just before serving, arrange curls on top of dacquoise.

EACH SERVING: ABOUT 365 CALORIES, 5g PROTEIN, 24g CARBOHYDRATE, 30g TOTAL FAT (16g SATURATED), 82mg CHOLESTEROL, 50mg SODIUM

STRAWBERRY-LEMON MERINGUE NESTS

Prep: 35 minutes plus chilling and cooling
Bake: 2 hours 30 minutes plus drying in oven
Makes 6 servings

3 large lemons
1 tablespoon cornstarch
6 tablespoons butter
1¼ cups sugar
4 large eggs, separated
¼ teaspoon cream of tartar

½ cup heavy or whipping
   cream
1 pint strawberries, hulled
   and each cut into quarters
1 tablespoon strawberry jam

◆ Prepare lemon curd: Grate 1 tablespoon peel and squeeze ½ cup juice from lemons. In 2-quart saucepan, with wire whisk, mix cornstarch, lemon peel, and lemon juice until smooth. Add butter and ¾ cup sugar; heat to boiling over medium heat. Boil 1 minute, stirring constantly.

◆ In small bowl, beat egg yolks lightly. Into yolks, beat small amount of hot lemon mixture; pour egg mixture back into lemon mixture in saucepan, beating rapidly. Reduce heat to low; cook, stirring constantly, 5 minutes, or until thick (do not boil). Pour into medium bowl; cover surface with plastic wrap. Refrigerate 3 hours, until chilled, or up to 3 days.

◆ Meanwhile, prepare meringue nests: Preheat oven to 225°F. Line large cookie sheet with foil. In small bowl, with mixer at high speed, beat egg whites and cream of tartar until soft peaks form. Sprinkle in remaining ½ cup sugar, 2 tablespoons at a time, beating well after each addition until sugar dissolves and whites stand in stiff, glossy peaks.

◆◆◆◆◆◆◆◆◆◆◆◆◆◆◆◆◆◆◆◆◆◆◆◆◆◆◆

PIPING MERINGUE STARS

For a dessert sensation, pipe any meringue mixture into stars: Preheat oven to 225°F. Line large cookie sheet with foil. Using 3-inch star-shape cookie cutter as a guide, with toothpick, trace star outlines on foil. Spoon two-thirds of meringue into decorating bag fitted with coupler and large star tip. Pipe meringue around outline of traced stars on foil; fill centers of stars with meringue. Change tip on decorating bag to medium star tip; spoon remaining meringue into bag.

Pipe slightly smaller star on top of each existing star. With spoon, form small indentation in center of each meringue star. Bake 2½ hours. Transfer meringues with foil to wire rack; cool completely. Top with lemon curd or whipped cream and fruit.

◆◆◆◆◆◆◆◆◆◆◆◆◆◆◆◆◆◆◆◆◆◆◆◆◆◆◆

◆ Spoon meringue into 6 mounds on cookie sheet. With back of spoon, form a well in center of each mound to create a nest. Bake 2½ hours. Turn oven off; leave nests in oven 1 hour to dry completely.

◆ Transfer nests with foil to wire rack; cool completely. With metal spatula, carefully loosen nests and remove from foil. Store in airtight container at room temperature until ready to use (up to 1 week).

◆ Just before serving, in small bowl, with mixer at medium speed, beat cream to stiff peaks. Gently fold into lemon curd. In medium bowl, toss strawberries with jam. Spoon lemon-curd mixture into nests; top with strawberry mixture.

Each serving: About 415 calories, 5g protein, 52g carbohydrate, 22g total fat (13g saturated), 200mg cholesterol, 165mg sodium

BERRIES AND CREAM MERINGUES

Prep: 25 minutes plus cooling *Bake: 45 minutes plus drying in oven*
Makes 8 servings

4 large egg whites
¼ teaspoon cream of tartar
¾ cup plus 1 tablespoon
   granulated sugar
1½ cups heavy or whipping
   cream
¼ teaspoon vanilla extract

2 tablespoons sweet Marsala
   wine (optional)
1 pint blueberries
½ pint raspberries
½ pint blackberries
Confectioners' sugar

◆ Preheat oven to 225°F. Line 2 large cookie sheets with foil. In small bowl, with mixer at high speed, beat egg whites and cream of tartar until soft peaks form. Sprinkle in ¾ cup granulated sugar, 2 tablespoons at a time, beating well after each addition until sugar completely dissolves and whites stand in stiff, glossy peaks.

◆ With small metal spatula, spread meringue on foil-lined cookie sheets into eight 6-inch rounds, about ½ inch apart. Bake 45 minutes. Turn oven off; leave meringues in oven 1 hour longer to dry completely.

◆ Transfer meringues with foil to wire racks; cool completely. With metal spatula, carefully loosen and remove meringues from foil. Store in airtight container at room temperature until ready to use (up to 1 week).

◆ Just before serving, in small bowl, with mixer at medium speed, beat heavy cream, vanilla, and remaining 1 tablespoon granulated sugar until soft peaks form. Beat in Marsala, if using. Spread whipped cream on meringues. Top with berries; sprinkle berries with confectioners' sugar.

Each serving: About 280 calories, 3g protein, 32g carbohydrate, 17g total fat (10g saturated), 61mg cholesterol, 45mg sodium

ICE-CREAM DESSERTS

Create impressive but easy desserts with store-bought ice cream and sorbets. Use to fill a cake roll or top a cookie-crumb crust, put it in the freezer – and relax.

CINNAMON ICE-CREAM ROLL

◆◆◆◆◆◆◆◆◆◆◆◆◆

Prep: 40 minutes plus cooling, freezing, and standing
Bake: 12 to 15 minutes
Makes 16 servings

⅔ cup cake flour (not self-rising)
1 teaspoon baking powder
½ teaspoon salt
About ⅓ cup unsweetened cocoa
½ teaspoon plus 2 tablespoons ground cinnamon
4 large eggs, separated
¾ cup plus 2 tablespoons sugar
¾ teaspoon vanilla extract
1 quart vanilla ice cream
1 cup heavy or whipping cream
Quick Chocolate Curls (see page 123) for garnish

1 Preheat oven to 375°F. Grease 15½" by 10½" jelly-roll pan; line pan with waxed paper. Set aside. Sift flour, baking powder, salt, ⅓ cup cocoa, and ½ teaspoon cinnamon through medium-mesh sieve into small bowl. In another small bowl, with mixer at high speed, beat egg whites until soft peaks form. Gradually sprinkle in ¼ cup sugar, beating until sugar completely dissolves and whites stand in stiff peaks.

2 In large bowl, with same beaters and with mixer at high speed, beat egg yolks, vanilla, and ½ cup sugar until very thick and lemon-colored.

3 With rubber spatula or wire whisk, fold in flour mixture and egg whites (this will take patience). Spread evenly in pan. Bake 12 to 15 minutes, until top springs back when lightly touched.

4 Sprinkle clean cloth kitchen towel with cocoa. When cake is done, immediately invert onto towel. Remove waxed paper. If you like, cut off crisp edges. From a narrow end, roll cake with towel, jelly-roll fashion. Cool cake completely, seam-side down, on wire rack, about 1 hour.

5 Place ice cream in large bowl; let stand at room temperature to soften slightly. Stir in remaining 2 tablespoons cinnamon. Unroll cooled cake; spread with ice cream. From same end, roll cake without towel. Place cake, seam-side down, on freezer-safe long platter. Freeze at least 4 hours, until firm. In small bowl, with mixer at medium speed, beat heavy cream and remaining 2 tablespoons sugar until stiff peaks form.

6 Spoon whipped cream over top of cake. (If not serving right away, freeze cake uncovered until whipped cream hardens. Wrap; return to freezer. To serve, let cake stand at room temperature 15 minutes for easier slicing.) Garnish with Quick Chocolate Curls.

EACH SERVING: ABOUT 200 CALORIES, 4g PROTEIN, 25g CARBOHYDRATE, 11g TOTAL FAT (6g SATURATED), 88mg CHOLESTEROL, 145mg SODIUM

SORBET-AND-CREAM CAKE

Prep: 30 minutes plus cooling, freezing, and standing   *Bake:* 10 minutes
Makes 20 servings

30 vanilla wafers	1 pint mango sorbet
4 tablespoons margarine or butter	1 pint lemon sorbet
½ teaspoon grated lime peel	1 ripe mango, peeled and thinly sliced, for garnish
2 pints vanilla ice cream	Fresh raspberries or strawberries for garnish
1 pint raspberry or strawberry sorbet	

◆ Preheat oven to 375°F. In food processor with knife blade attached or in blender at medium speed, blend vanilla wafers until fine crumbs form. (You should have about 1 cup crumbs.)

◆ In small saucepan, melt margarine over low heat; stir in lime peel. In 9" by 3" springform pan, with fork, stir wafer crumbs and margarine mixture until crumbs are moistened. With hand, press mixture firmly onto bottom of pan. Bake crust 10 minutes. Cool completely in pan on wire rack.

◆ While crust is cooling, place 1 pint vanilla ice cream and all sorbets in refrigerator 30 minutes to soften slightly.

◆ Spoon alternating scoops of softened vanilla ice cream and sorbets over crust in 2 layers; press mixture down to eliminate air pockets. Place pan in freezer about 30 minutes to harden mixture slightly.

◆ Meanwhile, place remaining vanilla ice cream in refrigerator to soften slightly.

◆ With metal spatula, evenly spread remaining vanilla ice cream over frozen layer. Cover and freeze at least 4 hours, until firm.

◆ To unmold, place warm dampened towels around side of pan for about 20 seconds to soften ice cream slightly. Remove side of pan and place cake on platter. (If you like, remove pan bottom also.) Cover cake and keep frozen if not serving right away; let stand at room temperature about 15 minutes for easier slicing. Before serving, garnish top of cake with mango slices and raspberries.

Each serving: About 160 calories, 1g protein, 23g carbohydrate, 8g total fat (2g saturated), 15mg cholesterol, 85mg sodium

VANILLA-PECAN ICE-CREAM TORTE

Prep: 20 minutes plus cooling, freezing, and standing   *Bake:* 8 minutes
Makes 16 servings

1 cup pecan halves, toasted and cooled	3 pints vanilla ice cream
20 gingersnap cookies	2 tablespoons plus 1 teaspoon pumpkin-pie spice
2 tablespoons sugar	
3 tablespoons margarine or butter, melted	

◆ Preheat oven to 375°F. Reserve 16 pecan halves for garnish. In food processor with knife blade attached or in blender at medium speed, blend remaining pecan halves with gingersnaps and sugar until mixture is finely ground.

◆ In 9-inch springform pan, with fork, stir cookie mixture and melted margarine until crumbs are moistened. With hand, press mixture firmly onto bottom of pan. Bake crust 8 minutes. Cool completely in pan on wire rack.

◆ While crust is cooling, let ice cream stand at room temperature 20 minutes to soften slightly. In large bowl, mix ice cream and pumpkin-pie spice until blended; spread over crust. Place pecan halves around top edge of torte. Cover torte and freeze at least overnight, or up to 1 week.

◆ To serve, let frozen torte stand at room temperature about 15 minutes for easier slicing. Remove side of pan.

Each serving: About 210 calories, 3g protein, 22g carbohydrate, 13g total fat (4g saturated), 22mg cholesterol, 125mg sodium

ICE-CREAM SPECIALS

For almost-instant desserts, layer ice cream, fruit, and sauce; top with crumbled cookies, chopped candy, or nuts

• Strawberry and vanilla ice cream layered with sliced strawberries, topped with crumbled macaroon cookies

• Peach ice cream with fresh raspberries, Blueberry Sauce (see page 54), and toasted slivered almonds

• Cinnamon ice cream (mix in 1 tablespoon ground cinnamon per pint of softened vanilla ice cream) with warmed maple syrup and pecans

HOMEMADE ICE CREAM

There's nothing difficult about making scrumptious ice cream yourself, whether it's with an old-fashioned hand-crank ice-cream maker or with an electric model. Our classic, custard-based Vanilla-Bean Ice Cream is irresistible; so are the easy variations on page 54. Alternatively, make our super-simple No-Cook Vanilla Ice Cream – just stir. To add crunch, stir in 1½ cups coarsely chopped Gold-Rush Nut Brittle (see page 96) or other chopped candy immediately *after* churning.

VANILLA-BEAN ICE CREAM

Prep: 5 minutes plus chilling and freezing   Cook: 15 to 20 minutes
Makes about 5 cups

1 vanilla bean or 1 tablespoon vanilla extract	4 large egg yolks
¾ cup sugar	⅛ teaspoon salt
3 cups half-and-half or light cream	1 cup heavy or whipping cream
	Butterscotch Sauce (optional, see page 54)

1 Chop vanilla bean into ¼-inch pieces. In blender, process vanilla bean and sugar until mixture is very finely ground; set aside. (If using vanilla extract, stir in with heavy cream in Step 4.) Prepare custard: In 3-quart saucepan, heat half-and-half to boiling. Meanwhile, in medium bowl, whisk egg yolks, salt, and vanilla-sugar until smooth.

2 Gradually whisk hot half-and-half into egg-yolk mixture.

3 Return mixture to saucepan and cook over medium heat, stirring constantly, just until mixture coats back of wooden spoon (do not boil, or mixture will curdle). Remove from heat.

4 Strain custard mixture through sieve into clean large bowl. Stir heavy cream into custard; refrigerate at least 2 hours, until chilled, or overnight.

5 Churn and freeze in ice-cream maker as manufacturer directs. Prepare Butterscotch Sauce, if you like. Serve ice cream with warm sauce.

NO-COOK VANILLA ICE CREAM

In large bowl, stir 2 cups half-and-half or light cream, 2 cups heavy or whipping cream, ¾ cup sugar, 1 tablespoon vanilla extract, and ⅛ teaspoon salt until sugar is completely dissolved. Pour mixture into ice-cream maker; churn and freeze as manufacturer directs. Makes about 6¾ cups.

Each ½ cup: 225 calories, 2g protein, 14g carbohydrate, 18g total fat (11g saturated), 64mg cholesterol, 50mg sodium

---

EACH ½ CUP: ABOUT 260 CALORIES, 4g PROTEIN, 19g CARBOHYDRATE, 19g TOTAL FAT (11g SATURATED), 145mg CHOLESTEROL, 70mg SODIUM

PEACH OR STRAWBERRY ICE CREAM

Prep: 20 minutes plus chilling and freezing   *Cook: 15 to 20 minutes*
Makes about 6 cups

Vanilla-Bean Ice Cream or No-
Cook Vanilla Ice Cream (see
page 53)
8 medium peaches, peeled
   and sliced (4 cups), or
   2 pints strawberries, hulled

½ cup sugar
2 tablespoons fresh lemon
   juice

Prepare Vanilla-Bean Ice Cream as directed in Steps
1 through 4 or prepare No-Cook Vanilla Ice Cream, but
omit vanilla and use only ½ cup sugar. In medium bowl,
mash peaches or strawberries with sugar and lemon juice;
cover and refrigerate 30 minutes. Before churning, stir fruit
mixture into ice-cream mixture; churn and freeze in ice-
cream maker as manufacturer directs.

**Each ½ cup: About 275 calories, 4g protein, 31g carbohydrate,
16g total fat (9g saturated), 120mg cholesterol, 55mg sodium**

CHOCOLATE ICE CREAM

Prep: 10 minutes plus chilling and freezing   *Cook: 15 to 20 minutes*
Makes about 6 cups

Vanilla-Bean Ice Cream or No-
Cook Vanilla Ice Cream (see
page 53)
3 squares (3 ounces)
   unsweetened chocolate

2 squares (2 ounces)
   semisweet chocolate
1 teaspoon vanilla extract

◆ Prepare Vanilla-Bean Ice Cream as directed in Steps
1 through 4 or prepare No-Cook Vanilla Ice Cream, but
omit vanilla and reserve ¼ cup heavy cream.

◆ In top of double boiler, melt unsweetened and semisweet
chocolate with reserved ¼ cup heavy cream; remove from
heat. Stir in vanilla.

◆ Stir 1 cup ice-cream
mixture into melted
chocolate; stir chocolate
mixture back into ice-
cream mixture. Churn
and freeze in ice-cream
maker as manufacturer
directs.

**Each ½ cup: About 280 calories,
4g protein, 21g carbohydrate,
21g total fat (12g saturated),
120mg cholesterol, 55mg sodium**

ICE-CREAM SAUCES

These no-fuss sauces are great over ice
cream and can be used for our Ice-
Cream Special ideas (see page 52).
Serve a selection with different ice-
cream flavors and let guests
assemble their own dessert.
These sauces are
equally delicious
with pound cake,
bread pudding,
dessert crepes, or
cream puffs.

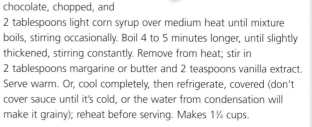

Hot fudge sauce

Blueberry sauce

Hot fudge sauce
In heavy 2-quart
saucepan, heat 1 cup
heavy or whipping
cream, ¾ cup sugar, 4 squares
(4 ounces) unsweetened
chocolate, chopped, and
2 tablespoons light corn syrup over medium heat until mixture
boils, stirring occasionally. Boil 4 to 5 minutes longer, until slightly
thickened, stirring constantly. Remove from heat; stir in
2 tablespoons margarine or butter and 2 teaspoons vanilla extract.
Serve warm. Or, cool completely, then refrigerate, covered (don't
cover sauce until it's cold, or the water from condensation will
make it grainy); reheat before serving. Makes 1¾ cups.

**Each ¼ cup: About 330 calories, 2g protein, 32g carbohydrate,
24g total fat (12g saturated), 47mg cholesterol, 55mg sodium**

Blueberry sauce
In 2-quart saucepan, stir ⅓ cup sugar,
2 teaspoons cornstarch, and ¼ cup cold water until smooth. Heat
to boiling over medium heat, stirring. Add 2 cups fresh or frozen
blueberries and heat to boiling, stirring. Reduce heat to low and
cook 1 minute longer. Remove from heat and stir in 1 teaspoon
fresh lemon juice. Serve warm. Makes 1¾ cups.

**Each ¼ cup: About 65 calories, 0g protein, 16g carbohydrate,
0g total fat, 0mg cholesterol, 5mg sodium**

Butterscotch sauce
In 3-quart saucepan, heat 1 cup packed
brown sugar, ½ cup heavy or whipping cream, ⅓ cup light corn
syrup, 2 tablespoons margarine or butter, 1 teaspoon distilled
white vinegar, and ⅛ teaspoon salt to boiling over high heat,
stirring occasionally. Reduce heat to low and cook 2 minutes.
Remove from heat and stir in 1 teaspon vanilla extract. Serve
warm. Makes 1⅓ cups.

**Each ¼ cup: About 355 calories, 1g protein, 60g carbohydrate,
13g total fat (6g saturated), 33mg cholesterol, 150mg sodium**

GRANITAS AND SORBETS

Fruity, refreshing, and fat-free, granitas and sorbets are made from similar mixtures of pureed fruit and sugar syrup, but granitas have a coarser texture (granita is derived from the verb "to granulate" in Italian). You don't even need an ice-cream maker: Just whirl up the sorbets in a food processor or, for the granitas, freeze in a metal pan (metal makes the mixture freeze faster). Any of the flavors here would make a light ending to a rich meal, perhaps with a crisp cookie on the side.

PEACH GRANITA

◆◆◆◆◆◆◆◆◆◆◆◆◆◆◆◆◆◆◆◆◆◆◆◆◆◆◆◆◆◆

Prep: 20 minutes plus freezing and standing
Makes about 8 cups

1 cup sugar
1¾ pounds peaches or nectarines (about 5 medium), unpeeled, cut into wedges

2 tablespoons fresh lemon juice
Almond-Anise Biscotti (optional, see page 90)

1 Prepare sugar syrup: In 1-quart saucepan, heat sugar and *1¼ cups water* to boiling over high heat, stirring occasionally. Reduce heat to medium; cook, stirring, 1 minute, or until sugar dissolves completely. Transfer to small bowl to cool. In blender at medium speed, blend peach wedges until smooth; pour into medium-mesh sieve set over medium bowl.

2 With spoon, press peach puree through sieve; you should have 3 cups puree. Into puree, stir lemon juice and syrup. Pour into 9" by 9" metal baking pan. Cover with foil or plastic wrap. Freeze 2 hours; stir with fork.

3 Freeze at least 3 hours longer, until fully frozen, or overnight. To serve, let stand 20 minutes at room temperature; with fork or spoon, scrape surface to create pebbly texture. Serve with biscotti, if you like.

MORE FRUIT GRANITAS

Raspberry or blackberry granita Prepare granita as above but substitute 3 pints raspberries or blackberries and 2 tablespoons fresh lime juice for peaches and lemon juice. Makes about 8 cups.

Each ½ cup: About 55 calories, 0g protein, 14g carbohydrate, 0g total fat, 0mg cholesterol, 0mg sodium

Raspberry granita

Watermelon granita Prepare granita as above but substitute 5½-pound piece watermelon, seeded and cut into chunks (about 9 cups), and 2 tablespoons fresh lime juice for peaches and lemon juice; when making the sugar syrup, use only ¾ cup water instead of 1¼ cups. Makes about 9 cups.

Each ½ cup: About 70 calories, 1g protein, 17g carbohydrate, 0g total fat, 0mg cholesterol, 0mg sodium

Watermelon granita

EACH ½ CUP: ABOUT 70 CALORIES, 0g PROTEIN, 18g CARBOHYDRATE, 0g TOTAL FAT, 0mg CHOLESTEROL, 0mg SODIUM

LEMON-ROSEMARY SORBET

Prep: 25 minutes plus standing and freezing
Makes about 4 cups

1¼ cups sugar
¼ cup light corn syrup
2 tablespoons coarsely chopped fresh rosemary
1⅓ cups fresh lemon juice (about 7 large lemons)

2 teaspoons grated lemon peel
Rosemary sprigs and lemon slices for garnish

◆ In 2-quart saucepan, heat sugar, corn syrup, and *4 cups water* to boiling over high heat, stirring occasionally until sugar dissolves. Remove saucepan from heat; stir in chopped rosemary. Cover pan and let stand 20 minutes.

◆ Pour mixture through sieve set over medium bowl; stir in lemon juice and peel. Pour lemon mixture into 9" by 9" metal baking pan; cover with foil or plastic wrap. Freeze, stirring occasionally, about 3 hours, until partially frozen.

◆ In food processor with knife blade attached, blend lemon mixture until smooth but still frozen. Return mixture to baking pan; cover and freeze at least 3 hours, or until firm.

◆ To serve, let sorbet stand at room temperature 10 to 15 minutes to soften slightly for easier scooping; garnish.

Each ⅓ cup: About 110 calories, 0g protein, 28g carbohydrate, 0g total fat, 0mg cholesterol, 5mg sodium

BLUEBERRY SORBET

Prep: 10 minutes plus freezing and standing
Makes about 3⅓ cups

½ cup sugar
2 tablespoons fresh lemon juice

1 bag (20 ounces) frozen unsweetened blueberries

◆ Prepare sugar syrup: In 1-quart saucepan, heat sugar, lemon juice, and *1 tablespoon water* to boiling over high heat. Reduce heat to low and cook, stirring occasionally, until sugar dissolves. Remove from heat.

◆ In food processor with knife blade attached, blend frozen blueberries until fruit resembles finely shaved ice, stopping processor occasionally to scrape down side. (If fruit is not finely shaved, sorbet will not be smooth.)

◆ With processor running, slowly pour hot sugar syrup in a thin stream through feed tube and process until mixture is smooth but still frozen. Spoon into freezer-safe container and freeze until firm.

◆ To serve, let sorbet stand at room temperature 10 to 15 minutes to soften slightly for easier scooping.

Each ⅓ cup: About 70 calories, 0g protein, 17g carbohydrate, 0g total fat, 0mg cholesterol, 0mg sodium

---

MORE FRUIT SORBETS

Peach sorbet Prepare as for Blueberry Sorbet (below left) but use ¼ cup sugar, 1 tablespoon fresh lemon juice, and 1 tablespoon water for sugar syrup, adding ½ teaspoon almond extract to cooked syrup; instead of blueberries, use 1 bag (20 ounces) frozen unsweetened peach slices. Makes about 3 cups.

Each ⅓ cup: About 50 calories, 0g protein, 13g carbohydrate, 0g total fat, 0mg cholesterol, 0mg sodium

Cantaloupe sorbet Prepare as for Blueberry Sorbet (left) but use ½ cup sugar, 2 tablespoons fresh lemon juice, and 1 tablespoon water for sugar syrup; instead of blueberries, use 1 small ripe cantaloupe (2 pounds), seeded, cut into small chunks, spread on jelly-roll pan, and frozen overnight. Makes about 4 cups.

Each ⅓ cup: About 55 calories, 1g protein, 15g carbohydrate, 0g total fat, 0mg cholesterol, 15mg sodium

Strawberry sorbet Prepare as for Blueberry Sorbet (left) but use ⅓ cup sugar, 1 tablespoon fresh lemon juice, and 1 tablespoon water for sugar syrup; instead of blueberries, use 1 bag (20 ounces) frozen unsweetened strawberries. Makes about 2⅓ cups.

Each ⅓ cup: About 65 calories, 0g protein, 17g carbohydrate, 0g total fat, 0mg cholesterol, 0mg sodium

Strawberry sorbet

PIES & TARTS

PIES AND TARTS

Simple or elegant, fruit-filled or fudgy, pies and tarts are wonderfully welcome after practically any meal. A light, flaky crust is a pie's crowning glory and surprisingly easy to make, as long as you use the right ingredients and follow our foolproof mixing and rolling techniques.

PERFECT PASTRY

• Start with cold ingredients (e.g. chilled margarine or butter, ice-cold water). The kitchen should be cool too.
• Generally, handle the dough as little as possible, or you'll overdevelop the gluten in the flour and make a tough crust.
• For best results, use a mix of fat – margarine or butter for flavor and color and shortening for flakiness.
• When cutting fat into the flour, work quickly so the fat remains firm and cold.
• Sprinkle in ice water just until the dough is moistened. Toss quickly and lightly with a fork; do not stir. (Use the least amount of water to avoid a tough crust.)
• Chilling dough for at least 30 minutes will make it easier to roll and also help prevent shrinkage. Wrap tightly so the edges don't dry out and crack when rolled.
• To prevent sticking, roll dough on a lightly floured surface; sprinkle surface with additional flour as necessary. Roll dough from the center forward and back; rotate the dough a quarter-turn and repeat rolling and rotating to make an even circle.
• If dough tears, just moisten the edges and press together. Or, brush a small piece of dough with water; use as a patch.
• When fitting dough into a pie plate, gently ease it onto the bottom with your fingertips or a small ball of dough, taking care to press out air pockets. Never stretch or pull the dough to fit, or the crust may shrink during baking.

WHICH PIE PAN?

Crisp, flaky crusts aren't dependent only on a good dough – the pan also makes a difference. For a crisp, well-browned crust, choose a glass pie plate, or a metal one with a dull finish (shiny pans are fine for crumb crusts). Use a regular pie plate (9 inches across by 1 inch deep) or a deep-dish one (9½ inches by 1½ to 2 inches) as directed so the filling won't overflow. For tarts, use a fluted pan with a removable bottom, which makes for easy removal of the tart.

BLIND BAKING

Crusts with moist fillings are often partially or completely baked before they're filled for crisp results. This is called "blind baking." Line the crust with foil and weight it with pie weights, dry beans, or uncooked rice to prevent puffing or slipping during baking. Cool completely before filling.

For tarts and pies, remove the foil and weights after the crust is set, then return to the oven to brown.

For tartlets, weight the crust with another tart pan before baking. Or, prevent puffing by piercing crust with a fork.

BETTER BAKING

• For non-soggy double-crust pies, cut slits in the top crust before baking so steam can escape during cooking.
• For easy handling – and to catch drips – bake the pie on a sheet of foil with crimped edges, or use a cookie sheet.
• Bake in the lower third of the oven so the bottom crust becomes crisp and the top doesn't overbrown (if pie still browns too quickly, just cover it loosely with foil).
• To check a custard pie for doneness, insert a knife about 1 inch from the center; it should come out clean. A starch-thickened fruit pie is ready when it bubbles in the center.
• Let pies cool before cutting so the filling can set.

NO-FUSS CRUMB CRUSTS

Cookie crumb crusts take no time to make – all you need is a blender or food processor. Or, crush cookies in a zip-tight bag with a rolling pin. Chocolate or vanilla wafers, gingersnaps, or graham crackers are a good base. For added richness, replace some of the cookies with ground nuts such as pecans, macadamias, or almonds, or with amaretti cookies. For spicy flavor, add a bit of ground ginger, cinnamon, or nutmeg.

Regular pie plate   Deep-dish pie plate

PIECRUSTS

Tender, flaky piecrust is a work of art – and surprisingly easy to master. For best results, chill the ingredients before mixing, and handle the pastry as little as possible (overworking develops the gluten in the flour, making the pastry tough). To create a glaze, brush the top crust (not the edge) with milk, cream, or slightly beaten egg white and sprinkle with sugar. Each piecrust takes about 10 minutes to prepare, plus chilling time.

PASTRY FOR 2-CRUST PIE

2¼ cups all-purpose flour
½ teaspoon salt
¼ cup shortening

½ cup cold margarine or butter, cut up

1 In large bowl, mix flour and salt . With pastry blender or two knives used scissor-fashion, cut in shortening and margarine until mixture resembles coarse crumbs.

2 Sprinkle in *4 to 6 tablespoons ice water*, a tablespoon at a time. Mix lightly with fork after each addition until dough is just moist enough to hold together.

3 Shape dough into 2 balls, one slightly larger. Wrap and refrigerate 30 minutes, or overnight (if chilled overnight, let stand at room temperature 30 minutes before rolling). On lightly floured surface, with floured rolling pin, roll larger ball 2 inches larger all around than inverted 9-inch pie plate.

4 Roll dough round gently onto rolling pin; gently ease into pie plate. Trim edge, leaving 1-inch overhang. Reserve trimmings for decorating pie, if you like. Fill piecrust.

5 Roll small ball of dough into 10-inch round. Cut several slashes; center over filling. Trim edge, leaving 1-inch overhang; fold overhang under. Make decorative edge (see page 60).

PASTRY FOR 1-CRUST PIE

1¼ cups all-purpose flour
¼ teaspoon salt
2 tablespoons shortening

4 tablespoons cold margarine or butter, cut up

Prepare pastry as directed for 2-Crust Pie, but in Step 2 sprinkle in *3 to 5 tablespoons ice water*, and in Step 3 make only 1 ball of dough.

PASTRY FOR 11-INCH TART

1½ cups all-purpose flour
½ teaspoon salt
2 tablespoons shortening

½ cup cold margarine or butter, cut up

Prepare pastry as directed for 2-Crust Pie, but in Step 2 sprinkle in *3 to 4 tablespoons ice water*, and in Step 3 make only 1 ball of dough and, after chilling, roll dough to a 14-inch round. Ease dough into 11" by 1" round tart pan with removable bottom. Fold overhang in and press against side of tart pan to form rim ⅛ inch above pan edge.

PASTRY FOR 9-INCH TART

1 cup all-purpose flour
¼ teaspoon salt
1 tablespoon shortening

6 tablespoons cold margarine or butter, cut up

Prepare pastry as directed for 2-Crust Pie, but in Step 2 sprinkle in only *2 to 3 tablespoons ice water*, and in Step 3 make only 1 ball of dough and, after chilling, roll dough to an 11-inch round. Use to line 9" by 1" round tart pan with removable bottom as directed for 11-inch tart.

FOOD PROCESSOR METHOD

In food processor with knife blade attached, combine flour, salt, shortening, and margarine. Process for 1 to 2 seconds, until mixture forms fine crumbs. Add smaller amount of *ice water* all at once; process for 1 to 2 seconds until dough leaves sides of bowl. Remove dough from bowl; with hands, shape into ball.

DECORATIVE PIE EDGES

From classic to creative, these borders are the perfect way to add a professional finish to homemade pies. The forked, fluted, sharp fluted, and rope edges are pretty on any pie, whether one- or two-crust. The appliqué leaf edge is best for one-crust pies (but you will need enough pastry for a two-crust). For neat results, chill the pastry so that it is firm (not hard) when you work with it.

◆ ◆ ◆ ◆ ◆ ◆ ◆ ◆ ◆ ◆ ◆ ◆

PREPARING PIE EDGES

1 Trim dough edge (or top crust for 2-crust pie) with kitchen shears to leave 1-inch overhang. (For forked or leaf edge, trim edge even with rim of pie plate; omit Step 2 below).

2 Fold overhang under; pinch to make stand-up edge. Shape decorative edge as desired (right).

◆ ◆ ◆ ◆ ◆ ◆ ◆ ◆ ◆ ◆ ◆ ◆

Forked edge Trim dough edge as in Step 1 (below left) even with rim of pie plate. With floured 4-tine fork, press dough to rim of plate; repeat around edge.

Fluted edge Push one index finger against outside edge of rim; with index finger and thumb of other hand, pinch to form ruffle. Repeat around edge, leaving ¼-inch space between each ruffle.

Sharp (or pinched) fluted edge Push one index finger against inside edge of rim; with index finger and thumb of other hand, pinch to make flute. Repeat around edge, leaving ¼-inch space between each flute.

Rope edge Press thumb into dough edge at an angle, then pinch dough between thumb and knuckle of index finger. Place thumb in groove left by index finger; pinch as before; repeat around edge.

Leaf edge Prepare Pastry for 2-Crust Pie (see page 59). Use larger ball of dough to line pie plate; trim even with rim. Roll smaller ball ⅛ inch thick. With knife or small cookie cutter, cut out leaves (see page 61). Lightly brush piecrust edge with water. Press shapes onto edge.

Double-crust pies

A double-crust pie, which lends itself to decorative edges and adornments of cutouts made from dough trimmings, is a beautiful – and delicious – way to encase a fruit filling. Be sure to cut a few slits in the top to allow the steam to escape. Always cool the pie for a short time as the recipe directs (even when serving it warm) so the filling can firm up for easier cutting.

DEEP-DISH APPLE PIE

Prep: 40 minutes plus chilling and cooling   Bake: 50 to 55 minutes
Makes 10 servings

Pastry for 2-Crust Pie (see page 59)

9 medium Golden Delicious or Newtown Pippin apples (about 3 pounds), peeled, cored, and cut into ⅛-inch-thick slices

½ cup sugar

3 tablespoons all-purpose flour

2 tablespoons coarsely chopped crystallized ginger

2 tablespoons margarine or butter, cut into small pieces

1 Prepare Pastry for 2-Crust Pie through chilling. Preheat oven to 425°F. In large bowl, toss apple slices with sugar, flour, and ginger.

2 Use larger ball of dough to line 9½-inch deep-dish pie plate. Spoon apple mixture into piecrust; dot with margarine.

3 Roll dough for top crust into 11-inch round. Place on filling as directed; make decorative edge (see page 60). Reroll trimmings. Make shapes (see below); brush with water. Place on pie. Place sheet of foil underneath pie plate; crimp foil edges to form a rim to catch drips during baking.

4 Bake pie 50 to 55 minutes, until apples are tender when pierced with a knife. Cover pie loosely with foil after 30 minutes to prevent overbrowning. Cool pie on wire rack 1 hour to serve warm. Or, cool completely to serve later.

DECORATIVE PASTRY SHAPES

Apple Roll out the dough trimmings. Use a small knife dipped in flour to cut a free-form apple shape.

Leaves Reflour knife; cut out leaves from remaining dough. Use back of the knife to mark veins in the leaves.

EACH SERVING: ABOUT 370 CALORIES, 3g PROTEIN, 53g CARBOHYDRATE, 17g TOTAL FAT (4g SATURATED), 0mg CHOLESTEROL, 240mg SODIUM

STRAWBERRY-RHUBARB PIE

Prep: 30 minutes plus chilling and cooling   Bake: 1 hour 35 to 45 minutes
Makes 10 servings

Pastry for 2-Crust Pie (see
   page 59)
¼ cup cornstarch
1 cup plus 1 tablespoon sugar
1 pint strawberries, hulled,
   each cut in half if large

1¼ pounds rhubarb, cut into
   ½-inch pieces (4 cups)
2 tablespoons margarine or
   butter, cut up

◆ Prepare Pastry for 2-Crust Pie through chilling. Preheat oven to 425°F. In large bowl, mix cornstarch and 1 cup sugar. Add strawberries and rhubarb; toss to combine.

◆ Use larger ball of dough to line 9-inch pie plate. Spoon fruit mixture into piecrust; dot with margarine. Roll top crust and place on filling as directed; make decorative edge (see page 60). Sprinkle with remaining 1 tablespoon sugar.

◆ Place sheet of foil underneath pie plate; crimp edges to form a rim to catch drips. Bake pie 15 minutes. Turn oven control to 375°F; bake 1 hour 20 to 30 minutes longer, until filling is bubbly in center. Cool pie on wire rack 1 hour to serve warm. Or, cool completely to serve later.

Each serving: About 355 calories, 4g protein, 49g carbohydrate, 17g total fat (4g saturated), 0mg cholesterol, 240mg sodium

PEAR-CRANBERRY PIE

Prep: 45 minutes plus chilling and cooling   Bake: 1 hour 20 to 30 minutes
Makes 10 servings

Pastry for 2-Crust Pie (see
   page 59)
3 tablespoons cornstarch
⅛ teaspoon ground cinnamon
¾ cup plus 1 tablespoon sugar
1½ cups cranberries, chopped

6 large fully ripe pears (about
   3 pounds), peeled, cored,
   and sliced
2 tablespoons margarine or
   butter, cut up

◆ Prepare Pastry for 2-Crust Pie through chilling. Preheat oven to 425°F. In large bowl, mix cornstarch, cinnamon, and ¾ cup sugar. Add cranberries and pears; toss to combine.

◆ Use larger ball of dough to line 9-inch pie plate. Spoon pear mixture into piecrust. Dot with margarine. Roll top crust and place on filling as directed; make decorative edge (see page 60). Sprinkle with remaining 1 tablespoon sugar.

◆ Place sheet of foil underneath pie plate; crimp foil edges to form a rim to catch drips. Bake pie 20 minutes. Turn oven control to 375°F; bake 60 to 70 minutes longer, until filling is bubbly in center. Cool pie on wire rack 1 hour to serve warm. Or, cool completely to serve later.

Each serving: About 400 calories, 3g protein, 61g carbohydrate, 17g total fat (4g saturated), 0mg cholesterol, 240mg sodium

HOME-STYLE PEACH AND CHERRY PIE

Prep: 50 minutes plus chilling and cooling   Bake: 1 hour 30 minutes
Makes 10 servings

Pastry for 2-Crust Pie (see
   page 59)
¾ cup packed light brown
   sugar
⅓ cup cornstarch
½ teaspoon salt
6 medium-size ripe peaches
   (about 2½ pounds), peeled,
   pitted, and thinly sliced

1 pound tart cherries,
   pitted (about 2 cups), or
   ½ (20-ounce) bag frozen
   pitted tart cherries, thawed
1 tablespoon milk
1 tablespoon granulated
   sugar

◆ Prepare Pastry for 2-Crust Pie through chilling. Preheat oven to 375°F. In large bowl, mix brown sugar, cornstarch, and salt. Add peaches and cherries; toss to combine.

◆ Use larger ball of dough to line 9½-inch deep-dish pie plate. Spoon fruit mixture into piecrust. Roll remaining dough into an 11-inch round; use to make lattice top (see page 72). Brush pastry with milk and sprinkle with granulated sugar.

◆ Place sheet of foil underneath pie plate; crimp foil edges to form a rim to catch drips during baking. Bake pie 1½ hours, or until filling is bubbly in center. Cover pie loosely with foil during last 40 minutes to prevent overbrowning. Cool pie on wire rack 1 hour to serve warm. Or, cool completely to serve later.

Each serving: About 375 calories, 4g protein, 59g carbohydrate, 15g total fat (3g saturated), 0mg cholesterol, 330mg sodium

SINGLE-CRUST PIES

A single crust can cradle luscious fruits, rich chocolate-nut creations, or silky custards. Be sure to mend any cracks that appear in the pastry during rolling: Moisten the torn edges, lay a patch of dough over the tear, and carefully press into position.

SWEET SUMMER PIE

◆◆◆◆◆◆◆◆◆◆◆◆

Prep: 55 minutes plus chilling and cooling
Bake: 1 hour
Makes 10 servings

Pastry for 1-Crust Pie (see page 59)
1 large orange
1 large lemon
4 large eggs, separated
⅛ teaspoon salt
⅔ cup plus ¼ cup sugar
⅓ cup all-purpose flour
8 medium nectarines (about 2½ pounds), peeled, pitted, and sliced
½ pint raspberries

1 Prepare Pastry for 1-Crust Pie through chilling. Grate 2 teaspoons peel and squeeze ⅓ cup juice from orange. Grate 1½ teaspoons peel from lemon, then squeeze enough juice to add to orange juice to equal ½ cup juice in total. In small bowl, with mixer at high speed, beat egg yolks, salt, and ⅓ cup sugar about 3 minutes, until thick and lemon-colored. Gradually beat in juice mixture and all of grated peel.

2 In 1-quart saucepan, cook yolk mixture over low heat, stirring constantly, 8 to 10 minutes, until thick (do not boil or mixture will curdle). Spoon into medium bowl; cool completely. Preheat oven to 425°F. In large bowl, mix flour and ⅓ cup sugar. Add nectarine slices; toss to combine. Gently stir in raspberries. Use pastry to line 9-inch pie plate; make decorative edge (see page 60).

3 Spoon fruit mixture into piecrust. Cover loosely with lightly greased foil; bake 45 minutes, or until bubbly in center and crust is lightly browned. Remove from oven. Turn oven control to 350°F.

◆◆◆◆◆◆◆◆◆◆◆◆◆◆◆◆◆◆◆◆◆◆◆◆◆◆◆◆◆◆◆◆◆◆◆◆◆◆◆

GRATING PEEL

When grating peel from oranges, lemons, or limes, avoid waste, messy scraping, and jammed grater holes by pressing a piece of plastic wrap over the fine side of the grater first. When you're finished, the peel will come off the wrap without any trouble – and the grater will be easier to clean.

4 In clean small bowl, with mixer at high speed, beat egg whites to soft peaks. Sprinkle in remaining ¼ cup sugar, beating until whites stand in stiff peaks. Fold whites into cooled yolk mixture, one-third at a time

5 Spread topping over filling right to edges. Return pie to oven; bake 15 minutes, or until topping is set and lightly browned. Cool pie completely on wire rack. Cover and refrigerate any leftovers.

◆◆◆◆◆◆◆◆◆◆◆◆◆◆◆◆◆◆◆◆◆◆◆◆◆◆◆◆◆◆◆◆◆◆◆◆◆◆◆

EACH SERVING: ABOUT 295 CALORIES, 6g PROTEIN, 49g CARBOHYDRATE, 10g TOTAL FAT (2g SATURATED), 85mg CHOLESTEROL, 160mg SODIUM

PEACH TARTE TATIN

Prep: 1 hour plus chilling
and cooling
Bake: 25 minutes
Makes 12 servings

Pastry for 1-Crust Pie (see
  page 59)
1 cup sugar
6 tablespoons margarine or
  butter
1 tablespoon fresh lemon juice

11 medium-size firm, slightly
  ripe peaches (about
  3¾ pounds), peeled, pitted,
  and each cut in half

◆ Prepare Pastry for 1-Crust Pie through chilling.

◆ In heavy 12-inch skillet with oven-safe handle, heat sugar, margarine, and lemon juice to boiling over medium-high heat. Place peaches in skillet, pitted side down. Cook 10 minutes. Carefully turn peaches; cook 8 to 12 minutes longer, until syrup is caramelized and thickened.

◆ Meanwhile, preheat oven to 425°F. Just before peaches are done, on lightly floured surface, with floured rolling pin, roll dough into a 14-inch round. Place dough on top of peaches in skillet; tuck edge under to form a rim. With knife, cut six ¼-inch slits in dough so steam can escape during baking. Bake 25 minutes, or until crust is golden.

◆ When tarte tatin is done, place large platter over top of skillet; carefully invert onto platter. Cool 1 hour to serve warm. Or, cool completely to serve later.

Each serving: 270 calories, 2g protein, 42g carbohydrate, 12g total fat (2g saturated), 0mg cholesterol, 155mg sodium

CHOCOLATE-PECAN PIE

Prep: 45 minutes plus chilling and cooling *Bake:* 1 hour 5 minutes
Makes 12 servings

Pastry for 1-Crust Pie (see
  page 59)
4 tablespoons margarine or
  butter
2 squares (2 ounces)
  unsweetened chocolate

¾ cup packed dark brown sugar
¾ cup dark corn syrup
1 teaspoon vanilla extract
3 large eggs
1¾ cups pecan halves
  (about 7 ounces)

◆ Prepare Pastry for 1-Crust Pie through chilling.

◆ Preheat oven to 425°F. Use pastry to line 9-inch pie plate. Make decorative edge (see page 60). Line pie shell with foil and fill with pie weights, dry beans, or uncooked rice.

◆ Bake piecrust 10 minutes. Remove foil with weights; bake 10 minutes longer, or until lightly golden. Cool piecrust on wire rack at least 10 minutes. Turn oven control to 350°F. Meanwhile, in heavy 1-quart saucepan, melt margarine and chocolate over low heat, stirring frequently. Cool slightly.

◆ In large bowl, with wire whisk, mix chocolate mixture, brown sugar, and next 3 ingredients until blended. Coarsely chop 1 cup pecan halves; leave remaining pecans as halves. Stir all pecans into chocolate mixture; pour into cooled crust.

◆ Bake pie 45 minutes, or until edges are set (center should jiggle slightly). Cool completely on wire rack. Cover and refrigerate any leftovers.

Each serving: About 390 calories, 5g protein, 42g carbohydrate, 24g total fat (4g saturated), 53mg cholesterol, 170mg sodium

GRANDMA'S SWEET-POTATO PIE

Prep: 1 hour 10 minutes plus chilling and cooling *Bake:* 40 minutes
Makes 10 servings

Pastry for 1-Crust Pie (see
  page 59)
4 medium sweet potatoes
  (about 2 pounds), unpeeled,
  or 2 cans (16 to 17 ounces
  each) sweet potatoes,
  drained
2 cups half-and-half or light
  cream

1 cup packed dark brown
  sugar
4 tablespoons margarine or
  butter, melted
1 teaspoon ground cinnamon
¾ teaspoon ground ginger
½ teaspoon ground nutmeg
½ teaspoon salt
3 large eggs

◆ Prepare Pastry for 1-Crust Pie through chilling.

◆ If using fresh sweet potatoes, in 3-quart saucepan, heat sweet potatoes and enough *water* to cover to boiling over high heat. Reduce heat to low. Cover and simmer 30 minutes, or until fork-tender; drain. Cool potatoes until easy to handle; peel and cut into chunks.

◆ Preheat oven to 400°F. In large bowl, with mixer at low speed, beat sweet potatoes until smooth. Add half-and-half and remaining ingredients; beat until well blended.

◆ Use pastry to line 9½-inch deep-dish pie plate. Make decorative edge (see page 60). Spoon sweet-potato mixture into piecrust.

◆ Bake pie 40 minutes, or until knife inserted 1 inch from edge comes out clean. Cool 1 hour to serve warm. Or, cool slightly, then refrigerate to serve later. Cover and refrigerate any leftovers.

Each serving: About 400 calories, 6g protein, 52g carbohydrate, 19g total fat (6g saturated), 82mg cholesterol, 320mg sodium

CRUMB-CRUST PIES

These foolproof crusts are simple to make. Cookie crumbs, melted margarine or butter, and sugar are simply mixed together and pressed into the pie plate – no rolling required. To set the mixture, the crust is briefly baked before filling. For firm, easy-to-cut slices, these pies should be chilled before serving.

STRAWBERRY-RHUBARB MOUSSE PIE

Prep: 20 minutes plus chilling and cooling   *Bake: 15 minutes*
Makes 10 servings

1 pound rhubarb, cut into 1-inch chunks (3½ cups)
1 cup sugar
2 envelopes unflavored gelatin
1 pint strawberries, hulled
1 tablespoon fresh lemon juice
6 tablespoons margarine or butter, melted

2 cups shortbread-style cookie crumbs (about thirty-six 1½-inch square cookies) or vanilla wafer crumbs
1 cup heavy or whipping cream
Mint sprigs and strawberry halves for garnish

1 In 2-quart saucepan, heat rhubarb, sugar, and *¼ cup water* to boiling over high heat, stirring constantly. Reduce heat to medium-low; cook 10 minutes, or until very tender. In food processor with knife blade attached, blend rhubarb mixture until smooth; return to saucepan. In small bowl, sprinkle gelatin over *½ cup cold water*; let stand 2 minutes to soften.

2 In bowl, with potato masher or fork, mash strawberries. Stir into rhubarb with gelatin and lemon juice; cook 3 minutes over low heat, until gelatin dissolves completely.

3 Pour rhubarb mixture into bowl; refrigerate, stirring occasionally, about 2½ hours, until mixture mounds slightly when dropped from a spoon. (Or, for quicker setting, place bowl with rhubarb mixture in a larger bowl of *ice water* and stir every 10 minutes for about 1 hour.)

4 Meanwhile, preheat oven to 350°F. In deep-dish 9½-inch pie plate, mix margarine with crumbs. Press onto bottom and up side of pie plate. Bake 15 minutes; cool on wire rack.

5 In medium bowl, with mixer at medium speed, beat cream to soft peaks. With rubber spatula, fold whipped cream into rhubarb mixture until blended. Spoon into piecrust. Refrigerate at least 3 hours, or overnight. Garnish.

WHIPPING CREAM

Heavy or whipping cream will double in volume when whipped, so use a bowl that is large enough. Soft peaks (right), when the cream forms gentle folds, are best for folding into other mixtures to add volume, as in our Strawberry-Rhubarb Mousse Pie. Stiff peaks (right), when the cream keeps its shape, can be used to top cream pies, frost cakes, or stack layers of pastry.

Soft peaks

Stiff peaks

EACH SERVING: ABOUT 315 CALORIES, 3g PROTEIN, 34g CARBOHYDRATE, 19g TOTAL FAT (8g SATURATED), 36mg CHOLESTEROL, 155mg SODIUM

DOUBLE BLUEBERRY PIE

Prep: 30 minutes plus cooling and chilling   Bake: 8 minutes
Makes 10 servings

30 gingersnap cookies	2 tablespoons cornstarch
2 tablespoons plus ½ cup sugar	3 pints blueberries
5 tablespoons margarine or butter, melted	Whipped cream (optional)

◆ Preheat oven to 375°F. In food processor with knife blade attached or in blender at high speed, process gingersnap cookies and 2 tablespoons sugar until fine crumbs form.

◆ In 9-inch pie plate, with fork, mix cookie crumbs with melted margarine. With hand, press mixture onto bottom and up side of pie plate, making a small rim. Bake crust 8 minutes. Cool on wire rack.

◆ Meanwhile, in 2-quart saucepan, mix cornstarch with *2 tablespoons cold water* until blended. Stir in half of blueberries and remaining ½ cup sugar; heat to boiling over medium-high heat, pressing blueberries against side of saucepan with back of spoon. Boil 1 minute, stirring constantly. Remove saucepan from heat; stir in remaining blueberries.

◆ Pour blueberry mixture into piecrust. Cover with plastic wrap and refrigerate at least 5 hours, or overnight. Serve with whipped cream, if you like.

Each serving: About 240 calories, 2g protein, 43g carbohydrate, 8g total fat (2g saturated), 0mg cholesterol, 210mg sodium

CHOCOLATE CREAM PIE

Prep: 25 minutes plus cooling and chilling   Bake: 8 minutes
Makes 10 servings

1¼ cups chocolate wafer cookie crumbs (24 cookies)	Chocolate Pudding (see page 46)
5 tablespoons margarine or butter, melted	1 cup heavy or whipping cream
2 tablespoons sugar	

◆ Preheat oven to 350°F. In 9-inch pie plate, with fork, mix cookie crumbs, melted margarine, and sugar. Press mixture onto bottom and up side of pie plate. Bake 8 minutes; cool on wire rack.

◆ Prepare Chocolate Pudding; pour warm pudding into piecrust. Place plastic wrap directly on surface to prevent skin from forming. Refrigerate at least 4 hours, or overnight. To serve, in medium bowl, with mixer at medium speed, beat cream until stiff peaks form. Spoon onto pie.

Each serving: About 430 calories, 7g protein, 40g carbohydrate, 29g total fat (12g saturated), 152mg cholesterol, 340mg sodium

BANANA CREAM PIE

Prep: 30 minutes plus cooling and chilling   Bake: 15 minutes
Makes 10 servings

8 tablespoons margarine or butter	⅓ cup cornstarch
2 cups shortbread-style cookie crumbs (about thirty-six 1½-inch square cookies) or vanilla wafer crumbs	¼ teaspoon salt
	3¾ cups milk
	5 large egg yolks
	1¾ teaspoons vanilla extract
	3 medium-size ripe bananas
¾ cup sugar	¾ cup heavy or whipping cream

◆ Preheat oven to 350°F. In small saucepan, melt 6 tablespoons margarine over low heat. In 9-inch pie plate, with fork, mix cookie crumbs with melted margarine. Press mixture onto bottom and up side of pie plate. Bake 15 minutes, or until golden; cool on wire rack.

◆ Prepare filling: In 3-quart saucepan, mix sugar, cornstarch, and salt; stir in milk until smooth. Cook over medium heat, stirring constantly, until mixture thickens and boils; boil 1 minute. In small bowl, beat egg yolks lightly; beat in small amount of hot milk mixture. Slowly pour yolk mixture back into milk, stirring rapidly. Cook over low heat, stirring constantly, 2 minutes, or until very thick.

◆ Remove from heat; stir in 1½ teaspoons vanilla and remaining 2 tablespoons margarine. Slice 2 bananas. Pour half of filling into piecrust. Arrange sliced bananas on top; spoon remaining filling over. Place plastic wrap directly on surface of filling; refrigerate at least 4 hours, or overnight.

◆ To serve, in small bowl, with mixer at medium speed, beat cream and remaining ¼ teaspoon vanilla to stiff peaks; spread over filling. Slice remaining banana; arrange around edge of pie. Cover and refrigerate any leftovers.

Each serving: About 410 calories, 6g protein, 42g carbohydrate, 25g total fat (10g saturated), 147mg cholesterol, 280mg sodium

FREE-FORM TARTS

These rustic-looking tarts suggest backroad bistros and homey farmhouse suppers. The dough is simply rolled into a circle and then folded up over the fruit mixture. To prevent leaking, pinch closed any cracks that form during assembly.

FARMSTAND CHERRY TART

◆◆◆◆◆◆◆◆◆◆◆◆◆

Prep: 45 minutes plus chilling and cooling
Bake: 45 to 50 minutes
Makes 6 servings

1½ cups all-purpose flour
⅓ cup plus 1 tablespoon yellow cornmeal
⅔ cup plus 1 teaspoon sugar
Salt
½ cup cold margarine or butter
2 tablespoons plus 1 teaspoon cornstarch
1½ pounds dark sweet cherries, pitted
1 large egg white

WHAT'S IN A NAME?

Galette is the French term for any round, flat, free-form tart that is baked on a cookie sheet. The pastry can be either a yeast dough or a simple unleavened pastry dough, as in the recipes here. A galette may be sweet or savory; possible toppings include jam, nuts, meat, or cheese, as well as fruit.

1 In medium bowl, mix flour, ⅓ cup cornmeal, ⅓ cup sugar, and ½ teaspoon salt. With pastry blender or two knives used scissor-fashion, cut in margarine until mixture resembles coarse crumbs.

2 Sprinkle in *4 to 5 tablespoons ice water*, 1 tablespoon at a time, mixing lightly with hand until dough comes together (dough will feel very dry at first). Shape into a ball.

3 Sprinkle large cookie sheet with remaining 1 tablespoon cornmeal. Place dampened towel under cookie sheet to prevent it from slipping while rolling dough. With floured rolling pin, roll dough on cookie sheet into a 13-inch round. With long metal spatula, gently loosen dough from cookie sheet. In large bowl, mix ⅓ cup sugar with cornstarch.

4 Sprinkle half of sugar mixture over center of dough, leaving a 2½-inch border all around. Add cherries to sugar mixture remaining in bowl; toss well.

5 Spoon cherry mixture over sugar on dough round. Fold dough up around cherries, leaving a 4-inch opening in center. Pinch to seal any cracks.

6 In cup, mix egg white and ⅛ teaspoon salt. Brush over dough; sprinkle with remaining 1 teaspoon sugar. Refrigerate 30 minutes, or until well chilled. Preheat oven to 425°F.

7 Place 2 sheets of foil under cookie sheet; crimp foil edges to form a rim to catch any drips during baking. Bake tart 45 to 50 minutes, until crust is golden and filling is gently bubbling, covering loosely with foil during last 10 minutes to prevent overbrowning. As soon as tart is done, with long metal spatula, loosen tart from cookie sheet. Cool tart 15 minutes on cookie sheet, then slide onto wire rack to cool completely.

EACH SERVING: ABOUT 460 CALORIES, 6g PROTEIN, 74g CARBOHYDRATE, 17g TOTAL FAT (3g SATURATED), 0mg CHOLESTEROL, 410mg SODIUM

LITTLE PEAR TARTS

Prep: 35 minutes plus chilling and cooling   Bake: 30 minutes
Makes 2 tarts (4 servings)

Pastry for 1-Crust Pie (see
  page 59)
3 small ripe pears (1¼ pounds),
  peeled, cored, and cut into
  ¼-inch-thick slices
2 tablespoons all-purpose flour
2 tablespoons dried currants
  or chopped raisins

4 teaspoons fresh lemon juice
½ teaspoon ground cinnamon
⅓ cup plus 6 teaspoons sugar
2 tablespoons milk
2 tablespoons chopped
  pecans

◆ Prepare Pastry for 1-Crust Pie through chilling, but shape dough into 2 equal balls. Preheat oven to 400°F. In large bowl, toss pear slices with flour, currants, lemon juice, cinnamon, and ⅓ cup sugar. Set aside.

◆ On lightly floured surface, with floured rolling pin, roll 1 dough ball into 10-inch round. Transfer to one half of large cookie sheet. Mound half of pear mixture in center of round; fold dough up around pears, leaving a 2½-inch opening in center.

◆ Repeat with remaining dough and pear mixture to make a second tart on same cookie sheet. Brush each crust with 1 tablespoon milk; sprinkle each with 2 teaspoons sugar.

◆ Place 2 sheets foil under cookie sheet; crimp foil edges to form a rim to catch any drips during baking. Bake tarts 20 minutes.

◆ In cup, mix pecans with remaining 2 teaspoons sugar; sprinkle over filling in centers of tarts. Bake 10 minutes longer, or until crust is browned. Cool tarts on cookie sheets on wire rack 10 minutes to serve warm. Or, slide tarts onto rack after 10 minutes and cool completely to serve later.

Each ½ tart: About 515 calories, 5g protein, 80g carbohydrate, 21g total fat (4g saturated), 1mg cholesterol, 270mg sodium

PEACH-BLUEBERRY TART

Prep: 30 minutes plus chilling and cooling   Bake: 40 minutes
Makes 8 servings

Pastry for 1-Crust Pie (see
  page 59)
2 tablespoons cornstarch
⅓ cup plus 2 tablespoons
  sugar
1 cup blueberries

6 large peaches (2 pounds),
  peeled, pitted, and each cut
  into 6 wedges
2 teaspoons fresh lemon juice
1 tablespoon margarine or
  butter, cut up

◆ Prepare Pastry for 1-Crust Pie through chilling. Preheat oven to 425°F. In large bowl, mix cornstarch and ⅓ cup sugar. Add blueberries, peaches, and lemon juice; toss to combine.

◆ On lightly floured surface, with floured rolling pin, roll dough to 14-inch round. Trim jagged edges; reserve scraps. Transfer round to large cookie sheet. Spoon fruit mixture with juices in center of round, leaving a 2-inch border. Dot fruit mixture with margarine. Fold dough up around fruit. Brush any cracks with *water*; patch with reserved scraps.

◆ Sprinkle dough and exposed fruit with remaining 2 tablespoons sugar. Place 2 sheets foil under cookie sheet; crimp foil edges to form rim to catch any drips during baking. Bake tart 40 minutes, or until bubbly in center. Cool on cookie sheet on wire rack 30 minutes to serve warm.

Each serving: About 270 calories, 3g protein, 42g carbohydrate, 11g total fat (2g saturated), 0mg cholesterol, 150mg sodium

APPLE GALETTE

Prep: 40 minutes plus chilling and cooling   Bake: 45 minutes
Makes 8 servings

Pastry for 1-Crust Pie (see
  page 59)
5 medium Golden Delicious
  apples (2 pounds)
¼ cup sugar

2 tablespoons margarine or
  butter, cut up
2 tablespoons apricot jam,
  melted

◆ Prepare Pastry for 1-Crust Pie through chilling. Preheat oven to 425°F. On lightly floured surface, with floured rolling pin, roll dough to 15-inch round. Transfer to large cookie sheet.

◆ Peel apples; cut each in half. With melon-baller, remove cores. Cut crosswise into ¼-inch-thick slices. Fan apple slices in concentric circles on dough round, leaving a 1½-inch border. Sprinkle apples evenly with sugar and dot with margarine. Fold dough up around apples.

◆ Place 2 sheets foil under cookie sheet; crimp edges to form a rim to catch any drips during baking. Bake galette 45 minutes, or until apples are tender. Place cookie sheet on wire rack. Brush apples with jam. Cool slightly to serve warm.

Each serving: About 270 calories, 2g protein, 40g carbohydrate, 12g total fat (3g saturated), 0mg cholesterol, 165mg sodium

TARTS

Bursting with colorful fruit, creamy custards, nuts, or silky chocolate mixtures, tarts make a dazzling dessert. Unlike a piecrust, a tart shell must be sturdy enough to stand on its own when removed from the pan.

PLUM FRANGIPANE TART

◆◆◆◆◆◆◆◆◆◆◆◆◆

Prep: 30 minutes plus chilling and cooling
Bake: 1 hour 10 to 25 minutes
Makes 12 servings

Pastry for 11-inch Tart (see page 59)
1 tube or can (7 to 8 ounces) almond paste, cut up
½ cup sugar
4 tablespoons margarine or butter, softened
¼ teaspoon salt
2 large eggs
2 teaspoons vanilla extract
¼ cup all-purpose flour
1¼ pounds ripe plums (about 5 large), pitted and each cut into 6 wedges

1 Prepare Pastry for 11-inch Tart and use to line tart pan as directed. Preheat oven to 425°F.

2 Line tart shell with foil and fill with pie weights, dry beans, or uncooked rice. Bake tart shell 15 minutes; remove foil with weights and bake 5 to 10 minutes longer, until golden. (If crust puffs up during baking, gently press it to tart pan with back of spoon.) Remove tart shell from oven; turn oven control to 375°F.

3 Meanwhile, prepare filling: In large bowl, with mixer at low speed, beat almond paste, sugar, margarine, and salt until crumbly. Increase speed to medium-high; beat 3 minutes, frequently scraping bowl with rubber spatula. (There may be some tiny lumps.) Add eggs and vanilla; beat until smooth. With wooden spoon, stir in flour until blended.

CRANBERRY-ALMOND TART

Prepare Plum Frangipane Tart as directed, but omit plums and bake almond filling only 20 minutes, until golden. Cool in pan on wire rack. In 2-quart saucepan over high heat, heat 1 cup cranberries, ¾ cup sugar, ⅓ cup water, and ½ teaspoon grated orange peel to boiling. Reduce heat to medium-low; simmer 5 minutes, until mixture thickens slightly and cranberries pop. Stir in additional 2 cups cranberries. Set aside until cool. When tart is cool, carefully remove side of pan; spoon cranberry topping over almond filling. Makes 12 servings.

Each serving: About 370 calories, 5g protein, 46g carbohydrate, 19g total fat (3g saturated), 36mg cholesterol, 280mg sodium

4 Pour filling into warm tart shell. Arrange plum wedges in concentric circles over filling. Bake tart 50 to 60 minutes, until golden. Cool tart completely in pan on wire rack. When tart is cool, carefully remove side from pan. Cover and refrigerate any leftovers.

EACH SERVING: ABOUT 335 CALORIES, 5g PROTEIN, 36g CARBOHYDRATE, 19g TOTAL FAT (3g SATURATED), 36mg CHOLESTEROL, 280mg SODIUM

RASPBERRY TART

Prep: 20 minutes plus chilling and cooling   *Bake: 50 to 60 minutes*
Makes 8 servings

Pastry for 9-inch Tart (see page 59)
⅔ cup sugar
¼ cup all-purpose flour
¼ teaspoon ground cinnamon
Four ½-pints raspberries
1 cup heavy or whipping cream (optional)

◆ Prepare Pastry for 9-inch Tart, but fit dough onto bottom and 1 inch up side of 9-inch springform pan. Preheat oven to 400°F.

◆ In small bowl, combine sugar, flour, and cinnamon; sprinkle half of sugar mixture over dough. Top with 4 cups raspberries; refrigerate remaining raspberries for topping. Sprinkle remaining sugar mixture evenly over raspberries in pastry. Bake tart on lowest oven rack 50 to 60 minutes, until raspberry mixture is bubbly.

◆ Cool tart completely in pan on wire rack. When tart is cool, carefully remove side of pan; top tart with reserved raspberries. To serve, pour 2 tablespoons cream on each plate, if you like; arrange a wedge of tart on cream.

Each serving: About 250 calories, 3g protein, 38g carbohydrate, 11g total fat (2g saturated), 0mg cholesterol, 165mg sodium

MIXED BERRY TART

Prep: 25 minutes plus chilling and cooling   *Bake: 22 to 27 minutes*
Makes 8 servings

Pastry for 9-inch Tart (see page 59)
1 cup milk
2 large egg yolks
⅓ cup granulated sugar
2 tablespoons cornstarch
2 teaspoons orange-flavor liqueur
1 teaspoon vanilla extract
3 cups assorted berries, such as blueberries, raspberries, and blackberries
Confectioners' sugar for garnish

◆ Prepare Pastry for 9-inch Tart; use to line tart pan as directed. Preheat oven to 425°F. Line tart shell with foil; fill with pie weights, dry beans, or uncooked rice. Bake 15 minutes. Remove foil with weights; bake 7 to 12 minutes longer, until golden. (If crust puffs up during baking, press it against tart pan with back of spoon.) Cool completely on rack.

◆ Meanwhile, prepare pastry cream: In 2-quart saucepan, heat milk to boiling over medium-high heat. In medium bowl, whisk egg yolks with granulated sugar until smooth; whisk in cornstarch. Gradually whisk hot milk into yolk mixture. Return to saucepan. Cook, whisking constantly, until mixture thickens and boils. Reduce heat to low and cook, whisking, 2 minutes. Remove from heat; stir in liqueur and vanilla. Pour into clean bowl; press plastic wrap directly onto surface to prevent skin from forming. Refrigerate at least 2 hours, until cold.

◆ When tart shell is cool, carefully remove side of pan. Whisk pastry cream until smooth; spread in tart shell. Spoon berries on top. Sift confectioners' sugar over berries. Cover and refrigerate any leftovers.

Each serving: About 250 calories, 4g protein, 30g carbohydrate, 13g total fat (3g saturated), 57mg cholesterol, 185mg sodium

FIG AND CUSTARD TART

Prep: 25 minutes plus chilling and cooling   *Bake: 34 to 42 minutes*
Makes 8 servings

Pastry for 9-inch Tart (see page 59)
1½ cups sour cream
⅓ cup sugar
2 tablespoons all-purpose flour
1 teaspoon vanilla extract
⅛ teaspoon salt
1 large egg
6 large or 12 small figs or 3 cups assorted berries
¼ cup apricot jam

◆ Prepare Pastry for 9-inch Tart and use to line tart pan as directed. Preheat oven to 425°F. Line tart shell with foil; fill with pie weights, dry beans, or uncooked rice. Bake 15 minutes. Remove foil with weights; bake 7 to 12 minutes longer, until golden. (If crust puffs up during baking, gently press it against tart pan with back of spoon.) Cool slightly on wire rack. Turn oven control to 400°F.

◆ In medium bowl, with wire whisk or fork, beat sour cream, sugar, flour, vanilla, salt, and egg until smooth and well blended; pour into baked tart shell. Bake 12 to 15 minutes, just until set. Cool tart completely in pan on wire rack. Cover and refrigerate 2 hours, or until cold.

◆ Carefully remove side of pan. Cut each fig into quarters, or halves if small. Arrange figs on tart. In small saucepan, melt apricot jam over low heat. Brush jam over figs. Cover and refrigerate any leftovers.

Each serving: About 335 calories, 4g protein, 36g carbohydrate, 20g total fat (8g saturated), 46mg cholesterol, 230mg sodium

LEMON TART

Prep: 20 minutes plus chilling and cooling   *Bake:* 52 to 57 minutes
Makes 8 servings

Pastry for 9-inch Tart (see page 59)
4 large lemons
4 large eggs
1 cup granulated sugar

⅓ cup heavy or whipping cream
Confectioners' sugar for garnish

◆ Prepare Pastry for 9-inch Tart and use to line tart pan as directed. Preheat oven to 425°F. Line tart shell with foil and fill with pie weights, dry beans, or uncooked rice.

◆ Bake tart shell 15 minutes. Remove foil with weights and bake 7 to 12 minutes longer, until golden. (If crust puffs up during baking, gently press it against tart pan with back of spoon.) Cool tart shell completely on wire rack. Turn oven control to 350°F.

◆ Grate 1½ teaspoons peel and squeeze ⅔ cup juice from lemons. In medium bowl, whisk together eggs, sugar, lemon peel, and lemon juice until well combined. Whisk in cream. Carefully pour lemon mixture into cooled tart shell.

◆ Bake on cookie sheet 30 minutes, or until barely set. Cool completely on wire rack.

◆ Carefully remove side of pan; just before serving, sprinkle with confectioners' sugar. Cover and refrigerate any leftovers.

Each serving: About 320 calories, 5g protein, 39g carbohydrate, 16g total fat (5g saturated), 120mg cholesterol, 200mg sodium

CHOCOLATE TRUFFLE TART

Prep: 20 minutes plus chilling and cooling   *Bake:* 42 to 47 minutes
Makes 12 servings

Pastry for 9-inch Tart (see page 59)
½ cup margarine or butter
6 squares (6 ounces) semisweet chocolate
¼ cup sugar

1 teaspoon vanilla extract
½ cup heavy or whipping cream
3 large eggs
White-chocolate hearts (see page 124) for garnish

◆ Prepare Pastry for 9-inch Tart and use to line tart pan as directed, but trim edge even with rim of pan. Preheat oven to 425°F. Line tart shell with foil and fill with pie weights, dry beans, or uncooked rice.

◆ Bake tart shell 15 minutes. Remove foil with weights and bake 7 to 12 minutes longer, until golden. (If crust puffs up during baking, gently press it against tart pan with back of spoon.) Cool tart shell in pan on wire rack 15 minutes. Turn oven control to 350°F.

◆ While crust is cooling, prepare filling: In heavy 1-quart saucepan, melt margarine and chocolate over low heat, stirring frequently. Stir in sugar and vanilla; remove from heat. In small bowl, with fork or wire whisk, lightly beat cream and eggs. Blend some warm chocolate mixture into egg mixture; stir egg mixture back into chocolate mixture until blended.

◆ Pour warm mixture into tart shell. Bake 20 minutes, or until just set (center will appear jiggly). While tart is baking, prepare white-chocolate hearts. Cool tart in pan on wire rack; refrigerate to serve cold. Carefully remove side of pan; garnish with hearts. Cover and refrigerate any leftovers.

Each serving: About 300 calories, 4g protein, 21g carbohydrate, 24g total fat (8g saturated), 67mg cholesterol, 220mg sodium

HOLIDAY NUT TART

Prep: 20 minutes plus chilling and cooling   *Bake:* 48 to 55 minutes
Makes 12 servings

Pastry for 11-inch Tart (see page 59)
½ cup packed light brown sugar
½ cup light corn syrup
3 tablespoons margarine or butter, melted

2 teaspoons vanilla extract
2 large eggs
1 can (10 to 11 ounces) salted deluxe mixed nuts (about 2 cups)
Whipped cream (optional)

◆ Prepare Pastry for 11-inch Tart and use to line tart pan as directed. Preheat oven to 375°F. Line tart shell with foil and fill with pie weights, dry beans, or uncooked rice.

◆ Bake tart shell 15 minutes; remove foil with weights and bake 8 to 10 minutes longer, until golden. (If crust puffs up during baking, gently press it against pan with back of spoon.)

◆ Meanwhile, in medium bowl, whisk together brown sugar and next 4 ingredients until smooth. Stir in nuts. Pour mixture into tart shell. Bake tart 25 to 30 minutes, until set and deep golden brown. Cool tart in pan on wire rack.

◆ Carefully remove side of pan. Serve tart with whipped cream, if you like. Cover and refrigerate any leftovers.

Each serving: About 405 calories, 7g protein, 35g carbohydrate, 26g total fat (5g saturated), 36mg cholesterol, 340mg sodium

LATTICE-TOPPED PECAN TART

Prep: 30 minutes plus chilling and cooling
Bake: 50 to 55 minutes
Makes 16 servings

Pastry for 2-Crust Pie (see page 59)	**1 cup sugar**
3 tablespoons margarine or butter	**1½ teaspoons vanilla extract**
	4 large eggs
1½ cups light corn syrup	**2½ cups pecans (10 ounces), coarsely chopped**

◆ Prepare Pastry for 2-Crust Pie through chilling. Preheat oven to 350°F. On lightly floured surface, with floured rolling pin, roll larger ball of dough to 14-inch round. Use to line 11" by 1½" tart pan with removable bottom. In 3-quart saucepan, melt margarine over low heat; remove from heat. Stir in corn syrup, sugar, and vanilla. Separate 1 egg; set yolk aside. With wire whisk or fork, beat remaining 3 eggs and egg white into margarine mixture just until blended. Stir in pecans; pour mixture into tart shell.

◆ In cup, mix remaining egg yolk with *2 teaspoons water*. Roll remaining dough into an 11-inch round. Make lattice top (see right); brush with yolk mixture. Bake tart 50 to 55 minutes, until knife inserted in filling 1 inch from edge comes out clean. Cool tart in pan on wire rack. To serve, carefully remove side of pan. Cover and refrigerate any leftovers.

Each serving: About 430 calories, 5g protein, 51g carbohydrate, 24g total fat (4g saturated), 53mg cholesterol, 195mg sodium

LATTICE-TOPPED FRUIT TART

Prep: 45 minutes plus chilling and cooling   *Bake: 55 to 60 minutes*
Makes 12 servings

Pastry for 2-Crust Pie (see page 59)	**3 tablespoons plus ⅔ cup sugar**
	Salt
3 medium Golden Delicious apples (about 1¼ pounds), peeled, cored, and cut into ½-inch cubes	**2 cups cranberries**
	½ cup golden raisins
	1 teaspoon vanilla extract
	2 tablespoons all-purpose flour
1 tablespoon margarine or butter	**1 large egg, lightly beaten**

◆ Prepare Pastry for 2-Crust Pie through chilling. On lightly floured surface, with floured rolling pin, roll larger ball of dough to 14-inch round. Use to line 11" by 1½" tart pan with removable bottom. Cover with plastic wrap and refrigerate.

◆ In 10-inch skillet, mix apples, margarine, 3 tablespoons sugar, and ¼ teaspoon salt; cover and cook over medium heat about 10 minutes, until very tender, mashing occasionally with fork. Uncover; increase heat to medium-high and cook, stirring frequently, until all liquid evaporates and apples form a thick puree. Remove skillet from heat; cool completely.

◆ Preheat oven to 375°F. In medium bowl, mix cranberries, raisins, vanilla, flour, remaining ⅔ cup sugar, and ¼ teaspoon salt. Spread apple puree evenly over bottom of tart shell. Top with cranberry mixture.

◆ Roll remaining dough into an 11-inch round. Make lattice top (see below); brush lightly with beaten egg.

◆ Bake tart 55 to 60 minutes, until filling begins to bubble and crust is golden. Cover with foil if necessary during last 30 minutes of baking to prevent overbrowning. Cool in pan on wire rack. To serve, carefully remove side of pan.

Each serving: About 315 calories, 3g protein, 47g carbohydrate, 14g total fat (3g saturated), 18mg cholesterol, 285mg sodium

◆◆◆◆◆◆◆◆◆◆◆◆◆◆◆◆◆◆◆◆◆◆◆◆◆◆◆◆◆

LATTICE TOP

1 With pastry wheel or knife, cut dough round into twenty ½-inch-wide strips. Place 10 strips, about ½ inch apart, over tart or pie filling; do not seal ends.

2 Fold every other strip back three-fourths of its length. Place center cross strip at right angle to first ones (place on a diagonal, if you like, for diamond lattice), and replace folded part of strips.

3 Now fold back alternate strips; place second cross strip in place, parallel to first and about ½ inch away. Replace folded part of strips.

4 Repeat to weave cross strips into lattice. Trim strips almost even with pan or dish; press to inside edge of crust to seal.

◆◆◆◆◆◆◆◆◆◆◆◆◆◆◆◆◆◆◆◆◆◆◆◆◆◆◆◆◆

TARTLETS

These dainty little desserts provide a festive end to dinner parties and holiday gatherings, not to mention tea parties. The delicate shells should be cooled in their pans. Do not fill them more than four hours in advance, or the pastry will get soggy. However, you can bake the pastry shells ahead and freeze them (just re-crisp before filling).

LEMON-RASPBERRY TARTLETS

◆ ◆ ◆ ◆ ◆ ◆ ◆ ◆ ◆ ◆ ◆ ◆

Prep: 40 minutes plus chilling and cooling
Bake: 15 minutes
Makes 6 tartlets (12 servings)

4 medium lemons
¾ cup sugar
¾ cup butter
1 tablespoon cornstarch
6 large egg yolks
Pastry for 2-Crust Pie (see page 59)
Three ½-pints raspberries

CORNSTARCH

Extracted from corn kernels, cornstarch thickens juicy pies, puddings, and sauces; it also may be mixed with flour in cookies, cakes, and pastry for extra-tender results. Dishes thickened with corn-starch are clear and glossy; those thickened with flour are opaque.

1 Prepare filling: Grate 1 tablespoon peel and squeeze ½ cup juice from lemons. In 2-quart saucepan, heat peel, juice, sugar, butter, and cornstarch over medium heat, stirring, until sugar dissolves and butter melts. In small bowl, beat egg yolks lightly. Beat small amount of lemon mixture into yolks; slowly pour egg mixture back into lemon mixture. Cook over low heat, stirring constantly, about 5 minutes, until thick enough to coat back of spoon.

2 Pour filling into a bowl; press plastic wrap directly onto surface to prevent skin from forming. Refrigerate 3 hours, or until well chilled. Meanwhile, prepare Pastry for 2-Crust Pie through chilling, but divide dough into 6 portions before refrigerating.

3 Press dough onto bottom and up sides of six 4-inch fluted tartlet pans.

4 Place tartlet pans in jelly-roll pan for easy handling. With fork, prick pastry all over. Refrigerate tartlet shells 20 minutes. Preheat oven to 400°F. Bake tartlet shells 15 minutes, or until golden.

5 Transfer tartlet pans to wire rack to cool. When tartlet shells are cool, carefully remove from pans. Spoon lemon filling into tartlet shells and top with raspberries. Cover and refrigerate any leftovers.

EACH ½ TARTLET: ABOUT 350 CALORIES, 3g PROTEIN, 34g CARBOHYDRATE, 24g TOTAL FAT (10g SATURATED), 31mg CHOLESTEROL, 295mg SODIUM

CHOCOLATE TARTLETS

Prep: 50 minutes plus chilling, cooling, and standing
Bake: 9 to 12 minutes
Makes 36

Pastry for 1-Crust Pie (see
  page 59)
3 tablespoons apricot jam
2 squares (2 ounces)
  semisweet chocolate
3 tablespoons plus ¼ cup
  heavy or whipping cream
1 tablespoon margarine or
  butter, cut up

1 teaspoon vanilla extract
1 teaspoon confectioners'
  sugar
Assorted berries, very thinly
  sliced kumquats, or shaved
  chocolate for garnish

◆ Prepare Pastry for 1-Crust Pie through chilling. Preheat oven to 425°F. On lightly floured surface, with floured rolling pin, roll dough less than ⅟₁₆ inch thick. With 2½-inch round cutter, cut out 36 pastry rounds (if necessary, reroll scraps). Fit into 3 dozen mini muffin-pan cups or 1¾-inch tartlet pans.

◆ Bake tartlets 9 to 12 minutes, until golden. Cool in pans on wire rack. Remove tartlet shells from pans; spoon ¼ teaspoon jam into each. In top of double boiler over simmering water, melt chocolate with 3 tablespoons cream. Remove from heat; stir in margarine until smooth. Stir in vanilla. Spoon mixture evenly into tartlets, covering jam. Let stand until set.

◆ In small bowl, with mixer at medium speed, beat remaining ¼ cup cream with confectioners' sugar to stiff peaks. Spoon small dollop of cream onto each tartlet; garnish.

Each tartlet: About 60 calories, 1g protein, 5g carbohydrate, 4g total fat (1g saturated), 4mg cholesterol, 35mg sodium

HAZELNUT TARTLETS

Prep: 1 hour plus chilling and cooling   Bake: 15 minutes
Makes 36

Pastry for 1-Crust Pie (see
  page 59)
1 cup (about 4 ounces)
  hazelnuts (filberts),
  toasted and skinned
  (see page 94)

1 cup confectioners' sugar
  plus extra for garnish
1 large egg
3 tablespoons margarine or
  butter, softened
1 teaspoon vanilla extract

◆ Prepare Pastry for 1-Crust Pie through chilling. Preheat oven to 400°F. In food processor with knife blade attached, process nuts with 1 cup confectioners' sugar until very finely ground. Add remaining ingredients; process until smooth.

◆ On lightly floured surface, with floured rolling pin, roll dough less than ⅟₁₆ inch thick. With 2½-inch round cutter, cut out 36 pastry rounds (if necessary, reroll scraps). Fit pastry into 3 dozen mini muffin-pan cups or 1¾-inch tartlet pans.

◆ Spoon hazelnut filling into tartlet shells. Bake tartlets 15 minutes, or until golden. Remove tartlets from pans and cool on wire rack. To serve, sift confectioners' sugar on top. Cover and refrigerate any leftovers.

Each tartlet: About 70 calories, 1g protein, 6g carbohydrate, 5g total fat (1g saturated), 6mg cholesterol, 40mg sodium

CREAM CHEESE AND FRUIT TARTLETS

Prep: 45 minutes plus chilling and cooling   Bake: 15 minutes
Makes 24

Pastry for 9-inch Tart (see
  page 59)
1 container (8 ounces) soft
  cream cheese
3 tablespoons sugar
1 tablespoon milk

¾ teaspoon vanilla extract
Kiwifruit, strawberries,
  canned mandarin-orange
  sections, and small seedless
  red and green grape halves
Mint leaves for garnish

◆ Prepare Pastry for 9-inch Tart through chilling. Preheat oven to 425°F.

◆ Divide dough in half. Roll one half into a 12-inch rope; cut rope into twelve 1-inch pieces. Repeat with other half of dough. Press each piece of dough evenly into bottom and up sides of twenty-four mini muffin-pan cups. Prick each tartlet shell several times with toothpick. Bake 15 minutes, or until golden. Cool tartlet shells 5 minutes in pans on wire rack. Remove shells from pans; cool completely on wire rack.

◆ Prepare filling: In small bowl, with fork, beat cream cheese, sugar, milk, and vanilla until blended. Spoon filling into tartlet shells. Top each tartlet with some fruit. Refrigerate until ready to serve; garnish.

Each tartlet: About 100 calories, 1g protein, 9g carbohydrate, 7g total fat (3g saturated), 11mg cholesterol, 85mg sodium

COOKIES & CAKES

A batch of fragrant, warm-from-the-oven cookies is a simple pleasure few can resist. Cookies come in six basic types: drop, shaped or molded, pressed, rolled, icebox, and bar (which includes brownies). Drop and bar cookies are made with a soft dough. All the others are made with a stiffer dough for ease of shaping. Although cookie making is not complicated, you'll achieve better results if you're ready with the best ingredients, equipment, and know-how. The following tips promise to help deliver delicious results.

MAKING AND SHAPING

• Avoid adding more flour than is necessary to a cookie dough or batter, or overmixing once the flour is added, or you'll have hard, tough cookies.
• For even baking, shape cookies to roughly the same thickness.
• For shaped or rolled cookies, chilled dough is easier to handle. Doughs made with butter chill to a firmer consistency and hold their shape better than doughs made with margarine or shortening.
• Roll out a small amount of cookie dough at a time; keep remainder covered with plastic wrap to keep it moist.

Icebox cookies can be shaped, chilled, and cut at your convenience. To bake, cut desired number of cookies in even slices from log, and arrange slightly apart on cookie sheets.

ABOUT COOKIE SHEETS

• Cookie sheets with only 1 or 2 turned-up edges allow for the best air circulation. If using a jelly-roll pan, invert it and place dough on the flip side.
• Cookie sheets should be at least 2 inches smaller in length and width than your oven, so air circulates.
• Grease cookie sheets only when a recipe calls for it. Some cookies have a high fat content, so greasing isn't always necessary. When greasing is required, use a light hand, and crumpled waxed paper for even spreading.

• Heavy-gauge metal cookie sheets with a dull finish result in the most evenly browned cookies. Aluminum is ideal. Dark-colored sheets can overbrown the bottoms of cookies.

BETTER BAKING

• If baking with margarine, make sure it contains 80 percent fat. Spreads (which may be labeled diet, whipped, liquid, or soft) have a high water content, which will result in cookies that are less tender and buttery.
• To make bar cookies easier to serve, and to aid cleanup, line the pan with foil before adding the batter; baked cookies can simply be lifted out of the pan, then cut.
• For best results, bake one sheet of cookies at a time on the center rack of the oven. If baking two at a time, switch sheets halfway through baking so the cookies bake evenly.
• When baking cookies in batches, cool the cookie sheet to room temperature before placing more cookies on it. A hot cookie sheet will melt the dough. If the recipe calls for greasing the sheet, regrease for each batch.
• To avoid overcooking, check cookies at the minimum baking time suggested in the recipe, and then watch them closely during their last few minutes in the oven.
• Straight from the oven, most drop cookies are too soft to handle. Let them cool slightly before transferring to a rack.
• To test bar cookies for doneness, insert a toothpick into the center of pan; it should come out clean (unless the recipe specifies otherwise). Other cookies are done when they're just firm at the edges.
• Bar cookies should be cooled in the pan before cutting, or they'll crumble.

STORING AND SHIPPING COOKIES

• To store cookie dough, place in an airtight container or plastic bag (wrap logs for icebox cookies first in plastic wrap); chill up to 1 week or freeze up to 6 months (if necessary, let stand at room temperature until easy to slice).
• To store cooled baked cookies, arrange a single layer in an airtight container; cover with waxed paper. Repeat layers; seal container. Store at room temperature up to 3 days.
• Freeze unbaked drop cookies directly on cookie sheets. Once cookies are frozen, transfer to heavy-duty zip-tight bags.
• To freeze baked cookies, place in zip-tight plastic bags, pressing out air. Or, place in airtight containers; for cushioning, layer with crumpled waxed paper. Freeze up to 3 months.
• Avoid mailing brittle cookies – chewy, soft drop cookies or bars will survive best. Line a sturdy cardboard box or tin with waxed paper or bubble wrap. Wrap cookies individually – or in pairs, back to back – with plastic wrap. Cushion each layer with crumpled newspaper. Fill empty spaces in the box with crumpled paper or bubble wrap; mark the package "fragile."

DROP COOKIES

These run the gamut from elegant, fragile Anise Wafers (see right) to cookie-jar favorites like oatmeal cookies. Drop cookies are formed by dropping spoonfuls of soft unchilled dough onto a cookie sheet. For even baking, distribute the dough in equal portions.

ANISE WAFERS

◆◆◆◆◆◆◆◆◆◆◆◆◆◆

Prep: 1 hour plus cooling
Bake: 5 to 7 minutes per batch
Makes about 2½ dozen

3 large egg whites
¾ cup confectioners' sugar
½ cup all-purpose flour
6 tablespoons butter, melted
¾ teaspoon anise extract
¼ teaspoon salt

ALMOND TUILES

Prepare batter as directed in Steps 1 through 3 above, but substitute ¼ teaspoon almond extract for anise extract and, before baking, sprinkle each cookie generously with a single layer of sliced almonds; you will need about ⅔ cup almonds (about 2½ ounces). Bake as directed in Step 4; but remove warm cookies from cookie sheet and drape over rolling pin to curve. When firm, transfer to wire racks. Makes about 2½ dozen.

Each cookie: About 50 calories, 1g protein, 4g carbohydrate, 3g total fat (2g saturated), 6mg cholesterol, 45mg sodium

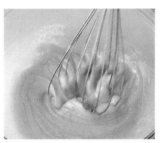

1 Preheat oven to 350°F. Grease large cookie sheet. In large bowl, with wire whisk, beat egg whites, confectioners' sugar, and flour until blended and smooth. Beat in remaining ingredients.

2 Drop 1 heaping teaspoon batter onto cookie sheet. Repeat to make 4 cookies in all, about 3 inches apart.

3 With small spatula, spread each cookie to a 3-inch round. (Do not place more than 4 on cookie sheet because, after baking, cookies must be shaped quickly before hardening.)

4 Bake cookies 5 to 7 minutes, until edges are golden. With pancake turner, quickly transfer 1 cookie to wire rack. Gently shape warm cookie to flute edges; leave on rack to cool. (If you like, omit shaping the cookies and cool flat.)

5 Repeat shaping with remaining cookies on cookie sheet. If cookies become too hard to shape, return cookie sheet to oven to soften cookies slightly. Repeat Steps 2 through 4 with remaining batter. (Batter will become slightly thicker upon standing.) Store cookies in tightly covered container.

EACH COOKIE: ABOUT 40 CALORIES, 1g PROTEIN, 4g CARBOHYDRATE, 2g TOTAL FAT (1g SATURATED), 6mg CHOLESTEROL, 45mg SODIUM

CHOPPING NUTS

Nuts can be tricky to keep in place while chopping. The best way: Using a chef's knife, hold down the tip of the knife with one hand while raising and lowering the handle with the other. Work the blade of the knife fanwise back and forth across the nuts.

JUMBO PECAN-DATE OATMEAL COOKIES

Prep: 30 minutes plus cooling
Bake: 20 to 25 minutes per batch
Makes about 2 dozen

1 cup margarine or butter, softened
¾ cup granulated sugar
¾ cup packed light brown sugar
1½ cups all-purpose flour
1 teaspoon baking soda
1 teaspoon vanilla extract
½ teaspoon salt
½ teaspoon ground cinnamon
2 large eggs
3 cups quick-cooking or old-fashioned oats, uncooked
2 cups pitted dates (10 ounces), chopped
1 cup pecans (about 4 ounces), chopped

◆ Preheat oven to 350°F. In large bowl, with mixer at medium speed, beat margarine and both sugars about 5 minutes, until light and creamy. Reduce speed to low; add flour and next 5 ingredients. Beat just until blended, occasionally scraping bowl with rubber spatula. With wooden spoon, stir in oats, dates, and pecans.

◆ Drop dough by level ¼ cups, about 3 inches apart, on ungreased large cookie sheet. Bake cookies 20 to 25 minutes, until golden. With pancake turner, transfer to wire rack to cool. Repeat with remaining dough. Store cookies in tightly covered container.

Each cookie: About 250 calories, 4g protein, 35g carbohydrate, 12g total fat (2g saturated), 18mg cholesterol, 195mg sodium

PEANUT-BRITTLE COOKIES

Prep: 25 minutes plus cooling
Bake: 15 to 20 minutes per batch
Makes about 1½ dozen

1 cup creamy peanut butter
½ cup margarine or butter, softened
½ cup packed light brown sugar
¼ cup granulated sugar
1 teaspoon baking soda
½ teaspoon vanilla extract
¼ teaspoon salt
1 large egg
1 cup all-purpose flour
8 ounces peanut brittle, coarsely chopped

◆ Preheat oven to 350°F. In large bowl, with mixer at medium speed, beat first 8 ingredients until blended, occasionally scraping bowl with rubber spatula. Reduce speed to low. Add flour; beat just until blended.

◆ Drop dough by heaping tablespoons, about 2 inches apart, on ungreased large cookie sheet. Top dough with chopped peanut-brittle pieces, gently pressing brittle halfway into dough.

◆ Bake cookies 15 to 20 minutes, until lightly browned. Cool 2 minutes on cookie sheet on wire rack; with pancake turner, transfer to wire rack to cool completely. Repeat with remaining dough and peanut brittle. Store cookies in tightly covered container.

Each cookie: About 245 calories, 6g protein, 26g carbohydrate, 14g total fat (3g saturated), 12mg cholesterol, 235mg sodium

DOUBLE-CHOCOLATE CHUNK COOKIES

Prep: 30 minutes plus cooling
Bake: 25 to 30 minutes per batch
Makes about 1½ dozen

1 package (12 ounces) semisweet chocolate chunks or 12 ounces coarsely chopped semisweet chocolate bars (2 cups)
1 cup margarine or butter, softened
⅔ cup packed light brown sugar
⅓ cup granulated sugar
1 teaspoon baking soda
2 teaspoons vanilla extract
½ teaspoon salt
1 large egg
2 cups all-purpose flour
2 cups walnuts (about 8 ounces), coarsely chopped

◆ In heavy small saucepan, heat 1 cup chocolate chunks over low heat, stirring frequently, until melted and smooth. Remove saucepan from heat; cool to room temperature.

◆ Preheat oven to 350°F. In large bowl, with mixer at low speed, beat margarine, both sugars, baking soda, vanilla, and salt until crumbly. Add melted chocolate and egg; beat until well blended, occasionally scraping bowl with rubber spatula. With wooden spoon, stir in flour, walnuts, and remaining chocolate chunks.

◆ Drop dough by level ¼ cups, about 3 inches apart, on ungreased large cookie sheet. Bake cookies 25 to 30 minutes, until edges are set but centers are still soft. With pancake turner, transfer cookies to wire rack to cool completely. Repeat with remaining dough. Store cookies in tightly covered container.

Each cookie: About 360 calories, 5g protein, 37g carbohydrate, 24g total fat (3g saturated), 12mg cholesterol, 255mg sodium

CHOCOLATE-ESPRESSO WALNUT CLUSTERS

Prep: 30 minutes plus cooling   Bake: 15 minutes per batch
Makes about 3 dozen

3 squares (3 ounces)
  unsweetened chocolate,
  melted
1 cup all-purpose flour
1 cup sugar
½ cup margarine or butter,
  softened
1 tablespoon instant espresso-
  coffee powder

2 teaspoons vanilla extract
1 teaspoon salt
½ teaspoon baking powder
2 large eggs
4 cups walnuts (about
  16 ounces), coarsely broken

◆ Preheat oven to 350°F. In large bowl, combine all ingredients except walnuts. With mixer at low speed, beat ingredients until well mixed, occasionally scraping bowl with rubber spatula. With wooden spoon, stir in walnuts.

◆ Drop dough by rounded tablespoons, about 1 inch apart, onto ungreased large cookie sheet. Bake 15 minutes, until set. Transfer to wire rack to cool. Repeat with remaining dough. Store cookies in tightly covered container.

Each cookie: About 160 calories, 3g protein, 11g carbohydrate, 12g total fat (2g saturated), 12mg cholesterol, 100mg sodium

FRUITCAKE COOKIES

Prep: 50 minutes plus cooling   Bake: 12 minutes per batch
Makes about 5½ dozen

1½ cups all-purpose flour
1 cup packed dark brown
  sugar
6 tablespoons margarine or
  butter, softened
½ teaspoon salt
½ teaspoon baking soda
½ teaspoon baking powder
½ teaspoon almond extract

2 large eggs
1 cup red candied cherries
  (8 ounces), coarsely
  chopped
½ cup green candied cherries
  (4 ounces), coarsely
  chopped
1 cup walnuts (about
  4 ounces), coarsely chopped

◆ Preheat oven to 400°F. In large bowl, with mixer at low speed, beat first 8 ingredients until well blended, occasionally scraping bowl with rubber spatula.

◆ Reserve ½ cup chopped red and green candied cherries. With spoon, stir walnuts and remaining candied cherries into cookie dough. Drop dough by heaping teaspoons, about 1 inch apart, onto ungreased large cookie sheet. Decorate tops of cookies with some of reserved cherries.

◆ Bake cookies 12 minutes, or until golden. With pancake turner, carefully transfer cookies to wire rack to cool. Repeat with remaining dough and candied cherries. Store cookies in tightly covered container.

Each cookie: About 60 calories, 1g protein, 10g carbohydrate, 2g total fat (0g saturated), 6mg cholesterol, 45mg sodium

MCINTOSH-OATMEAL COOKIES

Prep: 25 minutes plus cooling   Bake: 20 minutes per batch
Makes about 4 dozen

1½ cups sugar
1 cup margarine or butter,
  softened
1½ cups all-purpose flour
1 teaspoon baking soda
1 teaspoon ground cinnamon
1 teaspoon vanilla extract
½ teaspoon salt
2 large eggs

2 medium McIntosh apples,
  peeled, cored, and diced
  (about 2 cups)
3 cups quick-cooking or old-
  fashioned oats, uncooked
1 cup dark seedless raisins
¾ cup walnuts (about
  3 ounces), chopped

◆ Preheat oven to 350°F. In large bowl, with mixer at medium speed, beat sugar and margarine about 5 minutes, until light and creamy. Add flour, baking soda, cinnamon, vanilla, salt, and eggs; beat just until blended, occasionally scraping bowl with rubber spatula. With wooden spoon, stir in apples and remaining ingredients.

◆ Drop dough by heaping tablespoons, about 3 inches apart, onto ungreased large cookie sheet. Bake cookies 20 minutes, until golden. With pancake turner, transfer to wire rack to cool.

◆ Repeat with remaining dough. Store cookies in tightly covered container.

Each cookie: About 120 calories, 2g protein, 16g carbohydrate, 5g total fat (1g saturated), 9mg cholesterol, 95mg sodium

McIntosh-oatmeal cookies   Fruitcake cookies   Chocolate-espresso walnut clusters

LACY PECAN CRISPS

Prep: 40 minutes plus cooling   Bake: 6 to 8 minutes per batch
Makes about 5 dozen

1½ cups pecan halves (about 6 ounces)
6 tablespoons butter, softened
½ cup packed light brown sugar
⅓ cup light corn syrup
¾ cup all-purpose flour
½ teaspoon vanilla extract

◆ Preheat oven to 375°F. Grease large cookie sheet. Set aside 60 pecan halves; finely chop remaining pecans.

◆ In 2-quart saucepan, heat butter, brown sugar, and corn syrup to boiling over medium heat (do not use margarine, because it would separate from sugar during cooking); remove from heat. With wooden spoon, stir in chopped pecans, flour, and vanilla.

◆ Drop 1 level teaspoon mixture onto cookie sheet; top with a pecan half. Repeat to make 8 cookies, placing them about 3 inches apart. Bake cookies 6 to 8 minutes, until lightly browned.

◆ Remove cookie sheet from oven; let cool about 30 seconds to set slightly. With pancake turner, quickly loosen cookies and transfer to wire rack to cool completely. Repeat with remaining dough and pecan halves. Store cookies in tightly covered container.

Each cookie: About 45 calories, 0g protein, 5g carbohydrate, 3g total fat (1g saturated), 3mg cholesterol, 15mg sodium

COCONUT-ALMOND MACAROONS

Prep: 15 minutes plus cooling   Bake: 20 to 25 minutes per batch
Makes about 1½ dozen

1 bag (7 ounces) shredded coconut (2⅔ cups)
1 cup sliced natural almonds (about 4 ounces)
½ cup sugar
¼ teaspoon salt
4 large egg whites
1 teaspoon almond extract

◆ Preheat oven to 325°F. Grease large cookie sheet. In large bowl, with wooden spoon, mix coconut, almonds, sugar, and salt until combined. Stir in egg whites and almond extract until well blended.

◆ Drop mixture by heaping tablespoons, about 2 inches apart, on cookie sheet. Bake 20 to 25 minutes, until golden. With pancake turner, transfer cookies to wire rack to cool completely. Repeat with remaining dough. Store cookies in tightly covered container.

Each cookie: About 110 calories, 3g protein, 11g carbohydrate, 7g total fat (3g saturated), 0mg cholesterol, 45mg sodium

SESAME CRISPS

Prep: 20 minutes plus cooling   Bake: 8 minutes per batch
Makes about 3 dozen

6 tablespoons butter, softened
⅔ cup sugar
1 teaspoon vanilla extract
¼ teaspoon salt
¼ teaspoon baking powder
1 large egg
½ cup plus 2 tablespoons all-purpose flour
4 teaspoons white sesame seeds, toasted
4 teaspoons black sesame seeds (available in Asian markets; or, use all white sesame seeds)

◆ Preheat oven to 350°F. Grease large cookie sheet. In large bowl, with mixer at medium speed, beat first 5 ingredients until blended. Add egg; beat until well combined. With wooden spoon, stir in flour.

◆ Spoon half of dough into a small bowl; stir in toasted white sesame seeds. Stir black sesame seeds into dough remaining in large bowl. Drop doughs by rounded teaspoons, about 3 inches apart, onto cookie sheet. Bake cookies about 8 minutes, until set and edges are golden.

◆ Remove cookie sheet from oven; let cookies cool on sheet about 30 seconds to set slightly. With pancake turner, transfer to wire rack to cool completely. Repeat with remaining cookie doughs. Store cookies in tightly covered container.

Each cookie: About 45 calories, 1g protein, 5g carbohydrate, 2g total fat (1g saturated), 11mg cholesterol, 40mg sodium

Sesame crisps

Lacy pecan crisps

Coconut-almond macaroons

SHAPED AND PRESSED COOKIES

The dough for shaped cookies should be firm enough to be molded by hand. If it's too soft to handle, refrigerate it for 1 hour and try again. The dough for pressed cookies should be soft enough to be forced through a decorating bag or cookie press, but firm enough to hold its shape when baked.

WALNUT CRESCENTS

◆◆◆◆◆◆◆◆◆◆◆◆◆

Prep: 45 minutes plus chilling and cooling
Bake: 20 minutes per batch
Makes about 6 dozen

1 cup walnuts (about 4 ounces)
½ cup granulated sugar
1 cup butter, softened
2 cups all-purpose flour
½ cup sour cream
2 teaspoons vanilla extract
¼ teaspoon salt
½ cup confectioners' sugar

TEACAKES

Instead of shaping these rich, short cookies into crescents, in Step 4 simply roll the dough into 1-inch balls; bake and roll in confectioners' sugar as directed. If you like, substitute pecans or almonds for the walnuts. Or, try toasted, skinned hazelnuts (see page 94) and omit skillet-toasting in Step 1.

1 In 10-inch skillet, lightly toast walnuts over medium heat, shaking skillet frequently. Set skillet aside until walnuts are cool.

2 In food processor with knife blade attached, blend walnuts and ¼ cup granulated sugar until walnuts are very finely chopped. In large bowl, with mixer at low speed, beat butter and remaining ¼ cup granulated sugar until blended, occasionally scraping bowl with rubber spatula.

3 Increase speed to high; beat about 5 minutes, until light and fluffy. Reduce speed to low; gradually beat in flour, sour cream, vanilla, salt, and walnut mixture until blended. Divide dough in half; wrap each half in plastic wrap and refrigerate 1 hour, or until dough is firm enough to handle. (Or, place dough in freezer 30 minutes.) Meanwhile, preheat oven to 325°F.

4 Working with half of dough at a time, with lightly floured hands, shape dough by rounded teaspoons into 1" by ½" crescents. Place crescents, about 1½ inches apart, on ungreased large cookie sheet. Bake cookies 20 minutes, or until lightly browned around edges. Cool cookies on sheet on wire rack 2 minutes. Place confectioners' sugar in small bowl.

5 While still warm, gently roll cookies, one at a time, in confectioners' sugar to coat. Cool completely on wire rack. Repeat with remaining dough and confectioners' sugar. Store cookies in tightly covered container.

EACH COOKIE: ABOUT 55 CALORIES, 1g PROTEIN, 5g CARBOHYDRATE, 4g TOTAL FAT (2g SATURATED), 8mg CHOLESTEROL, 35mg SODIUM

ALMOND LOGS

Prep: 25 minutes plus cooling   Bake: 20 to 25 minutes per batch
Makes 2 dozen

2 tubes or cans (7 to 8 ounces each) almond paste, cut into 1-inch chunks	2 large egg whites
⅔ cup confectioners' sugar	2 cups sliced natural almonds (about 8 ounces)

◆ Preheat oven to 325°F. Grease and flour large cookie sheet. In small bowl, with mixer at low speed, beat almond paste until crumbly. Add confectioners' sugar and egg whites; beat until well blended (dough will be sticky and wet). Place sliced almonds on sheet of waxed paper. With lightly floured hands, roll 1 level tablespoon dough into a 3-inch-long log. Place dough log on almonds; gently press and stick almonds into dough to cover.

◆ Repeat with more dough and almonds to make 12 logs, placing logs on cookie sheet, about 1 inch apart, as they are formed. Bake cookies 20 to 25 minutes, until golden and set. Transfer to wire rack to cool. Repeat with remaining dough and almonds. Store cookies in tightly covered container.

Each cookie: About 140 calories, 4g protein, 13g carbohydrate, 8g total fat (1g saturated), 0mg cholesterol, 10mg sodium

GINGER MOLASSES COOKIES

Prep: 40 minutes plus cooling   Bake: 7 to 10 minutes per batch
Makes about 4 dozen

1 cup packed brown sugar	½ teaspoon salt
⅔ cup shortening	¼ teaspoon ground cloves
½ cup light molasses	1 large egg
¼ cup milk	3½ cups all-purpose flour
2 teaspoons baking powder	¼ cup granulated sugar
1½ teaspoons ground ginger	¼ cup crystallized ginger
1 teaspoon ground cinnamon	(about 1½ ounces), cut into
¾ teaspoon baking soda	¼-inch pieces (optional)

◆ Preheat oven to 350°F. In large bowl, with mixer at low speed, mix first 11 ingredients and 2 cups flour until blended. With wooden spoon, stir in remaining 1½ cups flour. Place sugar in small bowl. Roll cookie dough into 1½-inch balls; roll each ball in sugar to coat. Place 12 balls, 2 inches apart, on ungreased large cookie sheet.

◆ Gently press 1 piece of crystallized ginger, if using, into center of each ball on cookie sheet, flattening slightly. Bake 7 to 10 minutes, or until bottoms are lightly browned. Transfer to rack to cool. Repeat with remaining dough and crystallized ginger. Store cookies in tightly covered container.

Each cookie: About 85 calories, 1g protein, 14g carbohydrate, 3g total fat (1g saturated), 4mg cholesterol, 65mg sodium

CHOCOLATE-RASPBERRY ALMOND SPRITZ

Prep: 50 minutes plus cooling and chilling
Bake: 12 to 14 minutes per batch
Makes about 2½ dozen

½ cup blanched whole almonds (about 2 ounces)	¼ cup plus 2 tablespoons heavy or whipping cream
¾ cup sugar	6 squares (6 ounces) semisweet chocolate, finely chopped
2¼ cups all-purpose flour	
1 cup butter, softened	
1½ teaspoons almond extract	3 tablespoons seedless red raspberry jam
¼ teaspoon salt	
1 large egg	

◆ Preheat oven to 350°F. In food processor with knife blade attached, blend almonds with sugar, pulsing processor on and off, until almonds are finely ground. (Or, in blender, grind almonds with sugar in batches.)

◆ In large bowl, with mixer at low speed, beat almond mixture, flour, and next 4 ingredients just until blended, scraping bowl occasionally with rubber spatula. Spoon dough into large decorating bag with large star tip (about ¾ inch in diameter) or cookie press fitted with desired template.

◆ Pipe teardrop shapes (about 2" by 1½") or press through cookie press, 1 inch apart, onto ungreased large cookie sheet. Bake cookies 12 to 14 minutes, until lightly browned around edges. Cool slightly on cookie sheet. With pancake turner, transfer cookies to wire rack to cool completely. Repeat with remaining dough.

◆ Prepare filling: In 1-quart saucepan, heat cream to boiling over low heat. Place chocolate in small bowl with jam. Pour hot cream over chocolate mixture; let stand 1 minute. Stir until smooth. Refrigerate 15 to 18 minutes, until firm enough to spread. (If mixture becomes too firm, let stand at room temperature until slightly softened.)

◆ With small spatula, spread about 1 rounded teaspoon filling onto flat side of half of cooled cookies. Top with remaining cookies, flat-side down. Store cookies in refrigerator.

Each cookie: About 160 calories, 2g protein, 17g carbohydrate, 10g total fat (6g saturated), 28mg cholesterol, 85mg sodium

ROLLED COOKIES

These cookies are rolled out and cut into myriad shapes with decorative cutters, a pastry wheel, or a sharp knife. They require a firm dough that is often refrigerated (this relaxes the gluten and yields a more tender cookie). Cookies made with butter (instead of margarine or a spread) hold their shape best. Cut out the cookies as close to one another as possible to reduce excessive rerolling of the scraps.

TWO-TONE COOKIES

◆◆◆◆◆◆◆◆◆◆◆◆◆◆◆◆◆◆◆◆◆◆◆◆◆◆◆◆◆◆

Prep: 1 hour plus cooling   *Bake:* 12 to 15 minutes per batch
Makes 3 dozen

¾ **cup margarine or butter,** **softened**	½ **teaspoon salt**
⅔ **cup plus 3 teaspoons sugar**	1 **large egg**
1 **teaspoon baking powder**	2 **cups all-purpose flour**
1½ **teaspoons vanilla extract**	¼ **cup unsweetened cocoa**

1 Grease and flour 2 large cookie sheets. In large bowl, with mixer at low speed, beat margarine and ⅔ cup sugar until blended. Increase speed to high; beat until light and creamy. Reduce speed to low. Add baking powder, vanilla, salt, egg, 1½ cups flour, and *2 tablespoons water*; beat until blended.

2 Place half of dough in medium bowl; with wooden spoon, stir in remaining ½ cup flour. Stir cocoa into dough remaining in large bowl. On lightly floured surface, with floured rolling pin, roll vanilla dough ⅛ inch thick.

3 Preheat oven to 350°F. With floured 3-inch round scallop-shaped cookie cutter, cut vanilla dough into as many cookies as possible. Reserve trimmings. Place cookies on 1 cookie sheet, about ¼ inch apart. Repeat with chocolate dough, placing chocolate cookies on second cookie sheet.

4 With 1½-inch round scallop-shaped cookie cutter, cut out small round in center of each vanilla and chocolate cookie.

5 Fit a small vanilla cookie cutout into center of each chocolate cookie and a small chocolate cookie cutout into center of each vanilla cookie to make two-tone cookies.

6 Sprinkle cookies lightly with 2 teaspoons sugar. Bake cookies on 2 oven racks 12 to 15 minutes, until golden, rotating cookie sheets between upper and lower racks halfway through baking time. With pancake turner, transfer cookies to wire racks to cool. Gather trimmings, reroll, and cut out more cookies. Sprinkle cookies with remaining 1 teaspoon sugar and bake as above. Store cookies in tightly covered container.

EACH COOKIE: ABOUT 75 CALORIES, 1g PROTEIN, 9g CARBOHYDRATE, 4g TOTAL FAT (1g SATURATED), 6mg CHOLESTEROL, 90mg SODIUM

CLASSIC SUGAR COOKIES

Prep: 45 minutes plus chilling, cooling, and decorating
Bake: 12 to 15 minutes per batch   **Makes** *about 4 dozen*

¾ cup sugar	2 teaspoons vanilla extract
10 tablespoons butter, softened	1 large egg
1 teaspoon baking powder	2 cups all-purpose flour
½ teaspoon salt	Ornamental Frosting (optional, see below)
2 tablespoons milk	

◆ In large bowl, with mixer at low speed, beat first 4 ingredients until blended. Increase speed to high; beat until mixture is light and creamy. Reduce speed to low. Add milk, vanilla, and egg; beat until blended. (Mixture may appear curdled.)

◆ With wooden spoon, stir in flour until blended. Shape dough into 2 balls; flatten each slightly. Wrap each in plastic wrap and refrigerate 1 hour, or until firm enough to roll. (Or, place dough in freezer 30 minutes.)

◆ Preheat oven to 350°F. On lightly floured surface, with floured rolling pin, roll 1 piece of dough ⅛ inch thick, keeping remaining dough refrigerated.

◆ With floured assorted 3- to 4-inch cookie cutters, cut dough into as many cookies as possible; refrigerate trimmings. Place cookies, about 1 inch apart, on ungreased large cookie sheet.

◆ Bake cookies 12 to 15 minutes, until golden around edges. Transfer cookies to wire rack to cool. Repeat with remaining dough. Reroll trimmings; cut out more cookies and bake as above.

◆ When cookies are cool, prepare Ornamental Frosting, if you like, and use to decorate. Set cookies aside at least 1 hour to allow frosting to dry completely. Store cookies in tightly covered container.

Each cookie: About 55 calories, 1g protein, 7g carbohydrate, 3g total fat (2g saturated), 11mg cholesterol, 60mg sodium

DECORATING COOKIES

These frosted holiday cookies (made from Classic Sugar Cookies on this page and Gingerbread Cutouts, page 85) are pretty enough to be used as tree or wreath decorations. If you like, with skewer or toothpick, make 1 or 2 holes in top of each cookie before baking. Thread ribbon, string, or clear nylon fishing line through finished cookies for hanging.

ORNAMENTAL FROSTING In bowl, with mixer at medium speed, beat 1 package (16 ounces) confectioners' sugar, 3 tablespoons meringue powder, and ⅓ cup warm water about 5 minutes, until mixture is stiff and knife drawn through it leaves a clean-cut path.
 If you like, tint frosting with assorted food colorings as desired; keep covered with plastic wrap to prevent drying out. With small metal spatula, artists' paintbrushes, or decorating bags with small writing tips, decorate cookies with frosting. (Thin frosting with a little warm water if necessary to obtain the right consistency.) Makes about 3 cups.

Each tablespoon: About 40 calories, 0g protein, 9g carbohydrate, 0g total fat, 0mg cholesterol, 5mg sodium

HAZELNUT SPICE CUTOUTS

Prep: 45 minutes plus chilling and cooling
Bake: 10 to 12 minutes per batch   *Makes about 2 dozen*

½ cup (about 2 ounces) hazelnuts (filberts), toasted and skinned (see page 94), or walnuts	6 tablespoons margarine or butter, softened
½ cup packed light brown sugar	½ teaspoon ground cinnamon
	½ teaspoon vanilla extract
	¼ teaspoon ground allspice
1¼ cups all-purpose flour	¼ teaspoon salt
	1 large egg

◆ In food processor with knife blade attached or in blender at high speed, blend nuts with sugar until finely ground.

◆ In large bowl, with mixer at low speed, beat nut mixture with remaining ingredients just until mixed, occasionally scraping bowl with rubber spatula. Divide dough in half; pat each half into a 1-inch-thick disk. Wrap each half in plastic wrap and refrigerate 1 hour, or until firm enough to roll. (Or, place dough in freezer 30 minutes.)

◆ Preheat oven to 350°F. Grease large cookie sheet. On well-floured surface, with floured rolling pin, roll half of dough ⅛ inch thick. With floured assorted 3- to 4-inch cookie cutters, cut dough into as many cookies as possible; reserve trimmings.

◆ Place cookies, about 1 inch apart, on cookie sheet. Bake cookies 10 to 12 minutes, until edges are golden. Transfer cookies to wire rack to cool. Repeat with remaining dough. Reroll trimmings and cut out more cookies. Store cookies in tightly covered container.

Each cookie: About 80 calories, 1g protein, 10g carbohydrate, 5g total fat (1g saturated), 9mg cholesterol, 60mg sodium

TOASTED-WALNUT CRISPS

Prep: 30 minutes plus cooling   *Bake: 20 minutes*
Makes about 16

2 cups walnuts (8 ounces)	¾ cup margarine or butter, cut into small pieces
1⅓ cups all-purpose flour	
1 cup confectioners' sugar	1 tablespoon vanilla extract
2 tablespoons cornstarch	1 tablespoon milk
¼ teaspoon salt	1 tablespoon granulated sugar

◆ Reserve ⅓ cup walnuts for topping. In 12-inch skillet, toast remaining walnuts over medium heat, shaking skillet frequently, until golden brown; cool and chop walnuts.

◆ Preheat oven to 325°F. In large bowl, stir chopped toasted walnuts, flour, confectioners' sugar, cornstarch, and salt until well mixed. With hand, knead margarine and vanilla into flour mixture until well blended and mixture

holds together. On floured surface, with floured hands, gently knead dough 5 or 6 times, until smooth, sprinkling with extra flour if needed.

◆ With floured rolling pin, roll dough ¼ inch thick. With floured 3-inch fluted round cookie cutter, cut dough into as many rounds as possible; reserve trimmings. Place cookies on ungreased large cookie sheet, about 1 inch apart.

◆ Reroll trimmings and cut out more cookies. Brush cookies with milk; sprinkle with granulated sugar. Press 1 walnut into each. Bake 20 minutes, or until golden. Transfer to wire rack to cool. Store in tightly covered container.

Each cookie: About 240 calories, 3g protein, 18g carbohydrate, 18g total fat (3g saturated), 0mg cholesterol, 135mg sodium

GINGERBREAD CUTOUTS

Prep: 45 minutes plus cooling and decorating
Bake: 12 minutes per batch   *Makes about 3 dozen*

½ cup sugar	½ cup margarine or butter, cut into chunks
½ cup light molasses	
1½ teaspoons ground ginger	1 large egg, beaten
1 teaspoon ground allspice	3½ cups all-purpose flour
1 teaspoon ground cinnamon	Ornamental Frosting (optional, see page 84)
1 teaspoon ground cloves	
2 teaspoons baking soda	

◆ Preheat oven to 325°F. In 3-quart saucepan, heat first 6 ingredients to boiling over medium heat, stirring occasionally. Remove saucepan from heat; stir in baking soda (mixture will foam up in the pan). Stir in margarine until melted. With fork, stir in egg, then flour.

◆ On floured surface, knead dough until thoroughly mixed. Divide in half. Wrap half in plastic wrap; set aside.

◆ With floured rolling pin, roll remaining half of dough slightly less than ¼ inch thick. With floured assorted 3- to 4-inch cookie cutters, cut dough into as many cookies as possible; reserve trimmings. Place cookies, about 1 inch apart, on ungreased large cookie sheet.

◆ Bake cookies 12 minutes, or until edges begin to brown. Transfer to wire rack to cool. Repeat with remaining dough. Reroll trimmings and cut out more cookies.

◆ When cookies are cool, prepare Ornamental Frosting, if you like, and use to decorate. Set cookies aside at least 1 hour to allow frosting to dry completely. Store in tightly covered container.

Each cookie: About 90 calories, 1g protein, 14g carbohydrate, 3g total fat (1g saturated), 6mg cholesterol, 100mg sodium

LINZER WREATHS

Prep: 45 minutes plus chilling and cooling
Bake: 10 to 12 minutes per batch   Makes about 20

1 cup blanched whole
  almonds (about 4 ounces)
⅔ cup granulated sugar
1 teaspoon vanilla extract
2¼ cups all-purpose flour
½ teaspoon baking soda

1 cup margarine or butter,
  softened
¼ cup confectioners' sugar
⅔ cup seedless red raspberry
  jam

◆ In food processor with knife blade attached or in blender
at medium speed, blend almonds, ⅓ cup granulated sugar,
and vanilla until almonds are finely ground.

◆ In large bowl, stir together almond mixture, flour, baking
soda, and remaining ⅓ cup granulated sugar. With pastry
blender or two knives used scissor-fashion, cut in margarine
until mixture resembles coarse crumbs. With hand, knead
until dough forms a ball. Divide ball into 2 pieces; wrap each
in plastic wrap. Refrigerate 1 hour, or until firm enough to
roll. (Or, place dough in freezer 30 minutes.)

◆ Preheat oven to 350°F. On lightly floured surface, with
floured rolling pin, roll 1 piece of dough ⅛ inch thick; keep
remaining dough refrigerated. With floured 3-inch round
fluted cookie cutter, cut dough into as many rounds as
possible; reserve trimmings. With 1½-inch round fluted cutter,
cut out center of half of cookies. With pancake turner, place
cookies, about 1 inch apart, on ungreased large cookie sheet.

◆ Bake cookies 10 to 12 minutes, until lightly browned.
With pancake turner, transfer cookies to wire rack to cool
completely. Repeat with remaining dough. Gather trimmings
and cutout centers, reroll, and cut out more cookies.

◆ Sprinkle confectioners' sugar over cookies with cutout
centers. In small saucepan, heat jam over low heat until
melted. Brush whole cookies with jam and top with cutout
cookies. Store, between sheets of waxed paper, in tightly
covered container.

**Each cookie: About 220 calories, 3g protein, 27g carbohydrate,
12g total fat (2g saturated), 0mg cholesterol, 140mg sodium**

APRICOT-RASPBERRY RUGELACH

Prep: 1 hour plus chilling and cooling   Bake: 30 to 35 minutes
Makes 4 dozen

1 cup margarine or butter,
  softened
1 package (8 ounces) cream
  cheese, softened
1 teaspoon vanilla extract
¼ teaspoon salt
2 cups all-purpose flour
¾ cup granulated sugar
1 cup walnuts (about
  4 ounces), chopped

¾ cup dried apricots, chopped
¼ cup packed light brown
  sugar
1½ teaspoons ground
  cinnamon
½ cup seedless red raspberry
  jam
1 tablespoon milk

◆ In large bowl, with mixer at low speed, beat margarine
with cream cheese until blended and smooth. Beat in
vanilla, salt, 1 cup flour, and ¼ cup granulated sugar until
blended. With wooden spoon, stir in remaining 1 cup flour.

◆ Divide dough into 4 equal pieces. Wrap each piece in
plastic wrap; refrigerate at least 2 hours, until firm enough
to roll, or overnight.

◆ Prepare filling: In medium bowl, stir walnuts, apricots,
brown sugar, 6 tablespoons granulated sugar, and
½ teaspoon cinnamon until well mixed. Line 2 large cookie
sheets with foil; grease foil.

◆ Preheat oven to 325°F. On lightly floured surface, with
floured rolling pin, roll 1 piece of dough into a 9-inch
round; keep remaining dough refrigerated. Spread dough
with 2 tablespoons jam. Sprinkle with about ½ cup filling;
gently press filling onto dough.

◆ With pastry wheel or sharp knife, cut dough into
12 equal wedges. Starting at curved edge, roll up each
wedge, jelly-roll fashion. Place cookies on cookie sheet,
point-side down, about ½ inch apart. Repeat with remaining
dough, jam, and filling.

◆ In cup, mix remaining 2 tablespoons sugar with
remaining 1 teaspoon cinnamon. Brush rugelach with milk;
sprinkle with cinnamon-sugar.

◆ Bake rugelach on 2 oven racks 30 to 35 minutes, until
golden, rotating cookie sheets between upper and lower
racks halfway through baking time. Immediately remove to
wire racks to cool. Store in tightly covered container.

**Each cookie: About 115 calories, 1g protein, 12g carbohydrate,
7g total fat (2g saturated), 5mg cholesterol, 70mg sodium**

Linzer wreaths

Apricot-raspberry
rugelach

ICEBOX COOKIES

The beauty of these cookies, also called refrigerator or slice-and-bake cookies, is that you can have warm-from-the-oven treats anytime: Just prepare the dough and store, wrapped, in the refrigerator for up to 1 week (or freeze for up to 2 months), then bake cookies as you want them.

COCONUT BUTTONS

◆◆◆◆◆◆◆◆◆◆◆◆

Prep: 45 minutes plus chilling and cooling
Bake: 20 to 25 minutes per batch
Makes about 6½ dozen

1 cup butter, softened
½ cup sugar
2 tablespoons milk
1 teaspoon coconut extract
¾ teaspoon baking powder
½ teaspoon salt
2⅔ cups all-purpose flour
1½ cups flaked coconut, chopped
4 squares (4 ounces) semisweet chocolate
1 tablespoon shortening

COOKIE TIP

Although margarine and butter are equally suitable for most purposes, some cookie recipes, such as the one above, call for butter only. This is because the dough would spread too much during baking if made with margarine. Always use butter if the recipe specifically calls for it.

1 In large bowl, with mixer at medium-high speed, beat butter, sugar, milk, coconut extract, baking powder, and salt until light and creamy. With wooden spoon, stir in flour and chopped coconut (dough will be crumbly). With hands, squeeze dough together. Divide dough into 4 equal pieces. Shape each piece into a 10" by 1" log. Wrap each log in plastic wrap and slide onto small cookie sheet for easier handling. Refrigerate dough overnight, or freeze at least 2 hours, until firm enough to slice.

2 Preheat oven to 325°F. Cut 1 log into ½-inch-thick slices (keep remaining logs refrigerated). Place slices, 1 inch apart, on ungreased large cookie sheet. With toothpick, make 4 holes in each cookie to resemble a button.

3 Bake cookies 20 to 25 minutes, until lightly golden. Transfer to wire rack to cool. Repeat with remaining dough. When cookies are cool, in small heavy saucepan, melt chocolate with shortening over low heat, stirring frequently.

4 Dip bottom of each cooled cookie into melted chocolate so that chocolate comes slightly up side of cookie.

5 With small metal spatula, scrape excess chocolate from bottom of cookie, leaving a thin layer. Place cookies, chocolate-side down, on waxed paper; set aside to allow chocolate to set completely. Store finished cookies in tightly covered container.

EACH COOKIE: ABOUT 55 CALORIES, 1g PROTEIN, 6g CARBOHYDRATE, 3g TOTAL FAT (2g SATURATED), 6mg CHOLESTEROL, 45mg SODIUM

POPPY-SEED PINWHEELS

Prep: 40 minutes plus chilling and cooling
Bake: 8 to 10 minutes per batch   Makes about 7 dozen

2½ cups all-purpose flour	1 teaspoon salt
1 cup sugar	1 teaspoon vanilla extract
¾ cup margarine or butter, softened	2 large eggs
1 teaspoon baking powder	1 can (12 ounces) poppy-seed filling

◆ In large bowl, with mixer at low speed, beat all ingredients except poppy-seed filling until well blended, occasionally scraping bowl with rubber spatula. Divide dough in half; wrap each half in plastic wrap and refrigerate 1 hour, or freeze 30 minutes, until firm enough to handle.

◆ On sheet of waxed paper, with floured rolling pin, roll half of dough into a 12" by 8" rectangle; spread with half of filling. From a long side, roll dough jelly-roll fashion. Repeat with remaining dough and filling. Wrap in plastic wrap; refrigerate overnight or freeze at least 2 hours, until firm enough to slice.

◆ Preheat oven to 350°F. Grease large cookie sheet. Cut 1 log into ¼-inch-thick slices (keep remainder refrigerated). Place slices, about 1 inch apart, on cookie sheet. Bake 8 to 10 minutes, until edges are golden brown. Cool slightly on cookie sheet on wire rack. With pancake turner, transfer to wire rack to cool completely. Repeat with remaining dough. Store cookies in tightly covered container.

Each cookie: About 55 calories, 1g protein, 8g carbohydrate, 2g total fat (0g saturated), 5mg cholesterol, 55mg sodium

SPICY ALMOND SLICES

Prep: 25 minutes plus chilling and cooling
Bake: 10 to 12 minutes per batch   Makes about 6½ dozen

1 cup margarine or butter, softened	½ teaspoon ground cloves
1 cup granulated sugar	½ teaspoon ground nutmeg
¾ cup packed dark brown sugar	½ teaspoon salt
1 tablespoon ground cinnamon	2 large eggs
1 teaspoon baking soda	3½ cups all-purpose flour
1 teaspoon vanilla extract	2 cups sliced blanched almonds (about 8 ounces)

◆ In large bowl, with mixer at low speed, beat first 10 ingredients and 2 cups flour until well mixed. With wooden spoon, stir in almonds and remaining 1½ cups flour; mix thoroughly with hands, if necessary. (Dough will be stiff.)

◆ Divide dough in half. Shape each half into 10" by 3" by 1" brick; wrap each brick in plastic wrap. Refrigerate overnight or freeze at least 2 hours, until firm enough to slice. Preheat oven to 375°F. Cut 1 brick into ¼-inch-thick slices (keep remainder refrigerated).

◆ Place slices, 1 inch apart, on ungreased cookie sheet. Bake 10 to 12 minutes, until browned around edges. With pancake turner, transfer cookies to wire rack to cool. Repeat with remaining dough. Store in tightly covered container.

Each cookie: About 75 calories, 1g protein, 9g carbohydrate, 4g total fat (1g saturated), 5mg cholesterol, 60mg sodium

PECAN SQUARES

Prep: 30 minutes plus chilling and cooling
Bake: 12 to 15 minutes per batch   Makes about 5 dozen

¾ cup packed dark brown sugar	2 teaspoons vanilla extract
½ cup margarine or butter, softened	2½ cups all-purpose flour
1 large egg	½ teaspoon baking soda
2 tablespoons milk	½ teaspoon salt
	1¼ cups pecans (5 ounces), toasted and chopped

◆ In large bowl, with mixer at medium-high speed, beat brown sugar and margarine until light and fluffy. Add egg, milk, and vanilla; beat until smooth. With wooden spoon, stir in flour, baking soda, and salt. When flour is almost incorporated, stir in pecans. (Dough will be very stiff.)

◆ Divide dough in half. On lightly floured surface, shape each half of dough into an 8" by 1½" by 1½" bar, using pancake turner to help flatten sides. Wrap each bar in plastic wrap and slide onto small cookie sheet for easier handling. Refrigerate dough overnight or freeze at least 2 hours, until very firm.

◆ Preheat oven to 350°F. Grease large cookie sheet. Cut 1 bar into slightly less than ¼-inch-thick slices (keep remainder refrigerated). Place slices, about 1½ inches apart, on cookie sheet. Bake cookies 12 to 15 minutes, until browned around edges. Transfer cookies to wire rack to cool. Repeat with remaining dough. Store cookies in tightly covered container.

Each cookie: About 60 calories, 1g protein, 7g carbohydrate, 3g total fat (0g saturated), 4mg cholesterol, 50mg sodium

FROSTED PECAN SQUARES

Prepare Pecan Squares as above. In medium bowl, mix 2 cups confectioners' sugar and 2 tablespoons plus 2 teaspoons milk to make a thick icing, adding more milk if necessary. With small metal spatula or knife, spread some icing of top of each cooled cookie; top each with a toasted pecan half (you will need about 1¼ cups toasted pecan halves). Set aside to allow icing to dry.

Each cookie: About 90 calories, 1g protein, 11g carbohydrate, 5g total fat (1g saturated), 4mg cholesterol, 50mg sodium

BISCOTTI

Biscotti are irresistible Italian cookies that involve a unique cooking process. The dough is baked twice, first in a loaf shape, then again after the loaf is cut into slices. The result is a dry, crunchy cookie perfect for dipping into coffee or sweet wine. Flavors range from the traditional almond and anise to modern variations made with chocolate, ginger, or dried fruit.

CRANBERRY-HAZELNUT BISCOTTI

Prep: 1 hour plus cooling   Bake: 45 to 55 minutes
Makes about 4½ dozen

3¾ cups all-purpose flour	1⅓ cups (about 5½ ounces)
2 cups sugar	hazelnuts (filberts), toasted
1 teaspoon baking powder	and skinned (see page 94),
½ teaspoon salt	chopped
5 large eggs	½ cup dried cranberries or
2 teaspoons vanilla extract	currants

1 Preheat oven to 350°F. Grease and lightly flour 2 large cookie sheets. In large bowl, combine first 4 ingredients. Separate 1 egg; reserve white for glaze. In small bowl, with wire whisk or fork, beat 4 whole eggs, 1 egg yolk, vanilla, and *1 tablespoon water*. Pour egg mixture into flour mixture; with wooden spoon, stir until blended.

2 With hands, knead dough until it comes together (dough will be very stiff). Knead in hazelnuts and dried cranberries. Divide dough into 4 equal pieces.

3 On lightly floured surface, with floured hands, shape each piece of dough into an 11" by 2" log. Place 2 logs, about 4 inches apart, on each cookie sheet.

4 In cup, with fork, lightly beat reserved egg white. With pastry brush, brush logs with egg white. Bake logs on 2 oven racks 35 to 40 minutes, until toothpick inserted in center comes out clean, rotating cookie sheets between upper and lower racks halfway through baking time (logs will spread during baking and become loaf shaped). Cool loaves 10 minutes on cookie sheets on wire racks.

6 Place slices, cut-side down, on same cookie sheets in single layer. Bake slices on 2 oven racks 10 to 15 minutes, until golden, turning slices once and rotating cookie sheets between upper and lower racks halfway through baking time. Transfer biscotti to wire racks to cool completely. (Biscotti will harden as they cool.) Store in tightly covered container.

5 Transfer loaves to cutting board. With serrated knife, cut each loaf crosswise into ½-inch-thick diagonal slices.

EACH SERVING: ABOUT 85 CALORIES, 2g PROTEIN, 15g CARBOHYDRATE, 2g TOTAL FAT (0g SATURATED), 20mg CHOLESTEROL, 35mg SODIUM

CHOCOLATE BISCOTTI

Prep: 45 minutes plus cooling and chilling
Bake: 45 to 50 minutes   **Makes** *about 4 dozen*

1 cup sugar
1 cup margarine or butter, softened
2½ cups all-purpose flour
1 cup unsweetened cocoa
1 tablespoon baking powder
1 teaspoon instant-coffee granules
1 teaspoon vanilla extract
½ teaspoon salt
4 large eggs
8 squares (8 ounces) semisweet chocolate
¼ cup sliced almonds (1 ounce), toasted

◆ Preheat oven to 350°F. In large bowl, with mixer at medium speed, beat sugar and margarine until light and creamy. With mixer at low speed, beat in 1 cup flour and next 6 ingredients until blended. With wooden spoon, stir in remaining 1½ cups flour until blended. Divide dough in half. On ungreased large cookie sheet, with well-floured hands, shape dough into two 12" by 3" loaves, 3 inches apart. Bake loaves 25 to 30 minutes, until firm. Cool on cookie sheet on wire rack 20 minutes.

◆ Transfer loaves to cutting board. With serrated knife, cut each loaf crosswise into ½-inch-thick diagonal slices. Place slices, cut-side down, on 2 ungreased large cookie sheets in single layer. Bake on 2 oven racks 20 minutes, turning slices once and rotating cookie sheets between upper and lower racks halfway through cooking time. Transfer to wire racks to cool completely.

◆ In heavy small saucepan, melt chocolate over low heat until smooth, stirring frequently. With pastry brush, brush top of each biscotti with some melted chocolate; sprinkle some almonds on chocolate. Refrigerate biscotti 30 minutes, or until chocolate is set. Store in tightly covered container.

Each cookie: About 110 calories, 2g protein, 13g carbohydrate, 6g total fat (2g saturated), 18mg cholesterol, 105mg sodium

ALMOND-ANISE BISCOTTI

Prep: 25 minutes plus cooling
Bake: 55 minutes   **Makes** *about 7 dozen*

1 cup whole almonds (about 4 ounces)
1 tablespoon anise seeds, crushed
1 tablespoon anise-flavor aperitif or liqueur
2 cups all-purpose flour
1 cup sugar
1 teaspoon baking powder
⅛ teaspoon salt
3 large eggs

◆ Preheat oven to 325°F. Place almonds on jelly-roll pan. Bake 10 minutes, until lightly toasted. Cool; chop very coarsely. Meanwhile, in medium bowl, combine anise seeds and aperitif; let stand 10 minutes.

◆ Grease large cookie sheet. In large bowl, combine flour, sugar, baking powder, salt, and almonds. Whisk eggs into anise mixture. With wooden spoon, stir egg mixture into flour mixture. Divide dough in half.

◆ With floured hands, shape dough on cookie sheet into two 15-inch logs, 3 inches apart (dough will be sticky).

◆ Bake logs 40 minutes, or until golden and toothpick inserted in center of log comes out clean. Cool on cookie sheet on wire rack 10 minutes.

◆ Transfer logs to cutting board. With serrated knife, cut each crosswise into ¼-inch-thick diagonal slices.

◆ Place slices, cut-side down, on 2 ungreased cookie sheets in single layer. Bake on 2 oven racks 15 minutes, turning slices once and rotating cookie sheets between upper and lower racks halfway through baking time. Transfer to wire racks to cool completely. Store in tightly covered container.

Each cookie: About 30 calories, 1g protein, 5g carbohydrate, 1g total fat (0g saturated), 8mg cholesterol, 15mg sodium

GINGER BISCOTTI

Prep: 25 minutes plus cooling
Bake: 48 to 50 minutes
Makes *about 3½ dozen*

3 cups all-purpose flour
1 tablespoon ground ginger
2 teaspoons baking powder
¼ teaspoon salt
½ cup margarine or butter, softened
½ cup granulated sugar
½ cup packed brown sugar
3 large eggs
½ cup minced crystallized ginger (about 3 ounces)

◆ Preheat oven to 350°F. Grease large cookie sheet. In medium bowl, combine first 4 ingredients.

◆ In large bowl, with mixer at medium speed, beat margarine with both sugars until light and creamy. Beat in eggs, 1 at a time.

◆ With mixer at low speed, beat in flour mixture until blended. With wooden spoon, stir in crystallized ginger. Divide dough in half.

◆ With floured hands, shape dough on cookie sheet into two 12-inch logs, 3 inches apart.

◆ Bake 30 minutes, or until toothpick inserted in center of log comes out clean. Cool on cookie sheet on wire rack 10 minutes. Transfer logs to cutting board. With serrated knife, cut each crosswise into ½-inch-thick diagonal slices.

◆ Place slices, cut-side down, on 2 ungreased cookie sheets in single layer. Bake on 2 oven racks 18 to 20 minutes, until golden, turning slices once and rotating cookie sheets between upper and lower racks halfway through baking time. Transfer to wire racks to cool completely. Store in tightly covered container.

Each cookie: About 80 calories, 1g protein, 13g carbohydrate, 3g total fat (1g saturated), 15mg cholesterol, 70mg sodium

BROWNIES

Brownies are the most famous – and irresistible – breed of bar cookies. Whether they're dense and chewy or light and cakelike, studded with nuts or frosted, they continue to reign as one of America's best-loved desserts. If not using brownies within 3 days, cover tightly and freeze for future treats.

ALMOND CHEESECAKE BROWNIES

◆◆◆◆◆◆◆◆◆◆◆◆◆

Prep: 30 minutes plus cooling
Bake: 40 to 45 minutes
Makes 2 dozen

¾ **cup margarine or butter**
4 **squares (4 ounces) unsweetened chocolate**
4 **squares (4 ounces) semisweet chocolate**
2 **cups sugar**
6 **large eggs**
2½ **teaspoons vanilla extract**
1½ **cups all-purpose flour**
¾ **teaspoon baking powder**
½ **teaspoon salt**
1½ **packages (8 ounces each) cream cheese, slightly softened**
¾ **teaspoon almond extract**

1 Preheat oven to 350°F. Line 13" by 9" metal baking pan with foil; lightly grease foil. In heavy 3-quart saucepan, melt margarine and all chocolate over low heat, stirring frequently. Remove from heat. With wooden spoon, beat in 1½ cups sugar, then beat in 4 eggs and 2 teaspoons vanilla until well blended. Stir in flour, baking powder, and salt just until blended; set aside.

2 In small bowl, with mixer at medium speed, beat cream cheese until smooth; gradually beat in remaining ½ cup sugar. Beat in almond extract, remaining 2 eggs, and remaining ½ teaspoon vanilla just until blended.

3 Spread 1½ cups chocolate batter evenly in baking pan.

4 Spoon cream-cheese mixture in 6 large dollops on top of chocolate batter (cheese mixture will cover much of chocolate batter). Spoon remaining chocolate batter in 6 large dollops over and between cheese mixture.

5 With tip of knife, cut and twist through mixtures to create marble design. Bake 40 to 45 minutes, until toothpick inserted 2 inches from center comes out almost clean with a few moist crumbs attached. Cool brownies in pan on wire rack. When cool, cut brownies lengthwise into 4 strips, then cut each strip crosswise into 6 pieces.

EACH BROWNIE: ABOUT 260 CALORIES, 4g PROTEIN, 27g CARBOHYDRATE, 16g TOTAL FAT (7g SATURATED), 69mg CHOLESTEROL, 185mg SODIUM

CHOCOLATE AND PEANUT-BUTTER BROWNIES

Prep: 20 minutes plus cooling **Bake:** *25 to 30 minutes*
Makes 2 dozen

3 squares (3 ounces)
  semisweet chocolate
1 square (1 ounce)
  unsweetened chocolate
2½ cups all-purpose flour
1½ teaspoons baking powder
½ teaspoon salt
1¾ cups packed light brown
  sugar

1 cup creamy peanut butter
½ cup margarine or butter,
  slightly softened
3 large eggs
2 teaspoons vanilla extract
1 package (6 ounces)
  semisweet-chocolate pieces
  (about 1 cup)

◆ Preheat oven to 350°F. In heavy 1-quart saucepan, melt all chocolate squares over low heat, stirring frequently. Remove from heat. In medium bowl, mix flour, baking powder, and salt.

◆ In large bowl, with mixer at medium speed, beat brown sugar, peanut butter, and margarine about 2 minutes, until smooth. Reduce speed to low. Beat in eggs and vanilla until blended. Beat in flour mixture just until combined (dough will be stiff). Place one-third of dough (about 1¾ cups) in another large bowl. Stir in melted chocolate until blended; stir in ¾ cup semisweet-chocolate pieces.

◆ Pat half of remaining peanut-butter dough into ungreased 13" by 9" metal baking pan. Drop remaining peanut-butter dough and chocolate dough in random pattern on top; pat down with hand. Sprinkle with remaining chocolate pieces.

PRALINE-ICED BROWNIES

Prepare Classic Brownies (right). While brownies are cooling, prepare topping: In 2-quart saucepan, heat 5 tablespoons margarine or butter and ⅓ cup packed light brown sugar over medium-low heat about 4 minutes, until mixture melts and bubbles. Remove from heat. With wire whisk, beat in 3 tablespoons bourbon (or 1 tablespoon vanilla extract plus 2 tablespoons water), then beat in 2 cups confectioners' sugar until smooth. With metal spatula, spread topping over room-temperature brownies in pan. Sprinkle with ½ cup pecans (about 2 ounces), toasted and coarsely chopped. Cut brownies lengthwise into 8 strips; cut each strip crosswise into 8 pieces. Makes 64.

Each brownie: About 115 calories, 1g protein, 15g carbohydrate, 6g total fat (2g saturated), 20mg cholesterol, 65mg sodium

◆ Bake 25 to 30 minutes, until toothpick inserted in center comes out clean. Cool in pan on wire rack. When cool, cut lengthwise into 4 strips; cut each strip crosswise into 6 pieces.

Each brownie: About 265 calories, 5g protein, 34g carbohydrate, 14g total fat (3g saturated), 27mg cholesterol, 185mg sodium

COCOA BROWNIES

Prep: 10 minutes plus cooling **Bake:** *25 minutes*
Makes 16

½ cup margarine or butter
1 cup sugar
2 large eggs
1 teaspoon vanilla extract
½ cup all-purpose flour

½ cup unsweetened cocoa
¼ teaspoon baking powder
¼ teaspoon salt
1 cup coarsely chopped
  walnuts (4 ounces), optional

Preheat oven to 350°F. Grease 9" by 9" metal baking pan. In 3-quart saucepan, melt margarine over medium heat. Remove from heat; stir in sugar. With wooden spoon, stir in eggs, 1 at a time, and vanilla until well blended. In medium bowl, combine flour and next 3 ingredients; stir flour mixture into saucepan until blended. Stir in nuts, if using. Spread batter evenly in pan. Bake 25 minutes, or until toothpick inserted 2 inches from center comes out almost clean. Cool in pan on wire rack. When cool, cut brownies into 4 strips; cut each strip crosswise into 4 squares.

Each brownie: About 130 calories, 2g protein, 17g carbohydrate, 7g total fat (1g saturated), 27mg cholesterol, 115mg sodium

CLASSIC BROWNIES

Prep: 20 minutes plus cooling **Bake:** *35 minutes*
Makes 2 dozen

1 cup margarine or butter
4 squares (4 ounces)
  unsweetened chocolate
4 squares (4 ounces)
  semisweet chocolate

2¼ cups sugar
6 large eggs
2 teaspoons vanilla extract
½ teaspoon salt
1¼ cups all-purpose flour

Preheat oven to 350°F. Line 13" by 9" metal baking pan with foil; grease foil. In heavy 3-quart saucepan, melt margarine and all chocolate squares over low heat, stirring frequently. Remove from heat. With wire whisk, beat in sugar, then eggs, until well blended. Stir in vanilla, salt, then flour just until blended. Spread batter evenly in pan. Bake 35 minutes, or until toothpick inserted 2 inches from center comes out almost clean with a few moist crumbs attached. Cool brownies in pan on wire rack. When cool, cut length-wise into 4 strips; cut each strip crosswise into 6 pieces.

Each brownie: About 230 calories, 3g protein, 28g carbohydrate, 13g total fat (4g saturated), 53mg cholesterol, 150mg sodium

BAR COOKIES

Homey bar cookies are the easiest of all to make. Just spread the dough in a pan and bake, then cut the cookies to size – as big or as dainty as you like. Our selection includes tart-sweet Citrus Bars, traditional Shortbread enriched with hazelnuts, moist, dense Date-and-Nut Squares, and walnut-studded Blondies.

1 Preheat oven to 400°F. In food processor with knife blade attached, blend flour, shortening, margarine, ¼ cup sugar, and ¼ teaspoon salt, pulsing processor on and off until crumbs form. With processor running, add *2 to 3 tablespoons cold water* through feed tube, 1 tablespoon at a time, pulsing processor on and off until dough comes together.

2 Press dough onto bottom and ¼ inch up sides of ungreased 13" by 9" metal baking pan. With fork, prick dough all over. Bake 20 to 25 minutes, until golden; remove from oven. Turn oven control to 375°F.

3 Squeeze ⅓ cup juice from limes. Grate 2 teaspoons peel and squeeze ¼ cup juice from lemons. In medium bowl, whisk sour cream with eggs, remaining 1 cup sugar, and ⅛ teaspoon salt. Mix in lime and lemon juice and lemon peel.

CITRUS BARS

◆◆◆◆◆◆◆◆◆◆◆◆◆

Prep: 35 to 40 minutes plus cooling and chilling
Bake: 30 minutes
Makes 32

1¾ cups all-purpose flour
¼ cup shortening
4 tablespoons margarine or butter, cut up
1¼ cups sugar
Salt
3 limes
2 lemons
½ cup sour cream
5 large eggs
Confectioners' sugar for garnish

ORANGE BARS

For an easy variation, make Citrus Bars as above, but in Step 1, add 1 teaspoon grated orange peel to dough. In Step 3, substitute 1 teaspoon grated orange peel for lemon peel, and substitute ⅓ cup orange juice for lime juice.

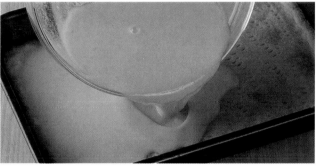

4 Pour citrus mixture over warm crust in baking pan; bake 15 minutes, or just until set (do not overbake, or surface of citrus filling may crack). Cool completely in pan on wire rack; refrigerate until well chilled.

5 When cool, sprinkle with confectioners' sugar. Cut lengthwise into 4 strips; cut each strip crosswise into 8 pieces. To store, cover pan and refrigerate.

EACH BAR: ABOUT 100 CALORIES, 2g PROTEIN, 13g CARBOHYDRATE, 5g TOTAL FAT (1g SATURATED), 35mg CHOLESTEROL, 55mg SODIUM

PREPARING HAZELNUTS

Toasting hazelnuts enhances their flavor and makes it easy to remove the bitter, papery skins. Preheat oven to 350°F. Spread hazelnuts in a jelly-roll or baking pan; bake 10 minutes, or until lightly toasted and skins begin to crack. Wrap hot hazelnuts in clean cloth towel. With hands, roll hazelnuts around, inside towel, to remove most of skins. Cool before using.

HAZELNUT SHORTBREAD

Prep: 45 minutes plus cooling   Bake: 50 to 60 minutes
Makes 3 dozen

1 cup (about 4 ounces) hazelnuts (filberts), toasted and skinned (see above)	1 cup butter, softened
	½ cup sugar
	½ teaspoon vanilla extract
2¼ cups all-purpose flour	¼ teaspoon salt

◆ Preheat oven to 300°F. In food processor with knife blade attached, finely chop hazelnuts with ¼ cup flour.

◆ In large bowl, with mixer at low speed, beat butter and sugar until light and creamy. Beat in vanilla, salt, hazelnut mixture, and remaining 2 cups flour just until blended. Pat dough evenly into ungreased 13" by 9" metal baking pan. With fork, prick dough all over.

◆ Bake shortbread 50 to 60 minutes, until lightly browned.

◆ While still warm, cut shortbread lengthwise into 3 strips; cut each strip crosswise into 12 pieces. Cool in pan on wire rack 10 minutes; remove pieces from pan. Cool shortbread completely on wire rack. Store in tightly covered container.

Each cookie: About 100 calories, 1g protein, 9g carbohydrate, 7g total fat (3g saturated), 14mg cholesterol, 65mg sodium

Blondies (below left), Hazelnut shortbread (below right), and Date and nut squares (bottom)

DATE AND NUT SQUARES

Prep: 15 minutes plus cooling   Bake: 30 to 35 minutes
Makes 16

1 cup packed light brown sugar	1 cup pecans (about 4 ounces), chopped
½ cup margarine or butter	1 cup pitted dates (5 ounces), chopped
1⅓ cups all-purpose flour	
1 teaspoon baking soda	2 large eggs

◆ Preheat oven to 350°F. Grease 9" by 9" metal baking pan. In 3-quart saucepan, heat brown sugar and margarine over medium-low heat, stirring occasionally, until melted and smooth. Remove saucepan from heat.

◆ With wooden spoon, beat in remaining ingredients until well blended. Spread batter evenly in pan.

◆ Bake 30 to 35 minutes, until toothpick inserted in center comes out clean. Cool in pan on wire rack. When cool, cut into 4 strips, then cut each strip crosswise into 4 squares. Store in tightly covered container.

Each cookie: About 220 calories, 3g protein, 30g carbohydrate, 11g total fat (2g saturated), 27mg cholesterol, 160mg sodium

BLONDIES

Prep: 15 minutes plus cooling   Bake: 35 minutes
Makes 1 dozen

1 cup walnuts, macadamia nuts, or pecans (about 4 ounces), coarsely chopped	6 tablespoons margarine or butter, softened
	1¼ teaspoons baking powder
1¼ cups all-purpose flour	½ teaspoon salt
½ cup granulated sugar	1½ teaspoons vanilla extract
½ cup packed light brown sugar	2 large eggs

◆ Preheat oven to 350°F. Grease 9" by 9" metal baking pan. Reserve ½ cup chopped nuts.

◆ In large bowl, with mixer at low speed, beat flour, remaining ingredients, and remaining ½ cup nuts until well blended, occasionally scraping bowl with rubber spatula.

◆ Spread batter evenly in pan; sprinkle reserved nuts on top. Bake 35 minutes, or until toothpick inserted in center comes out clean. Cool blondies in pan on wire rack.

◆ When cool, cut blondies into 3 strips; cut each strip crosswise into 4 pieces. Store in tightly covered container.

Each cookie: About 240 calories, 4g protein, 29g carbohydrate, 13g total fat (2g saturated), 36mg cholesterol, 220mg sodium

CANDY

Homemade candy is a holiday tradition. But you'll want to make these goodies year-round for birthdays, dinner parties, or even coffee-time treats.

TOFFEE ALMOND CRUNCH

◆◆◆◆◆◆◆◆◆◆◆◆◆◆

Prep: 1 hour plus cooling and standing
Cook: 30 minutes
Makes about 1¾ pounds

1¾ cups sugar
⅓ cup light corn syrup
1 cup margarine or butter
2 cups blanched slivered almonds (8 ounces), lightly toasted and finely chopped
2 squares (2 ounces) unsweetened chocolate
2 squares (2 ounces) semisweet chocolate
1 teaspoon shortening

1 Lightly grease 15½" by 10½" jelly-roll pan. In heavy 2-quart saucepan, heat sugar, corn syrup, and *¼ cup water* to boiling over medium heat, stirring occasionally until sugar dissolves. Stir in margarine. Set candy thermometer in place and continue cooking, stirring frequently, about 20 minutes, or until temperature reaches 300°F, or hard-crack stage (see below right). (Temperature will rise quickly once it reaches 220°F, so watch carefully.) Remove from heat.

4 Transfer candy in one piece from pan to cutting board. Spread chocolate over candy; sprinkle with reserved almonds, pressing them gently into chocolate. Set candy aside about 1 hour to allow glaze to set.

2 Reserve ⅓ cup almonds for sprinkling on chocolate glaze. Stir remaining almonds into hot syrup. Immediately pour mixture into jelly-roll pan; working quickly, with metal spatula, spread evenly. (Pan will become very hot.)

5 With knife, cut into hardened candy to break it into pieces. Store in layers, separated by waxed paper, in tightly covered container up to 1 month. (Note: This almond crunch is also delicious without the chocolate layer.)

3 Cool candy in pan on wire rack. Meanwhile, prepare glaze: Coarsely chop all chocolate. In heavy 1-quart saucepan, melt chopped chocolate and shortening over low heat, stirring frequently. Remove from heat; cool slightly.

TESTING CANDY

If you don't have a candy thermometer, use the cold-water test: Remove the syrup from the heat; drop a half spoonful into a cup or bowl of very cold water. Let stand 30 seconds.

Thread (230° to 234°F) Syrup forms a fine thread in the air as it falls from spoon

Soft ball (234° to 240°F) Syrup forms soft ball that flattens on removal from water

Firm ball (244° to 248°F) Syrup forms firm ball that does not flatten on removal from water

Hard ball (250° to 266°F) Syrup separates into hard, but not brittle, threads

Hard crack (300° to 310°F) Syrup separates into hard, brittle threads (above)

EACH OUNCE: ABOUT 185 CALORIES, 2g PROTEIN, 19g CARBOHYDRATE, 13g TOTAL FAT (3g SATURATED), 0mg CHOLESTEROL, 80mg SODIUM

CHOCOLATE-WALNUT FUDGE

Prep: 25 minutes plus chilling
Makes 36 pieces, about 2¼ pounds

1 pound bittersweet chocolate
  or 2 packages (8 ounces
  each) semisweet chocolate,
  coarsely chopped
1 can (14 ounces) sweetened
  condensed milk
1 cup walnuts (about
  4 ounces), coarsely chopped
1 teaspoon vanilla extract
⅛ teaspoon salt

◆ Line 8" by 8" metal baking pan with plastic wrap; smooth out as many wrinkles as possible. In heavy 2-quart saucepan, heat chocolate and condensed milk over medium-low heat, stirring constantly, until chocolate melts. Remove from heat; stir in remaining ingredients. Spoon chocolate mixture into pan; spread evenly. Refrigerate 3 hours, or until firm.

◆ Remove fudge from pan. Cut fudge into 6 strips; cut each strip crosswise into 6 pieces. Store in tightly covered container at room temperature up to 2 weeks.

Each piece: About 120 calories, 3g protein, 10g carbohydrate, 10g total fat (5g saturated), 4mg cholesterol, 20mg sodium

GOLD-RUSH NUT BRITTLE

Prep: 10 minutes plus cooling   *Cook:* 35 minutes
Makes about 1½ pounds

1½ cups sugar
1 cup light corn syrup
½ teaspoon salt
2 tablespoons margarine or
  butter
2 teaspoons vanilla extract
1 teaspoon baking soda
1 can (6 ounces) unsalted
  cocktail peanuts (1 cup)
1 cup sliced blanched
  almonds (about 4 ounces)
1 cup pecans (about 4 ounces)

◆ Grease large cookie sheet. In heavy 3-quart saucepan, heat sugar, corn syrup, salt, and *½ cup water* to boiling over medium heat, stirring occasionally until sugar dissolves.

◆ Set candy thermometer in place and continue cooking, stirring frequently, about 30 minutes, until temperature reaches 300°F, or hard-crack stage (see page 95).

◆ Remove saucepan from heat; stir in margarine, vanilla, baking soda, and all nuts. Immediately pour onto cookie sheet. With 2 forks, quickly lift and stretch nut mixture into about 14" by 12" rectangle.

◆ Cool brittle completely on cookie sheet on wire rack. With hands, break brittle into small pieces. Store in tightly covered container up to 1 month.

Each ounce: About 195 calories, 3g protein, 26g carbohydrate, 10g total fat (1g saturated), 0mg cholesterol, 120mg sodium

CHOCOLATE AND HAZELNUT TRUFFLES

Prep: 25 minutes plus chilling
Makes 32

8 ounces bittersweet
  chocolate or 6 squares
  (6 ounces) semisweet
  chocolate and 2 squares
  (2 ounces) unsweetened
  chocolate
½ cup heavy or whipping
  cream
3 tablespoons unsalted butter,
  softened and cut up
2 tablespoons coffee-,
  almond-, or orange-flavor
  liqueur (optional)
⅓ cup (about 1½ ounces)
  hazelnuts (filberts), toasted
  and skinned (see page 94),
  finely chopped
3 tablespoons unsweetened
  cocoa

◆ Line 8½" by 4½" metal loaf pan with plastic wrap. In food processor with knife blade attached, process chocolate until finely ground.

◆ In 1-quart saucepan, heat cream to boiling over medium-high heat. Add cream to chocolate in food processor and blend until smooth. Add butter, and liqueur, if using, and blend until incorporated. Spoon chocolate mixture into loaf pan; spread evenly. Refrigerate 3 hours, or until firm enough to handle.

◆ Spread hazelnuts and cocoa on separate sheets of waxed paper. Remove chocolate mixture from pan by lifting edges of plastic wrap and inverting mixture onto cutting board; discard plastic wrap. Cut chocolate mixture into 32 squares. Quickly roll each square into a ball.

◆ Roll half of truffles in chopped hazelnuts. Roll remaining truffles in cocoa. Refrigerate truffles up to 1 week. (Or, freeze in airtight container up to 1 month; remove from freezer 5 minutes before serving.)

Each truffle: About 65 calories, 1g protein, 3g carbohydrate, 7g total fat (4g saturated), 8mg cholesterol, 0mg sodium

Few desserts match the feeling of festivity evoked by a homemade cake. Satisfying to prepare and a pleasure to serve, a cake made from scratch is a supremely rewarding way to put your creative energies to work. Always follow the recipe accurately for reliable – and delicious – results.

WHY USE CAKE FLOUR?

Made from soft wheat, cake flour has a high starch content and low gluten content, which produces tender cakes. If you don't have cake flour and the recipe calls for it, you can use all-purpose flour; substitute 2 tablespoons cornstarch for the same amount of flour for each 1 cup cake flour specified. Or, use 1 cup minus 2 tablespoons all-purpose flour per 1 cup of cake flour.

LINING A CAKE PAN

Greasing and flouring cake pans prevents most cakes from sticking, but some batters require a lining of waxed paper as well.

Place pan on waxed paper. Use a pencil to trace around bottom rim; cut out circle.

Fit paper in greased pan; grease paper. Lightly dust with flour; tap to remove excess.

BUTTER VERSUS FOAM CAKES

Cakes come in two basic groups: butter and foam cakes. Butter cakes rely on fat for moisture and richness; they're loved for their flavor and velvety crumb. Chocolate, layer, and pound cakes are the most common varieties. The "creaming" stage is crucial; butter and sugar should be beaten together until they take on a pale color and fluffy consistency. To ensure that all of the dry ingredients are evenly dispersed, they should be well combined before they're added to the creamed mixture.

Foam cakes – light, airy chiffon and angel-food cakes – depend on beaten eggs or egg whites for volume and a delicate texture. Chiffon and sponge cakes contain both egg yolks and whites, and may include vegetable oil, margarine, or butter; angel-food cakes use only whites and contain no added fat. Adding cream of tartar to the egg whites before beating gives them better stability; beat until stiff peaks form when beaters are lifted. When combining ingredients, blend the foam gently so it won't deflate. Never grease the pan for an angel or chiffon cake; the batter needs to cling to the sides to rise. Before baking, cut through the batter in the pan with a rubber spatula to remove any air bubbles.

BAKING BASICS

• Before you begin preparing a recipe, set out all the ingredients, measuring when necessary.
• Room temperature eggs yield the best volume, but for safety, don't leave them out more than 30 minutes. Or, warm chilled eggs in a bowl of warm tap water 5 minutes before using.
• Use softened (not melted) butter; it's easier to beat.
• Although butter cakes can be mixed by hand, electric mixers provide the most even blending. Scrape the bowl often while beating so ingredients are mixed well.
• To avoid air bubbles, gently tap pans on the work surface after filling with batter.
• Bake cakes in the center of the oven. If making more than two layers, switch the position of pans halfway through baking.
• To prevent a cake from falling, leave the oven door shut during the first 15 minutes of baking.

HIGH-ALTITUDE BAKING

Most cake recipes require adjustment when prepared at high altitudes. The guidelines given in the chart below will help you avoid disasters. High-altitude cakes tend to stick to the pan, so grease and flour pans well, or line with waxed paper. Fill pans only half-full of batter, as these cakes may overflow.

RECIPE ADJUSTMENTS

INGREDIENT	3000 FEET	5000 FEET	7000 FEET
For each cup of liquid, add	1–2 tbsp liquid	2–4 tbsp liquid	3–4 tbsp liquid
For each teaspoon of baking powder, remove	⅛ tsp baking powder	⅛–¼ tsp baking powder	¼ tsp baking powder
For each cup sugar, remove	½–1 tbsp sugar	½–2 tbsp sugar	1–3 tbsp sugar

TESTING TIPS

The best bakers gauge doneness by how a cake looks, smells, sounds, and feels, in addition to the suggested cooking time. Begin testing for doneness about 10 minutes before the end of the recommended baking time. A fully baked cake should have a toasty aroma and (except for chocolate cakes) a deeply golden crust; any cracks on the surface should look dry. Most cakes will start to pull away from the sides of the pan; a toothpick inserted into the center of the cake should come out clean and dry, unless the recipe specifies otherwise. Alternatively, use the test illustrated below.

The secret's in the spring: Most cakes can be tested for doneness by pressing the top lightly with a finger. When the cake is fully baked, the top should spring back.

UNMOLDING AND COOLING

• Before unmolding, butter cakes should be cooled in their pans on a rack for approximately 10 minutes. Don't skimp on this resting period; it allows the cake to stabilize and further shrink from the side of the pan – and steam to build around the cake – making it easier to unmold.
• After the butter cake has rested in its pan, unmold it without delay so air can circulate around it freely, allowing it to cool more quickly and not become soggy.
• To unmold a butter cake, carefully run a small knife around the cake to loosen it from the side of the pan. Top cake with a wire cooling rack. Holding both the pan and the rack (if necessary, protect hands with a kitchen cloth or oven mitts), invert cake onto rack. Carefully remove pan and sandwich cake with second rack; flip cake, right-side up, onto second rack.
• Foam cakes call for a slightly different approach. Angel-food and chiffon cakes are too delicate to be removed from the pan until they're completely cooled. In addition, they must be cooled upside-down in the pan, which should be

Before unmolding the cake, carefully run a small knife around the edge to loosen it from the side of the pan.

To unmold cake, place cooling rack over pan; carefully invert cake. Remove pan and flip cake back onto second rack.

inverted onto the neck of a bottle or a funnel. This position prevents the cake from falling in the pan, while the bottle or funnel allows air to circulate evenly round the cake, and prevents the cake from touching the counter if it has risen above the rim of the pan. Sponge cakes are sturdier and can simply be cooled in the pan on a wire rack.
• To unmold a foam cake, carefully loosen it from the side of the pan with a long metal spatula or knife, pressing it firmly against the side of the pan (to avoid tearing the cake), and turn out onto a plate.

STORING CAKES

• All cakes should be cooled completely before they're frosted or stored.
• Because of their fat content, butter cakes stay fresh-tasting for 2 to 3 days. Foam cakes are best eaten within a day or 2 of preparation; they contain little fat and will dry out quickly.
• Keep cakes left in the pan tightly covered. Layer cakes and frosted tube cakes are best kept under an inverted large bowl.
• Always refrigerate cakes with fillings and frostings made with whipped cream, cream cheese, sour cream, yogurt, or eggs.
• Freeze frosted cakes, unwrapped, until firm, then wrap in plastic and aluminum foil and freeze up to 2 months.
• Freeze unfrosted butter cakes on a baking sheet just until firm. Wrap layers in plastic wrap, then foil, and freeze up to 4 months.
• Freeze foam cakes in a freezer bag for up to 3 months.

WHAT WENT WRONG?

Curdled batter Each egg was not thoroughly incorporated into the batter before the next was added; batter was beaten at too high a speed. This usually corrects itself when the dry ingredients are added.
Cake overflowed in pan Pan too small; too much leavening.
Tough, flat, and heavy texture Too much liquid; too much shortening; too much flour; batter under- or overbeaten.
Sunken middle Batter was overbeaten, creating excess aeration that cake was unable to contain; too much sugar, liquid, or baking powder was added to batter; oven door was opened before cake was set – or closed with too much force.
Peaked or cracked center A hard (high-gluten) flour was used instead of a softer flour (e.g., cake flour); batter was overbeaten after flour was added (this overactivates the gluten in flour, creating a tough cake); the oven was too hot, causing the cake to rise too quickly.
Cake did not rise properly Too much liquid; too much fat; too large a pan; oven too cool.
Dry crumb Too much baking powder; too long a baking time.
Crumbly texture Underbeaten; too much shortening.
Pale color Too little sugar; too short a baking time.
Tunnels in dough Too much egg; too little sugar; poor mixing; oven too hot.

CLASSIC LAYER CAKES

For family gatherings, birthdays, and other special occasions, there's nothing like the sheer romance of a layer cake made from scratch. The tender crumb and homemade taste simply can't compare with commercial mixes or store-bought cakes. Try timeless cakes, such as buttery Yellow or Rich Chocolate, or fanciful finales like the playful Checkerboard Cake.

CHECKERBOARD CAKE

◆◆◆◆◆◆◆◆◆◆◆◆◆◆◆◆◆◆◆◆◆◆◆◆◆◆◆◆◆◆◆

Prep: 40 minutes plus cooling   Bake: 25 to 30 minutes
Make 16 servings

1 cup margarine or butter, softened	Chocolate Butter Cream (see page 122)
2 cups sugar	
3½ cups cake flour (not self-rising)	Special equipment:
1¼ cups milk	2 large decorating bags, each with ½-inch opening or
1 tablespoon baking powder	⅛-inch writing tip (or use a
1 tablespoon vanilla extract	zip-tight plastic bag with
½ teaspoon salt	corner cut to make ½-inch
8 large egg whites	opening)
8 squares (8 ounces) semisweet chocolate, melted and cooled	

1 Preheat oven to 350°F. Grease three 8-inch round cake pans. Line bottoms of pans with waxed paper; grease paper. Dust pans with flour. In large bowl, with mixer at low speed, beat margarine and 1½ cups sugar until blended. Increase speed to high; beat about 5 minutes, until light and creamy. Reduce speed to low. Add flour and next 4 ingredients; beat just until combined. Increase speed to medium; beat 2 minutes, occasionally scraping bowl.

2 In another large bowl, with mixer at high speed, beat egg whites to soft peaks; gradually sprinkle in remaining ½ cup sugar, beating until stiff peaks form when beaters are lifted. Fold whites, one-third at a time, into flour mixture.

3 Spoon half of batter into medium bowl. Into batter in large bowl, fold melted chocolate. Spoon vanilla batter into a large decorating bag or zip-tight plastic bag with corner cut. Spoon chocolate batter into a second decorating bag.

4 Pipe 1½-inch-wide band of chocolate batter around inside edge of 2 cake pans. Pipe 1½-inch-wide band of vanilla batter next to each chocolate band; pipe enough chocolate batter to fill in center.

5 In third pan, repeat piping, alternating batters, but starting with vanilla around edge. Stagger pans on 2 oven racks, placing 2 on upper rack and 1 on lower rack, so that layers are not directly on top of one another.

6 Bake 25 to 30 minutes, until toothpick inserted in centers comes out clean. Cool in pans on wire racks 10 minutes. Run small knife around edges of pans to loosen cakes; invert onto racks. Remove waxed paper; cool completely. Prepare butter cream. Place one of the two identical layers on cake plate; spread with ½ cup butter cream. Top with the reverse-design layer. Spread with ½ cup butter cream; top with remaining layer. Frost side and top of cake with remaining butter cream. Store any leftover cake in refrigerator.

EACH SERVING: ABOUT 550 CALORIES, 6g PROTEIN, 72g CARBOHYDRATE, 29g TOTAL FAT (9g SATURATED), 3mg CHOLESTEROL, 430mg SODIUM

WHITE CHOCOLATE CAKE

Prep: 1 hour 15 minutes plus cooling   Bake: 25 minutes
Makes 16 servings

9 ounces white chocolate, Swiss confectionery bars, or white baking bars	1½ teaspoons vanilla extract
1½ cups milk	¾ teaspoon salt
1¼ cups sugar	3 large eggs
¾ cup margarine or butter, softened	Quick Chocolate Curls made with white chocolate (optional, see page 123)
3¼ cups cake flour (not self-rising)	Lemon Butter Cream (see page 122)
1½ teaspoons baking powder	⅔ cup seedless red raspberry jam

◆ In 2-quart saucepan, melt white chocolate with milk over low heat, stirring frequently, until mixture is smooth. Remove saucepan from heat; cool slightly.

◆ Preheat oven to 350°F. Grease and flour three 8-inch round cake pans.

◆ In large bowl, with mixer at low speed, beat sugar and margarine until blended. Increase speed to high; beat about 5 minutes, until light and creamy. Reduce speed to low; beat in flour, baking powder, vanilla, salt, eggs, and cooled white-chocolate mixture until blended, frequently scraping bowl with rubber spatula. Increase speed to medium; beat 2 minutes.

◆ Divide batter evenly among cake pans. Stagger pans on 2 oven racks, placing 2 on upper rack and 1 on lower rack, so that layers are not directly on top of one another. Bake 25 minutes, or until toothpick inserted in centers of layers comes out clean. Cool layers in pans on wire racks 10 minutes. Run small knife around edges of pans to loosen cakes; invert onto racks and cool completely.

◆ Meanwhile, prepare Quick Chocolate Curls, if you like, and refrigerate; prepare Lemon Butter Cream. With serrated knife, cut each layer horizontally in half to make 6 thin layers in all. Place 1 cake layer cut-side up on large cake plate. Spread with ⅓ cup butter cream. Top with second layer; spread with ⅓ cup jam. Repeat layering to make 3 layers of butter cream and 2 layers of jam in all, ending with sixth layer.

◆ Spread remaining butter cream over side and top of cake. With toothpick, carefully press chocolate curls, if using, into butter cream, completely covering cake. Store any leftover cake in refrigerator.

Each serving: About 550 calories, 6g protein, 70g carbohydrate, 28g total fat (9g saturated), 49mg cholesterol, 425mg sodium

RICH CHOCOLATE CAKE

Prep: 50 minutes plus cooling   Bake: 30 minutes
Makes 16 servings

2 cups all-purpose flour	2 cups sugar
1 cup unsweetened cocoa	1 cup margarine or butter, softened
2 teaspoons baking powder	4 large eggs
1 teaspoon baking soda	Fluffy White Frosting (see page 122) or other desired frosting
½ teaspoon salt	
1⅓ cups milk	
2 teaspoons vanilla extract	

◆ Preheat oven to 350°F. Grease three 8-inch round cake pans. Line bottoms of pans with waxed paper; grease paper. Dust pans with flour. In medium bowl, combine flour, cocoa, baking powder, baking soda, and salt; set aside. In measuring cup, mix milk and vanilla.

◆ In large bowl, with mixer at low speed, beat sugar and margarine until blended. Increase speed to high; beat about 2 minutes, until creamy. Reduce speed to medium-low; add eggs, 1 at a time, beating well after each addition. Alternately add flour mixture and milk mixture, beginning and ending with flour mixture; beat until batter is smooth, occasionally scraping bowl with rubber spatula.

◆ Divide batter evenly among cake pans. Stagger pans on 2 oven racks, placing 2 on upper rack and 1 on lower rack, so that layers are not directly on top of one another. Bake 30 minutes, or until toothpick inserted in centers of layers comes out almost clean. Cool in pans on wire racks 10 minutes. Run small knife around edges of pans to loosen cakes; invert cakes onto racks. Carefully remove waxed paper; cool cakes completely.

◆ Prepare frosting. Place 1 cake layer on cake plate; spread with ½ cup frosting. Top with second layer and ½ cup frosting. Place remaining cake layer on top. Frost side and top of cake with remaining frosting.

Each serving: About 345 calories, 5g protein, 54g carbohydrate, 14g total fat (3mg saturated), 56mg cholesterol, 375mg sodium

AMBROSIA LAYER CAKE

Prep: 1 hour 30 minutes plus chilling and cooling
Bake: 35 to 40 minutes
Makes 20 servings

4 large oranges
1 tablespoon fresh lemon
  juice
3 tablespoons cornstarch
2½ cups sugar
1¼ cups margarine or butter,
  softened
6 large egg yolks
2½ cups cake flour (not self-
  rising)
1½ teaspoons baking powder

1 teaspoon baking soda
¼ teaspoon salt
2 teaspoons vanilla extract
3 large eggs
1 cup buttermilk or soured
  milk
Fluffy White Frosting (see
  page 122)
1 cup flaked coconut
Orange-peel strips for garnish

◆ Grate 1 tablespoon peel and squeeze 1⅓ cups juice from oranges. In heavy 3-quart saucepan, mix orange peel and juice, lemon juice, cornstarch, and 1 cup sugar. Add ½ cup margarine; heat to boiling over medium heat, stirring. Boil 1 minute. In small bowl, beat egg yolks lightly. Into yolks, beat small amount of orange mixture; beat yolk mixture into orange mixture in saucepan. Cook over low heat, stirring constantly, 3 minutes, or until very thick. Pour filling into medium bowl; cover surface with plastic wrap to prevent skin from forming. Refrigerate 2 hours, or until well chilled.

◆ Meanwhile, preheat oven to 350°F. Grease and flour 13" by 9" metal baking pan. In medium bowl, combine flour, baking powder, baking soda, and salt.

◆ In large bowl, with mixer at low speed, beat remaining 1½ cups sugar and remaining ¾ cup margarine just until blended. Increase speed to high; beat 5 minutes, until light and creamy, scraping bowl often with rubber spatula. Reduce speed to low; add vanilla and whole eggs, 1 at a time, until blended. Alternately add flour mixture and buttermilk, beginning and ending with flour mixture; beat until batter is well mixed, occasionally scraping bowl.

◆ Spread batter in pan. Bake 35 to 40 minutes, until toothpick inserted in center of cake comes out clean. Cool in pan on wire rack 10 minutes. Run small spatula around edges of pan to loosen cake; invert onto rack to cool completely.

◆ Prepare Fluffy White Frosting. With serrated knife, cut cake horizontally in half. To remove top cake layer, carefully place cookie sheet in between cut layers and lift off top layer. Slide bottom layer onto serving platter; with metal spatula, spread with chilled filling. Carefully transfer top layer of cake onto bottom layer by gently sliding cake onto filling. Frost sides and top of cake with frosting. Sprinkle with coconut; garnish. Refrigerate until ready to serve.

Each serving: About 360 calories, 4g protein, 52g carbohydrate, 16g total fat (4g saturated), 96mg cholesterol, 300mg sodium

YELLOW CAKE

Prep: 45 minutes plus cooling   Bake: 23 to 28 minutes
Makes 16 servings

3 cups cake flour (not self-
  rising)
1 tablespoon baking powder
½ teaspoon salt
1 cup milk
2 teaspoons vanilla extract
2 cups sugar

1 cup margarine or butter,
  softened
4 large eggs
Orange Butter Cream (see
  page 122) or other desired
  frosting

◆ Preheat oven to 350°F. Grease three 8-inch round cake pans. Line bottoms of pans with waxed paper; grease paper. Dust pans with flour. In medium bowl, combine flour, baking powder, and salt; set aside. In measuring cup, mix milk and vanilla.

◆ In large bowl, with mixer at low speed, beat sugar and margarine until blended. Increase speed to high; beat 2 minutes, or until creamy. Reduce speed to medium-low; add eggs, 1 at a time, beating well after each addition. Alternately add flour mixture and milk mixture, beginning and ending with flour mixture; beat until batter is smooth, occasionally scraping bowl with rubber spatula.

◆ Divide batter evenly among pans. Stagger pans on 2 oven racks, placing 2 on upper rack and 1 on lower rack, so that layers are not directly on top of one another. Bake 23 to 28 minutes, until toothpick inserted in centers of layers comes out almost clean with a few moist crumbs attached. Cool in pans on wire racks 10 minutes. Run small knife around edges of pans to loosen cakes; invert onto racks. Remove waxed paper; cool completely.

◆ Prepare butter cream. Place 1 cake layer on cake plate; spread with ⅔ cup butter cream. Top with second cake layer and ⅔ cup butter cream. Place remaining cake layer on top. Frost side and top of cake with remaining butter cream. Store any leftover cake in refrigerator.

Each serving: About 475 calories, 5g protein, 59g carbohydrate, 25g total fat (6g saturated), 58mg cholesterol, 455mg sodium

CHOCOLATE BUTTERMILK CAKE

Prep: 30 minutes plus cooling   Bake: 30 minutes
Makes 16 servings

¾ cup unsweetened cocoa plus
   additional for dusting pans
2¼ cups all-purpose flour
1¾ cups sugar
1½ cups buttermilk or soured
   milk
1 cup vegetable oil

2 teaspoons baking soda
1½ teaspoons vanilla extract
1¼ teaspoons salt
3 large eggs
Chocolate Butter Cream (see
   page 122)

◆ Preheat oven to 350°F. Grease two 9-inch round cake pans. Dust pans with cocoa.

◆ In large bowl, mix flour, next 7 ingredients, and ¾ cup cocoa. With mixer at low speed, beat until mixed, frequently scraping bowl with rubber spatula. Increase speed to medium; beat 3 minutes, occasionally scraping bowl. Divide batter evenly between pans. Bake 30 minutes, or until toothpick inserted in centers of layers comes out clean. Cool layers in pans on wire racks 10 minutes. Run small knife around edges of pans to loosen cakes. Invert onto racks; cool completely. Prepare butter cream.

◆ Place 1 cake layer rounded-side down on cake plate; spread with ⅔ cup butter cream. Top with second layer, rounded-side up. Frost side and top of cake with remaining butter cream. Store any leftover cake in refrigerator.

Each serving: About 475 calories, 5g protein, 56g carbohydrate, 28g total fat (7g saturated), 41mg cholesterol, 465mg sodium

SPICE LAYER CAKE

Prep: 45 minutes plus cooling   Bake: 28 to 30 minutes
Makes 16 servings

1¾ cups all-purpose flour
1 teaspoon baking powder
¾ teaspoon ground cinnamon
½ teaspoon baking soda
½ teaspoon salt
½ teaspoon ground ginger
½ teaspoon ground nutmeg
Pinch ground cloves
1 cup sugar

½ cup margarine or butter,
   softened
2 large eggs
1 teaspoon vanilla extract
¾ cup buttermilk or soured
   milk
Vanilla Butter Cream (see
   page 122) or other desired
   frosting

◆ Preheat oven to 350°F. Grease three 8-inch round cake pans. Line bottoms with waxed paper; grease paper. Dust pans with flour. In bowl, mix flour and next 7 ingredients.

◆ In large bowl, with mixer at medium speed, beat sugar and margarine 5 minutes, or until light and creamy. Add eggs, 1 at a time, beating well after each addition. Beat in vanilla. With mixer at low speed, alternately add flour mixture and buttermilk, beginning and ending with flour; beat just until batter is smooth. Divide batter among pans. Stagger pans on 2 oven racks, placing 2 on upper rack and 1 on lower rack, so that layers are not directly on top of one another.

◆ Bake 28 to 30 minutes, until toothpick inserted in centers comes out clean. Cool in pans on wire racks 10 minutes. Run knife around edges of pans to loosen cakes; invert onto racks. Remove waxed paper; cool completely. Prepare butter cream. Place 1 layer on cake plate; spread with ⅔ cup butter cream. Top with second layer, ⅔ cup butter cream, and remaining layer. Frost side and top of cake with remaining butter cream. Store any leftover cake in refrigerator.

Each serving: About 340 calories, 4g protein, 40g carbohydrate, 19g total fat (4g saturated), 30mg cholesterol, 365mg sodium

BANANA LAYER CAKE

Prep: 40 minutes plus cooling   Bake: 30 minutes
Makes 16 servings

1 cup mashed fully ripe
   bananas (2 to 3 bananas)
¼ cup buttermilk or soured
   milk
1 teaspoon vanilla extract
2 cups cake flour (not self-
   rising)
1 teaspoon baking powder
½ teaspoon baking soda

¼ teaspoon salt
⅛ teaspoon ground nutmeg
1¼ cups sugar
½ cup margarine or butter,
   softened
2 large eggs
Cream-Cheese Frosting (see
   page 122)

◆ Preheat oven to 350°F. Grease three 8-inch round cake pans. Line bottoms with waxed paper; grease paper. Dust pans with flour. In bowl, mix bananas, buttermilk, and vanilla. In medium bowl, mix flour and next 4 ingredients.

◆ In large bowl, with mixer at medium speed, beat sugar and margarine 5 minutes, or until light and creamy. Add eggs, 1 at time, beating well after each addition. At low speed, alternately add flour mixture and banana mixture, beginning and ending with flour mixture; beat just until smooth.

◆ Divide batter among pans. Stagger pans on 2 oven racks, placing 2 on upper rack and 1 on lower rack, so layers are not directly on top of one another. Bake 30 minutes, or until toothpick inserted in centers comes out clean. Cool in pans on wire racks 10 minutes. Run knife around edges of pans to loosen cakes; invert onto racks. Remove waxed paper; cool completely. Prepare frosting. Place 1 layer on cake plate; spread with ½ cup frosting. Top with second layer, ½ cup frosting, and remaining layer. Frost side and top of cake with remaining frosting. Store any leftover cake in refrigerator.

Each serving: About 335 calories, 3g protein, 49g carbohydrate, 14g total fat (5g saturated), 39mg cholesterol, 265mg sodium

RICH CHOCOLATE CAKES AND TORTES

These dazzling desserts look as if they came from an expensive bakery, but our straightforward recipes make them easy to prepare. Each one promises a deep chocolate flavor, as well as a distinctive taste all its own. The mocha torte offers tiers of espresso cream and crunchy toasted almonds, Chocolate Truffle Cake boasts a dense, decadent texture, and the prune-nut torte is moist and fruity. Remember that chocolate can easily scorch when heated, so melt it carefully, over low heat, and stir it often.

TRIPLE-LAYER
MOCHA-ALMOND TORTE

◆◆◆◆◆◆◆◆◆◆◆◆◆◆◆◆◆◆◆◆◆◆◆◆◆◆◆◆◆

Prep: 45 minutes plus cooling   *Bake:* 45 to 50 minutes
Makes 16 servings

6 squares (6 ounces) semisweet chocolate	¼ cup all-purpose flour (yes, ¼ cup)
1 tablespoon plus 2 teaspoons instant espresso-coffee powder	1 teaspoon baking powder
	½ teaspoon salt
3 cups blanched whole almonds (about 12 ounces)	6 large eggs, separated
	½ teaspoon almond extract
¾ cup plus ⅓ cup sugar	2½ cups heavy or whipping cream

1 Preheat oven to 350°F. Grease 9" by 2½" springform pan. Line bottom of pan with waxed paper; grease paper. Dust with flour. In small saucepan, melt chocolate with 1 tablespoon espresso powder and ¼ *cup water* over low heat, stirring frequently, until smooth. Remove from heat.

2 In food processor with knife blade attached, or in blender in batches, grind 2 cups almonds with ¼ cup sugar. (Nuts should be finely ground but not pastelike.) Transfer nut mixture to medium bowl; stir in flour, baking powder, and salt.

3 In large bowl, with mixer at high speed, beat egg whites to soft peaks; sprinkle in ½ cup sugar, 2 tablespoons at a time, until whites stand in stiff peaks when beaters are lifted. In small bowl, with mixer at medium speed, beat yolks, chocolate mixture, and almond extract 3 minutes, frequently scraping bowl. Fold nut mixture and chocolate mixture into egg whites just until blended. Spread batter evenly in pan.

4 Bake 45 to 50 minutes, until toothpick inserted in center of cake comes out clean. Cool in pan on wire rack 10 minutes. Remove side and bottom of pan. Remove waxed paper; cool completely on rack.

5 Meanwhile, coarsely chop remaining 1 cup almonds. In small skillet, toast almonds over medium heat until golden. Cool. With serrated knife, cut cake horizontally into 3 layers. In cup, dissolve 2 teaspoons espresso powder in *1 tablespoon hot water.*

6 In large bowl, with mixer at medium speed, beat cream, remaining ⅓ cup sugar, and espresso mixture to stiff peaks. Place 1 cake layer on cake plate; spread with 1 cup cream. Top with second layer; spread with 1 more cup cream.

7 Top with third layer. Spread top and side of cake with remaining cream. Reserve 1 tablespoon almonds; press remaining almonds into side of cake. Garnish with reserved almonds. Refrigerate until ready to serve.

EACH SERVING: ABOUT 380 CALORIES, 9g PROTEIN, 27g CARBOHYDRATE, 29g TOTAL FAT (12g SATURATED), 131 mg CHOLESTEROL, 135mg SODIUM

CHOCOLATE TRUFFLE CAKE

Prep: 1 hour plus chilling overnight and standing   *Bake: 35 minutes*
Makes 24 servings

1 cup butter (do not use
  margarine)
14 squares (14 ounces)
  semisweet chocolate
2 squares (2 ounces)
  unsweetened chocolate

9 large eggs, separated
½ cup granulated sugar
¼ teaspoon cream of tartar
Confectioners' sugar for
  garnish

◆ Preheat oven to 300°F. Remove bottom from 9" by 3" springform pan and cover bottom with foil, wrapping foil around to the underside (this will make it easier to remove cake from pan). Replace bottom. Grease and flour foil bottom and side of pan.

◆ In heavy 2-quart saucepan, melt butter with all chocolate over low heat, stirring frequently. Pour chocolate mixture into large bowl.

◆ In small bowl, with mixer at high speed, beat egg yolks and granulated sugar about 5 minutes, until very thick and lemon-colored. With rubber spatula, stir egg-yolk mixture into chocolate mixture until blended.

◆ In another large bowl, with clean beaters, with mixer at high speed, beat egg whites and cream of tartar to soft peaks. With rubber spatula or wire whisk, gently fold beaten egg whites into chocolate mixture, one-third at a time.

◆ Spread batter evenly in pan. Bake 35 minutes. (Do not overbake; cake will firm on chilling.) Cool cake completely in pan on wire rack. Refrigerate overnight in pan.

◆ To remove cake from pan, run a hot knife around edge of cake; remove side of pan. Invert cake onto cake plate; unwrap foil on bottom and lift off bottom of pan. Carefully peel foil from cake.

◆ Let cake stand 1 hour at room temperature before serving. Just before serving, sprinkle confectioners' sugar through fine sieve over star stencil or doily for a pretty design (see page 124), or dust top of cake with confectioners' sugar. Store any leftover cake in refrigerator.

Each serving: About 200 calories, 4g protein, 15g carbohydrate, 16g total fat (9g saturated), 100mg cholesterol, 100mg sodium

CHOCOLATE, PRUNE, AND NUT TORTE

Prep: 1 hour plus chilling overnight   *Bake: 35 minutes*
Makes 12 servings

3 bittersweet chocolate bars
  (3 ounces each) or
9 squares (9 ounces)
  semisweet chocolate
6 large egg whites
½ cup granulated sugar

½ teaspoon vanilla extract
2 cups pitted prunes, diced
1½ cups pecans (about
  6 ounces), coarsely chopped
1 tablespoon confectioners'
  sugar

◆ Grease 10" by 2½" springform pan; line bottom of pan with waxed paper.

◆ Finely grate chocolate. (Or, in food processor with knife blade attached, process chocolate until ground.)

◆ Preheat oven to 425°F. In large bowl, with mixer at high speed, beat egg whites until soft peaks form. Beating at high speed, sprinkle in granulated sugar, 2 tablespoons at a time, beating well after each addition, until whites stand in stiff peaks when beaters are lifted. Beat in vanilla.

◆ With rubber spatula, gently fold prunes and pecans into beaten egg whites; gently but thoroughly fold in grated chocolate. Pour batter into pan, smoothing top. Bake 35 minutes, or until top of torte is deep brown and edge pulls away from side of pan.

◆ Cool torte in pan on wire rack 15 minutes; remove side of pan. Invert torte and remove bottom of pan; peel off waxed paper. Cool torte completely on rack. Cover and refrigerate torte overnight.

◆ Just before serving, cut six 12" by ½" strips of waxed paper. Place strips 1 inch apart on top of torte. Sprinkle top of torte with confectioners' sugar, then carefully remove waxed-paper strips. Store any leftover torte in refrigerator.

Each serving: About 305 calories, 6g protein, 34g carbohydrate, 21g total fat (7g saturated), 0mg cholesterol, 30mg sodium

CAKE ROLLS

Alluring spirals of cake and filling make cake rolls among the prettiest desserts around. Best made in advance, they're perfect for company.

WHITE-CHOCOLATE YULE LOG

◆◆◆◆◆◆◆◆◆◆◆◆◆

Prep: 1 hour 10 minutes plus cooling and chilling
Bake: 10 to 15 minutes
Makes 20 servings

10 large eggs, separated
1 cup granulated sugar
3 teaspoons vanilla extract
1 cup all-purpose flour
¼ cup confectioners' sugar plus additional for sprinkling
White-Chocolate Butter Cream (see page 122)
1 pint heavy or whipping cream (2 cups)
¼ cup unsweetened cocoa
½ teaspoon ground cinnamon
Chocolate Leaves (see page 123) and cranberries for garnish

1 Preheat oven to 350°F. Grease two 15½" by 10½" jelly-roll pans. Line pans with waxed paper; grease paper. In large bowl, with mixer at high speed, beat egg whites until soft peaks form. Beating at high speed, gradually sprinkle in ½ cup granulated sugar, 2 tablespoons at a time, beating until whites stand in stiff peaks when beaters are lifted.

2 In small bowl, with mixer at high speed, beat egg yolks, remaining ½ cup granulated sugar, and 2 teaspoons vanilla until very thick and lemon-colored; at low speed, beat in flour just until combined. With rubber spatula, fold yolk mixture into beaten whites.

3 Spread batter evenly in pans. Bake on 2 oven racks 10 to 15 minutes, until cakes spring back when lightly touched, rotating pans between upper and lower racks halfway through baking time.

4 Sprinkle large cloth kitchen towel with confectioners' sugar. When cakes are done, immediately run spatula around edges of pans to loosen cakes; invert onto towel, slightly over-lapping a long side of each.

5 Carefully peel off waxed paper. Starting from a long side, roll cakes with towel jelly-roll fashion. Cool completely, seam-side down, on wire rack. Meanwhile, prepare White-Chocolate Butter Cream; set aside.

6 In large bowl, with mixer at medium speed, beat cream, cocoa, cinnamon, ¼ cup confectioners' sugar, and remaining 1 teaspoon vanilla to stiff peaks. Unroll cake; spread with cocoa cream, leaving ½-inch border.

7 From same long side, roll cake without towel. Cut a 2-inch-thick diagonal slice from each end of roll; trim each to 2½ inches in diameter. Place cake, seam-side down, on long platter.

8 With metal spatula, spread some butter cream over roll. Place end pieces on top of roll to resemble cut branches. Spread remaining frosting over roll and branches. With four-tined fork, score frosting to resemble bark of tree. Refrigerate cake at least 2 hours before serving. Garnish with Chocolate Leaves and cranberries. Store any leftover cake in refrigerator.

EACH SERVING: ABOUT 360 CALORIES, 5g PROTEIN, 33g CARBOHYDRATE, 23g TOTAL FAT (14g SATURATED), 166mg CHOLESTEROL, 145mg SODIUM

FALLEN CHOCOLATE SOUFFLÉ ROLL

Prep: 30 minutes plus cooling and chilling   *Bake:* 15 minutes
Makes 16 servings

5 squares (5 ounces) semisweet chocolate	¾ teaspoon ground cinnamon
1 square (1 ounce) unsweetened chocolate	¼ teaspoon salt
1 teaspoon instant espresso-coffee powder, dissolved in 3 tablespoons hot water	⅛ teaspoon ground cloves
	1½ cups heavy or whipping cream
6 large eggs, separated	¼ cup coffee-flavor liqueur
¾ cup granulated sugar	5 tablespoons confectioners' sugar plus additional for sprinkling
1 teaspoon vanilla extract	

◆ Preheat oven to 350°F. Grease 15½" by 10½" jelly-roll pan. Line with waxed paper; grease paper. Dust pan with flour. In top of double boiler set over simmering water, melt all chocolate with espresso mixture, stirring often; set aside.

◆ In large bowl, with mixer at high speed, beat egg whites until soft peaks form. Beating at high speed, gradually sprinkle in ¼ cup granulated sugar, 1 tablespoon at a time, beating well after each addition, until whites stand in stiff peaks when beaters are lifted.

◆ In small bowl, with mixer at high speed, beat egg yolks with remaining ½ cup granulated sugar until very thick and lemon-colored. Reduce speed to low; beat in vanilla, cinnamon, salt, and cloves. With rubber spatula, fold chocolate mixture into yolk mixture. Gently fold one-third of whites into chocolate mixture; fold chocolate mixture into remaining whites.

◆ Spread batter evenly in pan. Bake 15 minutes, or until firm to the touch. Cover cake with clean, dampened kitchen towel; cool in pan on wire rack 30 minutes.

◆ In large bowl, with mixer at medium speed, beat cream until soft peaks form. Beat in coffee liqueur and 3 tablespoons confectioners' sugar, then beat until stiff peaks form.

◆ Remove towel from cake; sift 2 tablespoons confectioners' sugar over cake. Run small spatula around edges of pan. Cover cake with sheet of foil and a large cookie sheet; invert cake onto cookie sheet. Carefully peel off waxed paper.

◆ Spread whipped cream evenly over cake, leaving ½-inch border. Starting from a long side and using foil to help lift cake, roll cake jelly-roll fashion (cake may crack). Place, seam-side down, on long platter. Refrigerate at least 1 hour, until ready to serve. Just before serving, sprinkle confectioners' sugar on top.

Each serving: About 215 calories, 4g protein, 21g carbohydrate, 14g total fat (8g saturated), 110mg cholesterol, 65mg sodium

BLUEBERRY GINGERBREAD ROLL

Prep: 30 minutes plus cooling   *Bake:* 15 minutes
Makes 8 servings

1 cup all-purpose flour	¼ cup light molasses
½ cup granulated sugar	1 large egg
2 teaspoons ground ginger	3 tablespoons confectioners' sugar plus additional for sprinkling
1 teaspoon baking soda	
½ teaspoon baking powder	
½ teaspoon ground cinnamon	1 cup heavy or whipping cream
¼ teaspoon salt	1 teaspoon vanilla extract
¼ teaspoon ground nutmeg	2 cups blueberries
6 tablespoons margarine or butter, melted	

◆ Preheat oven to 350°F. Grease 15½" by 10½" jelly-roll pan. Line with waxed paper; grease paper. Dust pan with flour.

◆ In large bowl, combine flour and next 7 ingredients. In medium bowl, whisk together melted margarine, molasses, egg, and ⅓ *cup hot water.* Whisk molasses mixture into flour mixture just until smooth. Spread batter evenly in pan. Bake 15 minutes, or until top springs back when lightly touched.

◆ Meanwhile, sprinkle confectioners' sugar onto large cloth kitchen towel. Run small spatula around edges of pan; invert hot cake onto towel. Peel off waxed paper. Trim ¼ inch from edges of cake. Starting from a long side, roll cake jelly-roll fashion. Cool completely on wire rack.

◆ In medium bowl, with mixer at medium speed, beat cream with vanilla and 3 tablespoons confectioners' sugar until stiff peaks form. With rubber spatula, fold in blueberries. Unroll cooled cake (cake may crack); spread whipped cream evenly on top, leaving ½-inch border. Starting from same long side, roll up cake and transfer, seam-side down, to long platter. Refrigerate until ready to serve.

Each serving: About 350 calories, 3g protein, 40g carbohydrate, 20g total fat (9g saturated), 67mg cholesterol, 375mg sodium

ANGEL FOOD AND SPONGE CAKES

Angel food, its cousin the chiffon cake, and sponge cake share a light, springy texture. With virtually no fat, angel food cake is the most ethereal. Its delicate crumb is the result of perfectly beaten egg whites. Sponge and chiffon cakes get a bit more richness from egg yolks; chiffon, made with oil as well, is the richest of these airy wonders. All are delicious on their own, lightly glazed, or simply dusted with confectioners' sugar and served with fresh fruit.

CHOCOLATE ANGEL FOOD CAKE

Prep: 30 minutes plus cooling   *Bake: 30 to 35 minutes*
Makes 16 servings

1½ cups cake flour (not self-
   rising)
½ cup unsweetened cocoa
1⅔ cups egg whites
   (12 to 14 large egg whites)
1½ teaspoons cream of tartar

¾ teaspoon salt
1½ teaspoons vanilla extract
2 cups sugar
4 squares (4 ounces)
   semisweet chocolate
2 teaspoons shortening

1 Preheat oven to 375°F. Sift flour and cocoa through medium-mesh sieve into medium bowl. Set aside. In large bowl, with mixer at high speed, beat egg whites, cream of tartar, and salt until soft peaks form; beat in vanilla. Beating at high speed, gradually sprinkle in sugar, 2 tablespoons at a time, beating well after each addition, until whites stand in stiff peaks when beaters are lifted.

2 With rubber spatula or wire whisk, fold flour mixture into beaten whites just until flour mixture disappears. Do not overmix. Pour batter into ungreased 9- to 10-inch tube pan.

3 Bake 30 to 35 minutes, until cake springs back when lightly touched. Invert cake in pan on metal funnel or bottle; cool cake completely in pan.

4 Carefully run metal spatula around side of pan to loosen cake; remove from pan and place cake on cake plate.

5 Prepare chocolate glaze: In heavy small saucepan, melt semisweet chocolate with shortening over very low heat, stirring frequently, until smooth. Spread over top of cake, letting some run down side.

ANGEL FOOD CAKE TIPS

• Egg whites for beating are best at room temperature. The bowl in which you beat them should be perfectly dry and free from grease or any traces of yolk.

• Either over- or underbeating will cause loss of volume.

• For angel and chiffon cakes, never grease the pan; the batter must cling to the pan side as it bakes and cools. To cool, invert the pan over a funnel or bottle to let air circulate on all sides and prevent the cake from sinking.

• When loosening the cake from the pan, tightly press the spatula against the pan to avoid tearing the cake.

EACH SERVING: ABOUT 190 CALORIES, 4g PROTEIN, 39g CARBOHYDRATE, 3g TOTAL FAT (2g SATURATED), 0mg CHOLESTEROL, 145mg SODIUM

SUGAR 'N' SPICE ANGEL FOOD CAKE

Prep: 20 minutes plus cooling   Bake: 30 to 35 minutes
Makes 16 servings

1 cup cake flour (not self-rising)	1⅔ cups egg whites (12 to 14 large egg whites)
1 cup confectioners' sugar	1 teaspoon cream of tartar
1 teaspoon ground cinnamon	1 teaspoon vanilla extract
1 teaspoon ground ginger	¾ cup granulated sugar
¼ teaspoon ground allspice	¼ cup packed dark brown sugar
Salt	

◆ Preheat oven to 375°F. Sift flour, sugar, cinnamon, ginger, allspice, and ¼ teaspoon salt through medium-mesh sieve into medium bowl.

◆ In large bowl, with mixer at high speed, beat egg whites, cream of tartar, and ½ teaspoon salt until soft peaks form; beat in vanilla. Beating at high speed, sprinkle in granulated sugar and brown sugar, 2 tablespoons at a time, beating well after each addition, until whites stand in stiff peaks when beaters are lifted. With rubber spatula or wire whisk, fold in flour mixture just until flour mixture disappears. Do not overmix. Pour batter into ungreased 9- to 10-inch tube pan.

◆ Bake 30 to 35 minutes, until cake springs back when lightly touched. Invert cake in pan on funnel or bottle; cool completely in pan. Carefully run metal spatula around side of pan to loosen cake. Remove from pan; place on cake plate.

Each serving: About 115 calories, 3g protein, 25g carbohydrate, 0g total fat, 0mg cholesterol, 145mg sodium

VANILLA CHIFFON CAKE

Prep: 20 minutes plus cooling   Bake: 1 hour 15 minutes
Makes 16 servings

2¼ cups cake flour (not self-rising)	5 large egg yolks
1 tablespoon baking powder	1 tablespoon vanilla extract
1 teaspoon salt	7 large egg whites
1½ cups granulated sugar	½ teaspoon cream of tartar
½ cup vegetable oil	Confectioners' sugar for garnish

◆ Preheat oven to 325°F. In large bowl, combine flour, baking powder, salt, and 1 cup granulated sugar. Make a well in center and add oil, egg yolks, vanilla, and *¾ cup cold water*; whisk into flour mixture until smooth.

◆ In another large bowl, with mixer at high speed, beat egg whites and cream of tartar until soft peaks form. Beating at high speed, gradually sprinkle in remaining ½ cup granulated sugar, 2 tablespoons at a time, beating well after

each addition, until whites stand in stiff peaks when beaters are lifted. With rubber spatula, gently fold one-third of whites into yolk mixture; fold in remaining whites. Pour batter into ungreased 9- to 10-inch tube pan.

◆ Bake 1¼ hours, or until top springs back when lightly touched. Invert cake in pan on funnel or bottle; cool completely in pan. Carefully run metal spatula around side of pan to loosen cake; remove from pan and place on cake plate. Just before serving, sift confectioners' sugar on top.

Each serving: About 220 calories, 4g protein, 32g carbohydrate, 9g total fat (2g saturated), 67mg cholesterol, 250mg sodium

GOLDEN SPONGE CAKE

Prep: 20 minutes plus cooling   Bake: 15 to 20 minutes
Makes 8 servings

¾ cup all-purpose flour	1 tablespoon margarine or butter, melted
2 tablespoons cornstarch	Whipped cream and fresh fruit (optional)
3 large eggs	
½ cup sugar	

◆ Preheat oven to 375°F. Grease and flour 9" by 9" metal baking pan. In small bowl, combine flour and cornstarch. In large bowl, with mixer at high speed, beat eggs and sugar about 10 minutes, until thick and lemon-colored, occasionally scraping bowl with rubber spatula. With rubber spatula, fold in flour mixture until well blended; fold in melted margarine. Pour batter into pan.

◆ Bake 15 to 20 minutes, until cake is golden and springs back when lightly touched.

◆ Cool cake in pan on wire rack 10 minutes. Run small knife around edges of pan to loosen cake; invert onto rack to cool completely. Serve cake with whipped cream and fruit, if you like.

Each serving: About 135 calories, 3g protein, 23g carbohydrate, 3g total fat (1g saturated), 80mg cholesterol, 40mg sodium

FANCY DECORATED CAKES

These spectacular cakes are for grand celebrations. They rely on special frosting techniques that require a steady hand and a bit of patience. But your guests will agree – the stunning results are well worth the effort.

DOTTED SWISS ALMOND CAKE

◆◆◆◆◆◆◆◆◆◆◆◆◆◆◆◆◆◆◆◆◆◆◆◆◆◆◆◆◆

Prep: 1 hour plus cooling   Bake: 35 minutes
Makes 24 servings

2½ cups all-purpose flour
2½ teaspoons baking powder
½ teaspoon salt
½ cup margarine or butter, softened
1 tube or can (7 to 8 ounces) almond paste, cut up
1½ cups sugar
5 large egg whites
1 tablespoon vanilla extract
1¼ cups milk

Amaretto Butter Cream (see page 122)
6 tablespoons seedless red raspberry jam

Special equipment:
1 decorating bag with coupler
1 writing tip (⅛-inch opening)
1 writing tip (⅜-inch opening)

1 Preheat oven to 350°F. Grease two 8" by 8" metal baking pans. Line bottoms with waxed paper; grease paper. Dust pans with flour. In medium bowl, combine flour, baking powder, and salt; set aside. In large bowl, with mixer at low speed, beat margarine, almond paste, and sugar 2 to 3 minutes, until blended, scraping bowl often with rubber spatula.

2 Increase speed to medium; beat about 2 minutes, until well mixed, scraping bowl often (mixture may look crumbly). Gradually beat in egg whites and vanilla just until blended. Reduce speed to low; alternately add flour mixture and milk to almond-paste mixture, beginning and ending with flour mixture. Beat just until mixed.

3 Pour batter into pans. Bake 35 minutes, or until toothpick inserted in centers of cakes comes out clean. Cool layers in pans on wire racks 10 minutes. Run spatula around sides of pans to loosen cakes; invert onto racks. Remove waxed paper; cool completely. Prepare butter cream. Spoon 1 cup butter cream into decorating bag fitted with ⅛-inch writing tip; set aside.

4 With serrated knife, cut each cake layer horizontally in half. (Use ruler and toothpicks to mark halfway points.)

5 Place bottom half of 1 layer, cut side up, on cake plate; spread evenly with 2 tablespoons jam. Spread ⅓ cup butter cream on top of jam.

6 Repeat layering 2 times, then top with remaining cake layer. Spread remaining butter cream on top and sides of cake.

7 With butter cream in decorating bag, pipe clusters of small dots on top of cake.

8 With ⅜-inch writing tip, pipe rows of dots around bottom and top borders and down corners of cake. Store any leftover cake in refrigerator.

EACH SERVING: ABOUT 370 CALORIES, 4g PROTEIN, 40g CARBOHYDRATE, 22g TOTAL FAT (11g SATURATED), 43mg CHOLESTEROL, 180mg SODIUM

STRAWBERRY BASKET CAKE

Prep: 1 hour 15 minutes plus standing and cooling
Bake: 23 to 28 minutes   *Makes 20 servings*

Layers from Yellow Cake (see page 101)
2 pints heavy or whipping cream (4 cups)
1 tablespoon vanilla extract
1 envelope unflavored gelatin
⅔ cup confectioners' sugar
½ cup strawberry jam

2 pints strawberries

Special Equipment:
2 decorating bags
1 medium star tip (½-inch opening)
1 medium basket-weave tip (¾-inch opening)

◆ Prepare Yellow Cake. While cake layers are cooling, prepare frosting: In large bowl, combine cream and vanilla. In small saucepan, evenly sprinkle gelatin over *3 tablespoons cold water*; let stand 2 minutes to soften. Cook over medium-low heat, stirring frequently, about 3 minutes, until gelatin completely dissolves. (Do not boil.)

◆ Remove saucepan from heat; with mixer at medium-high speed, immediately begin beating cream mixture. Beat about 2 minutes, until thickened and soft peaks just begin to form. Beat in confectioners' sugar, then beat in dissolved gelatin in a thin, steady stream. Beat cream mixture until stiff peaks form but mixture is still soft and smooth; do not overbeat.

◆ Place 1 cake layer on cake plate; spread with half of jam, then spread with 1 cup frosting. Top with second cake layer, remaining jam, and 1 more cup frosting. Place remaining cake layer on top. Frost side and top of cake with a thin layer (about ⅛ inch thick) of frosting.

◆ Spoon about 1¼ cups frosting into decorating bag fitted with ½-inch medium star tip; set aside. Spoon about 2 cups of remaining frosting into decorating bag fitted with ¾-inch

medium basket-weave tip. Pipe basket-weave pattern around side of cake (see below). Add remaining frosting to decorating bag as necessary to complete basket weave.

◆ With frosting in bag with star tip, pipe decorative border around top edge of cake. Refrigerate cake until ready to serve. Just before serving, pile strawberries on top of cake. Remove berries before slicing cake; serve on the side.

Each serving: About 455 calories, 5g protein, 46g carbohydrate, 28g total fat (13g saturated), 110mg cholesterol, 270mg sodium

BASKET-WEAVE FROSTING

Creating the basket-weave effect for our celebration Strawberry Basket Cake is easier than it looks, and the results are stunning. If you're not sure of your piping skills, have a practice run on a sheet of waxed paper first, before you tackle the finished cake.

1 With basket-weave tip, serrated side of tip facing out, pipe vertical strip of frosting up side of cake.

2 Next, pipe 3 horizontal bars, evenly spaced, across vertical strip, extending ¾ inch to left and right sides of vertical strip.

3 Pipe another vertical strip of frosting to right of first one, just slightly overlapping ends of horizontal bars.

4 Starting at right edge of first vertical strip, pipe horizontal bars across second vertical strip in spaces between bars in first row, extending ¾ inch to right of second vertical strip. Repeat around cake to create a woven effect.

KIDS' CAKES

These whimsical creations are guaranteed crowd-pleasers at birthday parties and post-game celebrations. They're made from our simple layer cake recipes, then adorned with frostings and assorted candies. Your kids will love helping decorate – simply set out bowls of goodies and let their imaginations do the rest.

MONSTER SNAKE CAKE

◆◆◆◆◆◆◆◆◆◆◆◆◆

Prep: 1 hour 20 minutes plus cooling
Bake: 30 minutes
Makes 24 servings

2 layers from Rich Chocolate Cake (see page 100; freeze remaining layer for use another day) or 1 package cake mix for 2-layer cake, batter prepared as label directs

1 package (16 ounces) confectioners' sugar

1 cup margarine or butter, softened

5 tablespoons half-and-half or light cream

2 teaspoons vanilla extract

Green food-color paste

Candy garnishes: scallop-edged jelly candies, 1 small blue candy, ¼ cup multicolor nonmelting candy-coated chocolate pieces, and black, red, and white candy-coated licorice candies

1 Prepare Rich Chocolate Cake layers; cool as directed. (Or, if using cake mix, grease two 8-inch round cake pans. Line bottoms with waxed paper; grease paper. Dust pans with flour. Divide batter evenly between pans; bake and cool as label directs.)

2 While cakes are cooling, prepare frosting: In large bowl, with mixer at low speed, beat confectioners' sugar, margarine, half-and-half, and vanilla just until blended. Increase speed to medium and beat, frequently scraping bowl with rubber spatula, until frosting is smooth and an easy spreading consistency. Stir in enough green food-color paste to tint frosting bright green; set aside.

3 Cut 2½-inch round in center of each cake layer. Without removing round, cut each layer in half to make 4 C-shaped pieces and 4 small semicircles.

4 On cutting board or large piece of heavy cardboard covered with foil (finished cake is approximately 28" by 9"), place C-shaped pieces of cake end to end, alternating directions to create a curvy snake shape.

5 Place cut side of 1 cake semicircle against cut side of one end of snake to form tail. Repeat on other end for head. Place remaining 2 semicircles at head end of snake to form an open mouth. Frost side and top of cake.

6 Garnish cake: Cut all but 1 jelly candy in half. Place jelly-candy halves along top edge of cake for scales. Place whole jelly candy on head for eye, with blue candy in center for pupil. Use multicolor chocolate pieces to decorate body. Use black and red licorice candies for eyelashes and white licorice candies for teeth. Use brown candy-coated chocolate piece for nose. Store any leftover cake in refrigerator.

EACH SERVING: ABOUT 275 CALORIES, 2g PROTEIN, 37g CARBOHYDRATE, 14g TOTAL FAT (3g SATURATED), 26mg CHOLESTEROL, 255mg SODIUM

CIRCUS TRAIN

Prep: 2 hours plus cooling   Bake: 35 to 45 minutes
Makes 15 servings

Batter for Banana Layer Cake
  (see page 102)
Cream-Cheese Frosting (see
  page 122)
Toothpicks

Candy garnishes: multicolor
  décors, assorted licorice
  candies, gummy animals,
  and licorice whips and twists
Drinking straws

◆ Preheat oven to 350°F. Grease and flour five 5¼" by 2¾" mini-loaf pans (1½ cups capacity each) or 9" by 5" loaf pan.

◆ Prepare batter for Banana Layer Cake. Spread batter evenly in mini-loaf pans. Bake 35 minutes, or until toothpick inserted in centers of cakes comes out clean. Cool in pans on wire rack 10 minutes. Run spatula around sides of pans to loosen cakes; invert cakes onto rack and cool completely. (Or, if using 9" by 5" loaf pan, bake 45 minutes; cool as above. Cut cooled cake crosswise into five 1¾-inch-wide pieces.)

◆ While cake is cooling, prepare Cream-Cheese Frosting.

◆ To assemble: With serrated knife, cut rounded tops off 3 cakes; set aside. (Do not cut tops too thin.) For engine, from 1 of the same 3 cakes, cut a ½-inch-thick horizontal slice. Trim slice, rounding 2 corners of a short side; with toothpicks, attach to one end of cake for back of engine. Cut 1 rounded top crosswise in half. With toothpicks, attach half to bottom front of engine to resemble a cowcatcher. Cut 2-inch semicircle from second half of rounded top for front of train; with toothpicks, attach to top front of engine. Reserve remaining 2 rounded tops to make canopies.

◆ With small metal spatula, frost engine and cars and tops and sides of canopies. Sprinkle canopies with décors. Decorate engine and cars: Use round licorice candies for wheels; black licorice pieces for coal car; red licorice pieces for freight; assorted licorice candies for engine; and gummy animals for animal cars. Outline train borders with licorice whips. Attach canopies to animal cars with pieces of drinking straws. Assemble train on long board or tray, using licorice twists to attach cars. Store any leftover cake in refrigerator.

Each serving: About 355 calories, 3g protein, 53g carbohydrate, 15g total fat (5g saturated), 41mg cholesterol, 280mg sodium

GREAT-SPORT CUPCAKES

Prep: 1½ hours plus cooling   Bake: 25 minutes per batch
Makes 36

Batter for Rich Chocolate
  Cake (see page 100)
Vanilla Butter Cream (see
  page 122)
Black, red, orange, and yellow
  food-color paste

Special Equipment:
3 small decorating bags
3 writing tips (¹⁄₁₆-inch opening
  each)

◆ Preheat oven to 350°F. Line thirty-six 2½-inch muffin-pan cups with fluted paper liners. (If you do not have enough muffin-pan cups, bake cupcakes in batches.) Prepare batter; pour into cups. (Bake only as many cupcakes as 1 rack in center of oven can hold.) Bake 25 minutes, or until toothpick inserted in centers comes out almost clean. Cool in pans on wire racks 10 minutes. Remove from pans; cool completely on racks. Repeat with remaining batter.

◆ Prepare butter cream. Remove 1¼ cups butter cream; divide it among 3 cups. With food-color paste, tint one-third black and one-third red; leave one-third white. Cover with plastic wrap; set aside. Divide remaining butter cream among 3 more cups. With food-color paste, tint one-third orange and one-third yellow; leave one-third white. Frost 12 cupcakes with orange butter cream, 12 cupcakes with yellow butter cream, and 12 cupcakes with white butter cream.

◆ Spoon reserved black, red, and white butter creams into decorating bags, each fitted with a ¹⁄₁₆-inch writing tip. Pipe black butter cream onto each orange cupcake for basketballs. Pipe red butter cream onto each white cupcake for baseballs. Pipe white butter cream onto each yellow cupcake for tennis balls. Store any leftover cupcakes in refrigerator.

Each cupcake: About 210 calories, 3g protein, 25g carbohydrate, 12g total fat (3g saturated), 26mg cholesterol, 225mg sodium

DRIED FRUIT AND NUT CAKES

Studded with dried and candied fruits and nuts, these dense, moist cakes have a rich, concentrated flavor that improves with time. A perennial favorite for the holidays, these cakes are also great for housewarming gifts and special brunches, or with afternoon coffee.

CHRISTMAS FRUITCAKE

◆◆◆◆◆◆◆◆◆◆◆◆◆◆◆◆◆◆◆◆◆◆◆◆◆◆◆◆◆◆◆

Prep: 30 minutes plus cooling and chilling   Bake: 1 hour 30 minutes
Makes 36 servings

1 cup pitted prunes, each cut in half
1 package (10 ounces) dried figs (1 cup), chopped
1 package (6 ounces) dried apricots (1 cup), chopped
½ (10-ounce) package pitted dates (1 cup)
2 cups pecans (about 8 ounces)
1 cup green candied cherries (8 ounces)
1 cup red candied cherries (8 ounces)
½ cup candied pineapple wedges (4 ounces)
½ cup diced candied lemon peel (4 ounces)
1 cup sugar
1 cup margarine or butter
2 cups all-purpose flour
2 teaspoons baking powder
1 teaspoon salt
1 teaspoon vanilla extract
5 large eggs
¼ cup brandy (optional)
¼ cup apricot jam, melted
Dried fruit, green and red candied cherries, and pecans for garnish
Wide ribbon for decoration

1. Preheat oven to 325°F. Grease 10-inch tube pan. Line bottom with foil; grease foil. In large bowl, combine first 9 ingredients. In another large bowl, with mixer at low speed, beat sugar and margarine just until blended. Increase speed to high; beat until light and creamy. Add flour, baking powder, salt, vanilla, and eggs. Reduce speed to low; beat until just blended, frequently scraping bowl.

2. Stir batter into fruit mixture until fruit is evenly distributed. Spoon batter into pan. Bake fruitcake 1½ hours, or until toothpick inserted near center of cake comes out clean.

3. Remove fruitcake from oven. With skewer, poke holes in warm cake and drizzle with brandy, if using. Cool cake completely in pan on wire rack.

4. Run small knife around edge of pan to loosen cake; remove from pan and carefully peel off foil. Wrap fruitcake tightly in plastic wrap or foil; refrigerate overnight so cake will be firm and easy to slice. Store in refrigerator up to 4 weeks.

5. To serve, brush fruitcake with half of melted jam; garnish with dried fruit, candied cherries, and pecans. Brush fruit and pecans with remaining jam. If you like, wrap ribbon around cake to decorate; secure with double-sided tape. To serve, slice cake very thin.

MINIATURE FRUITCAKE LOAVES

Prepare fruitcake as above, but spoon batter into six 5¾" by 3¼" mini-loaf pans and bake 50 to 60 minutes. Poke holes in warm cakes and drizzle with ½ cup brandy, if using; brush cakes with melted jam and garnish with fruit and pecans as directed.

EACH SERVING: ABOUT 255 CALORIES, 3g PROTEIN, 42g CARBOHYDRATE, 10g TOTAL FAT (2g SATURATED), 30mg CHOLESTEROL, 155mg SODIUM

COATING NUTS AND FRUIT WITH FLOUR

Tossing chopped nuts and dried or fresh fruit with a small amount of flour helps keep them separate – and suspended – in a cake batter. Otherwise, these ingredients tend to clump together and may sink to the bottom of the pan during baking.

APRICOT-PECAN FRUITCAKE

Prep: 20 minutes plus cooling   *Bake:* 1 hour 10 to 20 minutes
Makes 24 servings

2½ packages (6 ounces each) dried apricots (2½ cups), cut into ½-inch pieces
2 cups coarsely chopped pecans (about 8 ounces) plus ⅔ cup pecan halves (about 3 ounces)
1 tablespoon plus 2 cups all-purpose flour
1¼ cups sugar
1 cup margarine or butter, softened
5 large eggs
½ cup brandy
1 tablespoon vanilla extract
2 teaspoons baking powder
1 teaspoon salt
⅓ cup apricot jam, melted and strained

◆ Preheat oven to 325°F. Grease 9- to 10-inch tube pan.

◆ In medium bowl, toss dried apricot pieces and chopped pecans with 1 tablespoon flour until coated; set aside.

◆ In large bowl, with mixer at low speed, beat sugar and margarine until blended. Increase speed to high; beat about 2 minutes, until light and creamy, frequently scraping bowl with rubber spatula.

◆ Reduce speed to low; add eggs, brandy, vanilla, baking powder, salt, and remaining 2 cups flour; beat mixture until well blended, occasionally scraping bowl. Stir in dried-apricot mixture.

◆ Spoon batter into pan. Arrange ⅔ cup pecan halves on top of batter in 2 concentric circles. Bake cake 1 hour 10 to 20 minutes, until toothpick inserted near center of cake comes out clean.

◆ Cool cake in pan on wire rack 10 minutes. Run small knife around edge of pan to loosen cake; remove cake from pan and cool completely on rack.

◆ To serve, brush top of cake with melted apricot jam. Or, wrap and refrigerate cake up to 1 week; brush with jam before serving.

Each serving: About 295 calories, 4g protein, 32g carbohydrate, 17g total fat (2g saturated), 44mg cholesterol, 235mg sodium

SPICE AND NUT CAKE

Prep: 20 minutes plus cooling   *Bake:* 50 to 60 minutes
Makes 12 servings

Unsweetened cocoa for dusting
1 cup margarine or butter, softened
½ cup packed dark brown sugar
1 teaspoon vanilla extract
2 large eggs
3 cups all-purpose flour
1 cup buttermilk, soured milk, or plain low-fat yogurt
¾ cup dark molasses
1 tablespoon ground ginger
2 teaspoons baking soda
1½ teaspoons ground cinnamon
1 teaspoon salt
¾ teaspoon ground allspice
1½ cups walnuts (about 6 ounces), coarsely chopped
1 cup pitted prunes, coarsely chopped
Confectioners' sugar for garnish

◆ Preheat oven to 350°F. Grease 10-inch Bundt pan; dust with cocoa. In large bowl, with mixer at low speed, beat margarine and next 3 ingredients until blended. Increase speed to high; beat about 5 minutes, until light and fluffy.

◆ Reduce speed to low; add flour and next 7 ingredients. Beat until well blended, frequently scraping bowl with rubber spatula. Stir in walnuts and prunes.

◆ Spoon batter into pan, spreading evenly with back of spoon. Bake cake 50 to 60 minutes, until toothpick inserted near center of cake comes out clean.

◆ Cool cake in pan on wire rack 10 minutes. Remove cake from pan and cool completely on rack. Just before serving, sift confectioners' sugar through sieve over cake.

Each serving: About 480 calories, 7g protein, 57g carbohydrate, 26g total fat (4g saturated), 36mg cholesterol, 605mg sodium

APPLE, CARROT, AND SPICE CAKES

Chopped or shredded fruits and vegetables lend a subtle sweetness, moisture, and luscious texture to these varied cakes. Except for our apple upside-down cake, which is most delicious warm, all these cakes keep well.

CARROT CAKE

◆◆◆◆◆◆◆◆◆◆◆◆◆

Prep: 40 minutes plus cooling
Bake: 55 to 60 minutes
Makes 20 servings

2½ cups all-purpose flour
2 teaspoons baking soda
2 teaspoons ground cinnamon
1 teaspoon baking powder
1 teaspoon salt
½ teaspoon ground nutmeg
4 large eggs
1 cup granulated sugar
¾ cup packed light brown sugar
1 cup vegetable oil
1 tablespoon vanilla extract
3 cups lightly packed shredded carrots (about 6 medium)
1 cup walnuts (about 4 ounces), chopped
¾ cup dark seedless raisins
1 can (8 to 8¼ ounces) crushed pineapple in unsweetened juice
Cream-Cheese Frosting (see page 122)

1 Preheat oven to 350°F. Grease 13" by 9" metal baking pan. Line bottom with waxed paper; grease paper. Dust pan with flour. In medium bowl, combine flour, baking soda, cinnamon, baking powder, salt, and nutmeg.

2 In large bowl, with mixer at medium-high speed, beat eggs until blended. Gradually add granulated sugar, then brown sugar; beat 2 minutes, frequently scraping bowl with rubber spatula. Beat in oil and vanilla. Reduce speed to low; add flour mixture and beat about 1 minute, until smooth, frequently scraping bowl.

3 Fold in carrots, walnuts, raisins, and pineapple with its juice.

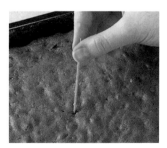

4 Pour batter into pan. Bake 55 to 60 minutes, until toothpick inserted in center of cake comes out clean, with a few moist crumbs attached. Cool cake in pan on wire rack 10 minutes. Invert cake onto rack and remove waxed paper. Cool cake completely on rack.

5 Prepare frosting. Transfer cake to large platter or tray. With metal spatula, spread frosting over sides and top of cake. Store any leftover cake in refrigerator.

ZUCCHINI CAKE

Prepare Carrot Cake as above, but substitute 3 cups shredded zucchini (about 2 medium) for carrots and add ⅛ teaspoon ground cloves to flour mixture. Omit pineapple. Garnish with chopped walnuts.

Each serving: About 415 calories, 5g protein, 51g carbohydrate, 22g total fat (5g saturated), 52mg cholesterol, 340g sodium

EACH SERVING: ABOUT 425 CALORIES, 5g PROTEIN, 54g CARBOHYDRATE, 22g TOTAL FAT (5g SATURATED), 52mg CHOLESTEROL, 345mg SODIUM

APPLE-WALNUT BUNDT CAKE

Prep: 25 minutes plus cooling   *Bake: 1 hour 15 minutes*
Makes 16 servings

3 cups all-purpose flour	3 medium Golden Delicious
1¾ cups granulated sugar	or Granny Smith apples
1 cup vegetable oil	(about 1¼ pounds), peeled,
½ cup apple juice	cored, and coarsely
1 teaspoon baking soda	chopped
1 teaspoon ground cinnamon	1 cup walnuts (about
2 teaspoons vanilla extract	4 ounces), coarsely chopped
¾ teaspoon salt	1 cup golden raisins
¼ teaspoon ground nutmeg	Confectioners' sugar for
3 large eggs	garnish

◆ Preheat oven to 350°F. Grease and flour 10-inch Bundt pan. In large bowl, with mixer at low speed, beat flour and next 9 ingredients until well mixed, frequently scraping bowl with rubber spatula. Increase speed to medium; beat 2 minutes, occasionally scraping bowl. Stir in apples, walnuts, and raisins.

◆ Spoon batter into pan, spreading evenly. Bake 1¼ hours, or until cake pulls away from side of pan and toothpick inserted near center of cake comes out clean. Cool cake in pan on wire rack 10 minutes. Remove from pan and cool completely on rack. Just before serving, sprinkle with confectioners' sugar.

Each serving: About 405 calories, 5g protein, 55g carbohydrate, 20g total fat (3g saturated), 40mg cholesterol, 195mg sodium

APPLESAUCE-APPLE UPSIDE-DOWN CAKE

Prep: 25 minutes plus cooling   *Bake: 35 to 40 minutes*
Makes 8 servings

¾ cup margarine or butter,	1½ teaspoons baking soda
softened	1 teaspoon ground cinnamon
3 medium Granny Smith	½ teaspoon salt
apples (about 1¼ pounds),	¼ teaspoon ground nutmeg
peeled, cored, and each cut	Pinch ground cloves
into 8 wedges	⅔ cup granulated sugar
½ cup packed brown sugar	2 large eggs
2 cups all-purpose flour	1 cup applesauce

◆ Preheat oven to 350°F. In 10-inch skillet with oven-safe handle (or wrap handle in double thickness of foil), melt ¼ cup margarine over medium-high heat. Add apples and brown sugar and cook, stirring occasionally, 8 minutes, or until apples are tender. Remove from heat.

◆ In medium bowl, combine flour and next 5 ingredients. In large bowl, with mixer at medium speed, beat remaining ½ cup margarine with granulated sugar until light and

creamy. Beat in eggs, 1 at a time. Reduce speed to low; alternately add flour mixture and applesauce, beginning and ending with flour mixture, beating just until smooth.

◆ Spoon batter evenly over apples in skillet. Bake 35 to 40 minutes, until cake springs back when lightly touched and toothpick inserted in center comes out clean. When cake is done, invert platter over cake. Quickly invert skillet to unmold cake; replace any apples left in skillet. Cool 30 minutes to serve warm.

Each serving: About 455 calories, 5g protein, 70g carbohydrate, 19g total fat (4g saturated), 53mg cholesterol, 590mg sodium

GINGERBREAD

Prep: 15 minutes plus cooling   *Bake: 55 minutes*
Makes 9 servings

½ cup sugar	1 teaspoon ground cinnamon
½ cup margarine or butter,	½ teaspoon baking powder
softened	½ teaspoon baking soda
2 cups all-purpose flour	½ teaspoon salt
1 cup light or dark molasses	¼ teaspoon ground cloves
1 tablespoon ground ginger	1 large egg

◆ Preheat oven to 325°F. Grease 9" by 9" metal baking pan. Line bottom of pan with waxed paper; grease paper. Dust pan with flour. In large bowl, with mixer at low speed, beat sugar and margarine until blended. Increase speed to high; beat 1 minute, or until creamy. Reduce speed to low; beat in flour, remaining ingredients, and ¾ *cup hot water* until blended. Increase speed to high; beat 1 minute, occasionally scraping bowl with rubber spatula. Pour batter into pan.

◆ Bake 55 minutes, or until toothpick inserted in center of gingerbread comes out clean. Cool gingerbread in pan on wire rack 10 minutes. Invert onto rack. Remove waxed paper and serve warm, or cool completely to serve later.

Each serving: About 325 calories, 4g protein, 55g carbohydrate, 11g total fat (2g saturated), 24mg cholesterol, 345mg sodium

POUND CAKES

Dense and velvety, with a fine crumb, traditional pound cakes are leavened simply by beating air into the batter. The original pound cakes were made with a pound each of butter, sugar, flour, and eggs. Modern versions, with the addition of baking powder and liquid, are a bit lighter in texture. Try our lovely Southern pound cake, imbued with bourbon, go Italian-style with crunchy cornmeal, or just enjoy the classic, vanilla. Pound cakes keep well and, in fact, are better the next day.

BOURBON-BROWN SUGAR POUND CAKE

◆◆◆◆◆◆◆◆◆◆◆◆

Prep: 25 minutes plus cooling
Bake: 1 hour 20 to 25 minutes
Makes 24 servings

3 cups all-purpose flour
¾ teaspoon salt
½ teaspoon baking powder
½ teaspoon baking soda
¾ cup milk
2 teaspoons vanilla extract
¼ cup plus 2 tablespoons bourbon whiskey
1½ cups packed dark brown sugar
½ cup plus ⅓ cup granulated sugar
1 cup margarine or butter, softened
5 large eggs
2 tablespoons orange juice

1 Preheat oven to 325°F. Grease and flour 10-inch Bundt pan or fluted tube pan. In medium bowl, combine flour, salt, baking powder, and baking soda.

2 In measuring cup, mix milk, vanilla, and ¼ cup bourbon. In large bowl, with mixer at medium speed, beat brown sugar and ½ cup granulated sugar until free of lumps. Add margarine and beat 5 minutes, or until light and creamy. Add eggs, 1 at a time, beating well after each addition. Reduce speed to low; alternately add flour mixture and milk mixture, beginning and ending with flour mixture.

3 Pour batter into pan. Bake 1 hour 20 to 25 minutes, until cake springs back when lightly touched and toothpick inserted near center comes out clean. Cool cake in pan on wire rack 10 minutes. Remove cake from pan.

4 In small bowl, mix orange juice, remaining 2 tablespoons bourbon, and remaining ⅓ cup granulated sugar; brush mixture all over warm cake. Cool cake completely on rack. To serve, slice very thin.

EACH SERVING: ABOUT 230 CALORIES, 3g PROTEIN, 32g CARBOHYDRATE, 9g TOTAL FAT (2g SATURATED), 45mg CHOLESTEROL, 215mg SODIUM

VANILLA POUND CAKE

Prep: 20 minutes plus cooling   *Bake: 1 hour to 1 hour 10 minutes*
Makes 16 servings

2¼ cups granulated sugar
1½ cups margarine or butter, softened
1 tablespoon vanilla extract
¾ teaspoon salt

6 large eggs
3 cups cake flour (not self-rising)
Confectioners' sugar for garnish

◆ Preheat oven to 325°F. Grease and flour 10-inch Bundt pan. In large bowl, with mixer at low speed, beat granulated sugar and margarine just until blended. Increase speed to high; beat about 5 minutes, until light and creamy.

◆ Add vanilla, salt, and eggs. Reduce speed to low; beat until well blended, frequently scraping bowl with rubber spatula. Increase speed to high; beat 3 minutes, occasionally scraping bowl. With wire whisk, fold in flour just until smooth.

◆ Spoon batter into pan. Bake 60 to 70 minutes, until toothpick inserted near center of cake comes out clean. Cool in pan on wire rack 10 minutes. Remove from pan; cool completely on rack. Sprinkle with confectioners' sugar.

Each serving: About 365 calories, 4g protein, 45g carbohydrate, 19g total fat (4g saturated), 80mg cholesterol, 320mg sodium

CORNMEAL POUND CAKE

Prep: 20 minutes plus cooling   *Bake: 1 hour 5 minutes*
Makes 10 servings

1 cup all-purpose flour
½ cup yellow cornmeal
½ teaspoon baking powder
¼ teaspoon salt
1 cup margarine or butter, softened

1 cup sugar
4 large eggs
1 teaspoon grated orange peel
1 teaspoon vanilla extract

◆ Preheat oven to 325°F. Grease and flour 9" by 5" loaf pan or 6-cup fluted tube pan. In medium bowl, combine flour and next 3 ingredients. In large bowl, with mixer at medium speed, beat margarine with sugar 5 minutes, or until light and creamy. Add eggs, 1 at a time, beating well after each addition. Beat in orange peel and vanilla. Reduce speed to low; beat in flour mixture just until combined.

◆ Pour batter into pan. Bake 1 hour 5 minutes, or until cake pulls away from sides of pan and toothpick inserted in center comes out clean. Cool cake in pan on wire rack 10 minutes. Remove cake from pan and cool completely on rack. To serve, slice very thin.

Each serving: About 340 calories, 4g protein, 35g carbohydrate, 20g total fat (4g saturated), 85mg cholesterol, 315mg sodium

---

POPPY SEEDS

The tiny, bluish-gray seeds of a poppy plant lend a nutty taste and crunchy bite to a variety of cakes, breads, pastries, creamy dressings, salads, and noodle dishes. Because of their high oil content, poppy seeds can turn rancid quickly, so store them in an airtight container in the freezer.

LEMON-POPPY-SEED POUND CAKE

Prep: 25 minutes plus cooling   *Bake: 1 hour 30 minutes*
Makes 16 servings

2 cups all-purpose flour
2 tablespoons poppy seeds
½ teaspoon baking powder
¼ teaspoon baking soda
¼ teaspoon salt
3 large lemons

¾ cup margarine or butter, softened
1¾ cups sugar
4 large eggs
1 teaspoon vanilla extract
½ cup sour cream

◆ Preheat oven to 325°F. Grease and flour 9" by 5" loaf pan or 6-cup fluted tube pan. In medium bowl, combine flour and next 4 ingredients. Grate 1 tablespoon peel and squeeze 3 tablespoons juice from lemons.

◆ In large bowl, with mixer at medium speed, beat margarine with 1½ cups sugar about 5 minutes, until light and creamy. Add eggs, 1 at a time, beating well after each addition. Beat in lemon peel and vanilla. Reduce speed to low; alternately add flour mixture and sour cream, beginning and ending with flour mixture.

◆ Spoon batter into pan. Bake 1½ hours, or until toothpick inserted in center of cake comes out clean. Cool cake in pan on wire rack 10 minutes. Remove from pan. In small bowl, mix lemon juice and remaining ¼ cup sugar. Brush mixture over top and sides of warm cake. Cool completely on rack. To serve, slice very thin.

Each serving: About 255 calories, 4g protein, 34g carbohydrate, 12g total fat (3g saturated), 56mg cholesterol, 190mg sodium

CHEESECAKES

Few desserts are as popular as a rich, sumptuous cheesecake. So we've come up with recipes to suit every occasion. Purists will adore our Classic Cheesecake, a dense-textured delight that makes any get-together more festive. For variety, try the crunchy pecan and brown sugar topping as a delicious finishing touch. For dinner parties, Pumpkin-Swirl Cheesecake entices with mellow fall flavors and a dramatic design. Tart-sweet Lime Cheesecake is cool and creamy.

PUMPKIN-SWIRL CHEESECAKE

Prep: 30 minutes plus standing, cooling, and chilling
Bake: 1 hour 10 minutes
Makes 16 servings

8 cinnamon graham crackers (5" by 2½" each) or 1 cup graham-cracker crumbs
2 tablespoons margarine or butter, melted
3 packages (8 ounces each) cream cheese, softened
1 cup sugar
⅓ cup brandy
2 teaspoons vanilla extract

4 large eggs
1 can (16 ounces) solid-pack pumpkin (not pumpkin-pie mix)
2 tablespoons cornstarch
1 teaspoon ground cinnamon
½ teaspoon ground allspice
½ teaspoon salt
1 container (8 ounces) sour cream

1 Preheat oven to 325°F. In food processor with knife blade attached or in blender, process graham crackers until fine crumbs form. In 9" by 3" springform pan, with fork, stir graham-cracker crumbs and melted margarine until evenly moistened. With hand, press mixture onto bottom of pan. Bake crust 10 minutes. Cool crust completely in pan on wire rack.

2 Meanwhile, in large bowl, with mixer at medium speed, beat cream cheese until smooth; gradually beat in sugar. Reduce speed to low; beat in brandy, vanilla, and eggs just until blended, scraping bowl often with rubber spatula. In medium bowl, mix pumpkin, cornstarch, cinnamon, allspice, and salt. Stir half of cream-cheese mixture into pumpkin mixture until blended. Stir sour cream into remaining cream-cheese mixture.

3 Reserve ½ cup pumpkin mixture. Pour remaining pumpkin mixture onto crust. Carefully pour cream-cheese mixture on top of pumpkin layer.

4 Spoon dollops of reserved pumpkin mixture onto cream-cheese layer. With knife, cut and twist through cream-cheese layer for swirl effect.

5 Bake cheesecake 1 hour, or until edges are set (center will jiggle). Turn off oven; let cheesecake remain in oven 1 hour. Remove cheesecake from oven. Run small knife around edge of pan to loosen cheesecake (this helps prevent cracking during cooling). Cool completely in pan on wire rack. Cover and refrigerate cheesecake at least 6 hours, or until well chilled. To serve, remove side of pan.

EACH SERVING: ABOUT 300 CALORIES, 6g PROTEIN, 21g CARBOHYDRATE, 21g TOTAL FAT (12g SATURATED), 107mg CHOLESTEROL, 255mg SODIUM

CLASSIC CHEESECAKE

Prep: 30 minutes plus chilling, standing, and cooling
Bake: 50 minutes   Makes 20 servings

¾ cup margarine or butter, softened
1¼ cups plus 2 tablespoons all-purpose flour
1¼ cups sugar
5 large eggs
2 teaspoons grated lemon peel
4 packages (8 ounces each) cream cheese, softened
3 tablespoons milk

◆ In small bowl, with mixer at medium speed, beat margarine, 1¼ cups flour, ¼ cup sugar, 1 egg yolk, and 1 teaspoon lemon peel until well mixed. Shape dough into ball; wrap with plastic wrap. Refrigerate 1 hour.

◆ Preheat oven to 400°F. Press one-third of dough onto bottom of 10" by 2½" springform pan. Bake 8 minutes, or until golden; cool on wire rack. Turn oven control to 475°F.

◆ In large bowl, with mixer at medium speed, beat cream cheese just until smooth; gradually beat in remaining 1 cup sugar. Reduce speed to low; beat in remaining 1 egg white and 4 eggs, milk, remaining 2 tablespoons flour, and remaining 1 teaspoon lemon peel. Beat 5 minutes. Press remaining dough around side of pan to within 1¼ inches of top; pour filling into dough.

◆ Bake 12 minutes. Turn oven control to 300°F; bake 30 minutes longer, until edges are set (center will jiggle). Turn off oven; let cheesecake remain in oven 30 minutes. Remove cheesecake from oven and cool in pan on wire rack. Refrigerate at least 6 hours, or until well chilled. To serve, carefully remove side of pan.

Each serving: About 320 calories, 6g protein, 20g carbohydrate, 24g total fat (12g saturated), 104mg cholesterol, 230mg sodium

LIME CHEESECAKE

Prep: 25 minutes plus cooling and chilling
Bake: 50 minutes   Makes 16 servings

8 honey graham crackers (5" by 2½" each) or 1 cup graham-cracker crumbs
½ cup walnuts (about 2 ounces), very finely chopped
⅓ cup margarine or butter, melted
¾ teaspoon ground cinnamon
3 medium limes
2 packages (8 ounces each) cream cheese, softened
4 large eggs
1 container (16 ounces) sour cream
1¼ cups sugar
1 teaspoon vanilla extract
½ teaspoon salt
Lime slices for garnish

◆ Preheat oven to 350°F. In food processor with knife blade attached or in blender, process graham crackers until fine crumbs form. In 9" by 2½" springform pan, with fork, mix graham-cracker crumbs, chopped walnuts, melted margarine, and cinnamon until well blended. Press mixture onto bottom and 1½ inches up side of pan; set aside.

◆ Grate 1 tablespoon peel and squeeze ⅓ cup juice from limes; set aside. In large bowl, with mixer at medium speed, beat cream cheese and eggs until smooth. Reduce speed to low; beat in sour cream, sugar, vanilla, salt, lime juice, and grated lime peel until well blended. Pour cream-cheese mixture into graham-cracker crust.

◆ Bake cheesecake 50 minutes. (Center may jiggle slightly.) Cool in pan on wire rack. Refrigerate cheesecake at least 6 hours, or until well chilled. To serve, carefully remove side of pan; garnish cheesecake with lime slices.

Each serving: About 315 calories, 5g protein, 22g carbohydrate, 24g total fat (11g saturated), 97mg cholesterol, 250mg sodium

NUT-AND-CRUMB-TOPPED CHEESECAKE

Prepare topping: In medium bowl, with fingertips, mix 1 cup pecans (about 4 ounces), chopped, ⅔ cup all-purpose flour, ½ cup packed brown sugar, 6 tablespoons margarine or butter, 2 tablespoons granulated sugar, and ½ teaspoon vanilla extract until mixture is crumbly. Prepare Classic Cheesecake as above, but before baking, sprinkle with topping. Bake as directed (if top browns too quickly, cover loosely with foil). Let stand in oven, cool, and refrigerate as directed. To serve, carefully remove side of pan. In small bowl, with mixer at medium speed, beat ½ cup heavy or whipping cream, 1 tablespoon brown sugar, and ½ teaspoon vanilla extract until stiff peaks form. Spoon whipped cream into decorating bag fitted with ½-inch star tip; pipe pretty design around top edge of cheesecake. Garnish with pecan halves, if you like.

Each serving: About 445 calories, 7g protein, 32g carbohydrate, 33g total fat (14g saturated), 112mg cholesterol, 275mg sodium

FROSTING AND DECORATING

Using a decorating bag and assorted tips, it's easy to pipe frosting or whipped cream into a vast range of whimsical shapes and playful designs. You may want to practice piping on a sheet of waxed paper before you decorate your cake.

FILLING A DECORATING BAG

Place coupler base in decorating bag. Attach desired tip with ring.

Stand bag in measuring cup or sturdy glass. Fold bag over to make cuff; fill halfway with frosting.

Shake down frosting and twist bag shut. Hold bag closed with one hand; use writing hand to guide tip.

WRITING TIP

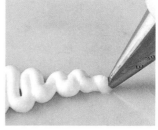

Piping dots Hold bag fitted with small writing tip at a 90° angle, with tip just above cake. Gently squeeze bag, keeping tip in frosting, until the dot forms. Stop pressure and lift tip.

Smoothing dots If the tip leaves a small "tail" at the top of the dot, gently smooth it with finger dipped in confectioners' sugar or cornstarch.

Squiggles and lettering Use thinned frosting for a smooth flow. With tip at a 45° angle, touch surface to secure frosting then lift slightly to form squiggles. To finish, stop pressure and lift tip.

STAR TIP

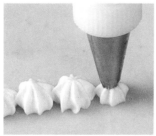

Stars With star tip at 90° angle and just above cake, squeeze to form star, then lift slightly, keeping tip in frosting. Stop pressure and lift tip.

Rosettes Position star tip as for stars, but as you squeeze, move tip up in a circular motion. Stop pressure and lift tip.

Ropes Holding bag at a 45° angle, pipe a C. Tuck tip under bottom portion of C; repeat, overlapping curves to form a rope.

A SELECTION OF OTHER TIPS

5-POINT STAR Use this smaller star to pipe small rosettes and fancy borders.

BASKET This tip forms the ridged lines that create the woven design for our basket cake.

PETAL With a wider opening at one end, petal tubes are used to make petals, ribbons, and bows.

LEAF The open "V" of this tube gives leaves, veins, and pointed tips.

EASY FROSTINGS

FLUFFY WHITE FROSTING In top of double boiler, over simmering water, with mixer at high speed, beat 2 large egg whites, 1 cup sugar, ¼ cup water, 2 teaspoons fresh lemon juice, 1 teaspoon light corn syrup, and ¼ teaspoon cream of tartar 7 to 10 minutes, until soft peaks form. Remove double-boiler top from bottom; beat 7 to 10 minutes longer, until stiff peaks form. Makes about 3 cups.

Each tablespoon: About 15 calories, 0g protein, 4g carbohydrate, 0g total fat, 0mg cholesterol, 5mg sodium

CREAM-CHEESE FROSTING In large bowl, with mixer at low speed, beat 3 cups confectioners' sugar, 2 packages (3 ounces each) cream cheese, softened, 6 tablespoons margarine or butter, softened, and 1½ teaspoons vanilla extract just until blended. Increase speed to medium. Beat 1 minute, or until smooth and fluffy, frequently scraping bowl. Makes about 2½ cups.

Each tablespoon: About 60 calories, 0g protein, 8g carbohydrate, 3g total fat (1g saturated), 5mg cholesterol, 35mg sodium

CHOCOLATE BUTTER CREAM In large bowl, with mixer at low speed, beat 2 cups confectioners' sugar, ¾ cup margarine or butter, softened, and 1 teaspoon vanilla extract until almost combined. Add 4 squares (4 ounces) semisweet chocolate, melted and cooled, and 2 squares (2 ounces) unsweetened chocolate, melted and cooled. Increase speed to high; beat about 1 minute, or until light and fluffy. Makes about 2½ cups.

Each tablespoon: About 70 calories, 0g protein, 7g carbohydrate, 5g total fat (2g saturated), 0mg cholesterol, 40mg sodium

WHITE-CHOCOLATE BUTTER CREAM In large bowl, with mixer at low speed, beat 1 cup butter, softened (do not use margarine), 3 tablespoons milk, 2 cups confectioners' sugar, and 6 ounces white chocolate, Swiss confectionery bars, or white baking bars, melted and cooled, just until mixed. Increase speed to high; beat 2 minutes, or until light and fluffy, scraping bowl often with rubber spatula. Makes about 2½ cups.

Each tablespoon: 85 calories, 0g protein, 8g carbohydrate, 6g total fat (4g saturated), 13mg cholesterol, 50mg sodium

VANILLA BUTTER CREAM In 2-quart saucepan, mix 1 cup sugar and ½ cup all-purpose flour until evenly combined. Gradually stir in 1⅓ cups milk until smooth. Cook over medium-high heat, stirring often, until mixture thickens and boils. Reduce heat to low; cook 2 minutes, stirring constantly. Remove from heat; cool completely. In large bowl, with mixer at medium speed, beat 1 cup margarine or butter, softened, until creamy. Gradually beat in milk mixture. Beat in 1 tablespoon vanilla extract. Makes about 3¼ cups.

Each tablespoon: About 55 calories, 0g protein, 5g carbohydrate, 4g total fat (1g saturated), 1mg cholesterol, 45mg sodium

LEMON BUTTER CREAM Prepare Vanilla Butter Cream as above, but replace vanilla extract with 1 tablespoon grated lemon peel.

ORANGE BUTTER CREAM Prepare Vanilla Butter Cream as above, but replace vanilla extract with 1 teaspoon grated orange peel.

AMARETTO BUTTER CREAM

Prep: 20 minutes   *Cook:* 10 minutes
Makes about 4 cups

1 cup sugar
4 large egg whites
2 cups unsalted butter, softened (no substitutions)

¼ cup amaretto liqueur or
½ teaspoon almond extract
Pinch salt

◆ In 1-quart saucepan, heat ¾ cup sugar and ⅓ *cup water* to boiling over high heat without stirring. Cover and cook 2 minutes longer. Uncover; set candy thermometer in place and continue cooking, without stirring, until temperature reaches 248° to 250°F, or hard-ball stage (see page 95). Remove from heat.

◆ Just before syrup is ready (temperature will be about 220°F), in large bowl, with mixer at high speed, beat egg whites until foamy. Gradually beat in remaining ¼ cup sugar and continue beating until soft peaks form.

◆ With mixer at low speed, slowly pour hot syrup in thin stream into beaten egg whites. Increase speed to high; beat 15 minutes longer, or until mixture forms stiff peaks and is cool to the touch.

◆ When mixture is cool, reduce speed to medium. Gradually add softened butter, 1 tablespoon at a time, beating after each addition. (If butter cream appears to curdle, increase speed to high and beat until mixture comes together, then reduce speed to medium and continue adding softened butter.) When butter cream is smooth, reduce speed to low; beat in amaretto and salt until incorporated.

Each tablepoon: About 65 calories, 0g protein, 4g carbohydrate, 6g total fat (4g saturated), 16mg cholesterol, 10mg sodium

CAKE GARNISHES

These elegant finishing touches transform home-style cakes into distinctive desserts. Arrange them to form a border or design, or simply scatter them on top. The chocolate decorations can be made ahead and stored in an airtight container, between layers of waxed paper, in the refrigerator. Stenciling with confectioners' sugar should be done shortly before serving, or the cake's moisture may dissolve the sugar.

CHOCOLATE CURLS

1 Melt 1 package (6 ounces) semisweet chocolate pieces and 2 tablespoons shortening (see page 124).

2 Scrape mixture onto cookie sheet with no sides; spread to cover evenly. Refrigerate 10 minutes, or until firm but not brittle.

3 Place cookie sheet on damp cloth (to keep it from slipping). Holding back of pancake turner at 45° angle, scrape chocolate into curls (if chocolate softens or sticks to pancake turner, chill several minutes). Transfer to jelly-roll pan; refrigerate until ready to use).

QUICK CHOCOLATE CURLS

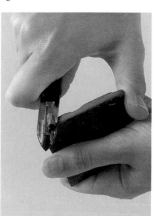

Hold a 1-ounce square semi-sweet or white chocolate between palms of hands to warm, 5 minutes. Slowly and firmly draw vegetable peeler along smooth bottom of square for wide curls, or along sides for short curls. Refrigerate in jelly-roll pan until ready to use. With toothpick, place curls on cake.

LEAVES FOR GARNISHES

The following nontoxic leaves, available from the florist, are safe to use and sturdy enough for making chocolate leaves: gardenia, grape, lemon, orange, magnolia, nasturtium, and rose. Be sure to wash these nontoxic leaves in warm, soapy water; rinse and dry leaves thoroughly before using them.

Do not use the following toxic leaves or let come in contact with chocolate or any other food: amaryllis, azalea, caladium, daffodil, delphinium, dieffenbachia, English ivy, holly, hydrangea, jonquil, larkspur, laurel, lily of the valley, mistletoe, narcissus, oleander, poinsettia, and rhododendron.

CHOCOLATE LEAVES

1 Melt ½ cup semisweet chocolate pieces and 2 teaspoons shortening (see page 124). Meanwhile, rinse and dry 6 medium nontoxic leaves (see above).

2 With clean paintbrush, pastry brush, or small metal spatula, spread layer of melted chocolate on underside of each leaf.

3 Refrigerate chocolate-coated leaves 30 minutes, or until firm. With cool hands, carefully peel each leaf from chocolate.

GRATED CHOCOLATE

For an easy decoration to garnish the top or sides of cake, run a block of semisweet chocolate over the large holes of a grater.

MELTING CHOCOLATE

Melt semisweet chocolate (with shortening, if called for) in top of double boiler over simmering water, stirring occasionally. Or, melt in heavy 1-quart saucepan over very low heat, stirring constantly. White chocolate should always be melted in top of a double boiler over barely simmering water; stir constantly until smooth.

MAKING A PARCHMENT CONE

1 Cut 12" by 12" square of baking parchment; cut in half into 2 triangles. Lay one triangle on flat surface, wide side at top. Fold left-hand point down to bottom point.

2 Take right-hand point; wrap completely round folded left-hand point, forming cone. Both points should meet at bottom point of original triangle.

3 Grasp all thicknesses of paper where original three points meet and fold point in to secure cone. Fill cone not more than two-thirds full and fold top over to seal. Snip off tip to desired size opening.

FEATHERING

1 Frost cake. Before frosting sets, melt 2 ounces semi-sweet chocolate (see above). Spoon into parchment cone, small decorating bag with small writing tip, or zip-tight bag (cut one corner off); pipe spiral on top of cake, working outward from center.

2 Immediately run tip of paring knife through spiral, working from center to edge of cake. Repeat, working from center, to mark cake in 8 segments. Divide each segment again, this time working from edge to center for feathered effect.

CHOCOLATE SHAPES

1 With pencil, draw outline of 12 hearts or other shapes, each 1½ inches across, on piece of waxed paper. Place waxed paper, pencil-side down, on cookie sheet; tape to cookie sheet. Melt 1½ ounces chocolate or white chocolate.

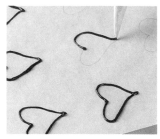

2 Spoon warm chocolate into parchment cone, small decorating bag with small writing tip, or zip-tight plastic bag (cut one corner off); pipe in continuous line (not too thin, or shape will be fragile) over each tracing to form 12 shapes in all.

3 Refrigerate at least 15 minutes, or until set. Carefully peel off shapes and transfer to cake. (Create your own designs by making other shapes, such as leaves, scrolls, or flowers.)

QUICK PIPING BAG

If you don't have a decorating bag, just use a zip-tight plastic bag with corner cut off. With rubber spatula, scrape melted chocolate into bag. Seal bag, then snip off one corner with scissors to make a small opening.

STENCILING

1 Cut lightweight cardboard or manila file folder at least 1 inch larger all around than cake. With mat knife or single-edge razor blade, cut out stars, triangles, or other shapes of different sizes.

2 Place stencil over unfrosted cake. Sift unsweetened cocoa, confectioners' sugar, or cinnamon-sugar over top. After decoration has been evenly dispersed in cutout holes, carefully lift off stencil to reveal design.

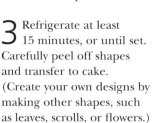

GLOSSARY

Beat To briskly whip or stir a mixture with a spoon, whisk, or electric mixer until it is smooth and light.

Blend To combine two or more ingredients until smooth or uniformly mixed. Blending can be done with a spoon, or an appliance such as an electric mixer or a blender.

Blind bake To bake a piecrust before it's filled to create a crisper crust. To prevent puffing and slipping during baking, the pastry is lined with foil and filled with pie weights, dry beans, or uncooked rice; these are removed shortly before the end of baking time to allow the crust to brown.

Boil To heat a liquid until bubbles break vigorously on the surface. You can reduce sauces by boiling them. Never boil custard sauces (they'll curdle).

Caramelize To heat sugar in a skillet until it becomes syrupy and deep amber brown. Sugary toppings on desserts like crème brûlée can also be caramelized (by heating under the broiler until melted), as can onions (by sautéing slowly until deep golden and very tender).

Core To remove the core or center of various fruits. Coring eliminates small seeds or tough and woody centers (as in pineapple).

Cream To beat a fat, such as margarine or butter, alone or with sugar, until it's fluffy and light in color. This technique whips air into the fat, creating light-textured baked goods. An electric mixer makes short work of creaming.

Crimp To pinch or press dough edges – especially piecrust edges – to create a decorative finish and/or to seal two layers of dough so the filling doesn't seep out during baking. The edges of a parchment or foil packet may also be crimped to seal in food and its juices during cooking.

Curdle To coagulate, or separate, into solids and liquids. Egg- and milk-based mixtures are susceptible to curdling if they're heated too quickly or combined with an acidic ingredient, such as lemon juice or tomatoes.

Cut in To work a solid fat, such as shortening, butter, or margarine, into dry ingredients by using a pastry blender or two knives used scissor-fashion. The fat and flour should form pea-size nuggets or coarse crumbs for flaky pastry.

Dice To cut food into small cubes of about ¼ inch.

Dot To scatter bits of margarine or butter over a pie, or other dish before baking. This adds extra richness and flavor and helps promote browning.

Drizzle To slowly pour a liquid, such as melted butter or a glaze, in a fine stream, back and forth, over food.

Dust To sprinkle very lightly with a powdery ingredient, such as confectioners' sugar (on cakes and pastries) or flour (in a greased cake pan).

Emulsify To bind liquids that usually can't blend smoothly. The trick is to add one liquid to the other in a slow stream while mixing vigorously. You can also use natural emulsifiers – egg yolks – to bind mixtures like sauces.

Fold To incorporate a light, airy mixture (such as beaten egg whites) into a heavier mixture (a cake batter). To fold, use a rubber spatula to cut through the center of the mixture. Scrape across the bottom of the bowl and up the nearest side. Give the bowl a quarter turn, and repeat just until blended.

Knead To work dough until it's smooth, either by pressing and folding with the heels of the hands or in a food processor or an electric mixer with a dough hook.

Leavening Any agent that causes a dough or batter to rise. Common leaveners include baking powder, baking soda, and yeast. Natural leaveners are air (when beaten into eggs) and steam (in popovers and cream puffs).

Liqueur A sweet, high-alcohol beverage made from fruits, nuts, seeds, spices, or herbs infused with a spirit, such as brandy or rum. Traditionally served after dinner as a mild digestive, liqueurs can also be used in cooking.

Marinate To flavor and/or tenderize a food by letting it soak in a liquid that may contain an acid ingredient (e.g., lemon juice, wine, or vinegar), oil, herbs, and spices.

Mince To chop or cut food into tiny, irregular pieces.

Pare To cut away the skin or rind of a fruit or vegetable. You can use a vegetable peeler or a paring knife – a small knife with a 3- to 4-inch blade.

Pasteurize To sterilize milk by heating, then rapidly cooling it. Most milk sold in the U.S. is pasteurized, which both destroys bacteria that can cause disease and improves shelf life. Ultrapasteurized (UHT) milk is subjected to very high temperatures – about 300°F – and vacuum-packed for extended storage. It will keep without refrigeration for up to 6 months, but must be refrigerated once it's opened. Ultrapasteurized cream, however, is not vacuum-packed and should be refrigerated even when unopened.

Pinch The amount of a powdery ingredient you can hold between your thumb and forefinger – about ¹⁄₁₆ teaspoon.

Pipe To force a food (typically frosting or whipped cream) through a pastry tip to use as a decoration or garnish, or to shape dough, such as that for éclairs. You can also use a zip-tight plastic bag with a corner snipped off.

Poach To cook food in gently simmering liquid; the surface should barely shimmer. If you plan to use the cooking liquid for a sauce afterward, poach in a pan just large enough to hold the food. That way, you can add less liquid and avoid diluting flavors.

Prick To pierce a food in many or a few places. You can prick a food to prevent buckling – an empty piecrust before it's baked, for example.

Puree To form a smooth mixture by whirling food, usually a fruit or vegetable, in a food processor or blender, or straining through a food mill.

Reduce To rapidly boil a liquid, especially a sauce, so a portion cooks off by evaporation. This creates a thicker sauce with a deeper, more concentrated flavor. If you use a wide pan, the liquid will evaporate faster.

Shred To cut, tear, or grate food into narrow strips

INDEX

ADDITIONAL CREDITS

Food preparation Eric Treuillé,
Kathy Man, Maddalena Bastianelli
Additional art direction
Cherry Ramsayer
Photographers' assistant
Margaret-Ann Hugo
IT Manager John Clifford
Typesetting Sue Hill
Additional editorial assistance
Jennifer Rylaarsdam
Additional nutrition advice
Antonina Smith
Proofreading Pamela Ellis
Index Madeline Weston

EDITOR'S ACKNOWLEDGMENTS

Many thanks to members of the food industry for their patient help
and information.

Thanks also to Delia Hammock, Sharon Franke, Mary Ann Svec,
Marianne Marinelli, Lisa Troland, Lynda Gunn, Karen Kolnsberg,
and Mary O'Connor of the Good Housekeeping Institute for their
myriad contributions.

Finally, to our indefatigable copy editor, Judith Sutton, our thanks
and admiration.